The Triune God

The Triune God

An Essay in Postliberal Theology

WILLIAM C. PLACHER

Westminster John Knox Press
LOUISVILLE • LONDON

Book design by Drew Stevens
Cover design by Mark Abrams
Cover art: Georges Rouault, Christ on the Road to Emmaus *© 2006 Artists Rights Society (ARS), New York / ADAGP, Paris. Courtesy of The Bridgeman Art Library*

First edition
Published by Westminster John Knox Press
Louisville, Kentucky

This book is printed on acid-free paper that meets the American National Standards Institute Z39.48 standard. ♾

PRINTED IN THE UNITED STATES OF AMERICA

07 08 09 10 11 12 13 14 15 16—10 9 8 7 6 5 4 3 2 1

Library of Congress Cataloging-in-Publication Data is on file at the Library of Congress, Washington, D.C.

ISBN-13: 978-0-664-23060-9
ISBN-10: 0-664-23060-1

This book is dedicated with gratitude to three institutions:

The Religion Division of the Lilly Endowment,
The Center of Theological Inquiry,
and Westminster John Knox Press.

Contents

Preface

Of books I have written developing my own theological ideas, I had thought of *Unapologetic Theology* as an introduction on theological method, *Narratives of a Vulnerable God* as a general survey of the application of that method to a range of theological topics, *The Domestication of Transcendence* as a doctrine of God, and *Jesus the Savior* as my attempt at a Christology. My friend and former student Alex Wimberly therefore urged that I next needed to write a book about the Holy Spirit. But the more I thought about it, the more I came to realize that in addressing how we come to believe, *Unapologetic Theology* was already implicitly a book about the Spirit—and would have been better if it had been explicitly such. If I had already written on the Spirit as well as a doctrine of God and a Christology, it was time to connect them in a book on the Trinity. In this book, then, I am trying to tie together a good bit of what I have written before, and I have not hesitated to repeat myself when I think I got it right the first time. Another friend and former student, Derek Nelson, worries that I am too cautious about presenting my own theology. Maybe this book will help. It is, at any rate, as close to "my theology" as I can get right now.

My general project, I suppose, has been to connect a radical view of God's transcendence with a narrative Christology. I think that is possible only through a strong doctrine of the Holy Spirit. There are lots of things Calvinists are not much good at when it comes to the Trinity, but I think our tradition has a great deal of insight to offer when it comes to the Holy Spirit.

I have subtitled the book with reference to "postliberal theology," a term coined by one of my teachers, George Lindbeck, and preeminently exemplified by another, Hans Frei. Readers familiar with their work will see Frei's influence in much of my Christology, and Lindbeck's in what I say about religious language. After I had written a first draft, though, I realized to my surprise how often I had cited Hans Urs von Balthasar at key junctures. I do not know what it means for a pragmatic, midwestern American Presbyterian to be so influenced by a

Catholic who said he drew his most important insights from a woman mystic who claimed to have received the stigmata, but there it is.

Stephanie Egnotovich, my editor at Westminster John Knox Press, has once again improved nearly every paragraph of my book with her thoughtful suggestions. Students in my seminar on contemporary theology read a manuscript and made helpful comments; thanks to Kyle Coffey, John Garrett, Peter Joslyn, Jacob Juncker, Wayne Lewis, Bryan Roesler, Jason Simons, Austin Somers, Adrian Starnes, and Cory Zwickel.

Readers and reviewers of my books have been most generous over the years. If I have any complaint, it is that when I struggle really hard to make complicated ideas clear, some conclude that clear ideas cannot possibly be very complicated. Oh well.

The week I received the page proofs for this book, my mother died, two weeks short of her ninety-first birthday. Louise Placher was a gifted artist, an elementary school teacher so excellent that her students remembered her as their favorite over sixty years later, and a compassionate social worker for the Red Cross, radicalized politically by her work with soldiers' families during the Vietnam War. Her kindness communicated itself to all who knew her, even in the dementia of her last two years, and she modeled for her son that love which the doctrine of the Trinity implies lies at the very core of all things.

W.C.P.

1
The Unknowable God

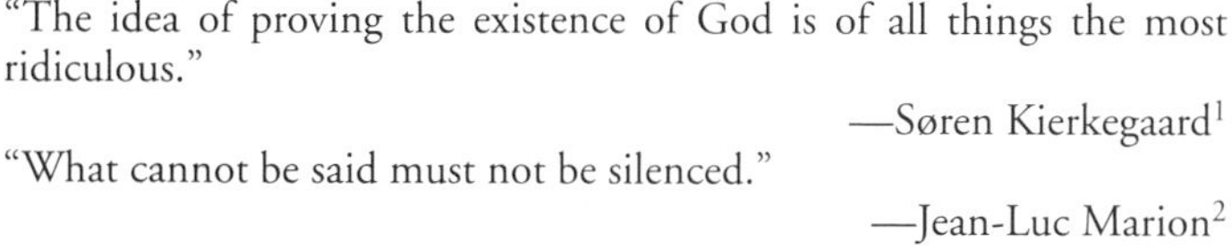

"The idea of proving the existence of God is of all things the most ridiculous."

—Søren Kierkegaard[1]

"What cannot be said must not be silenced."

—Jean-Luc Marion[2]

Several years ago, I took a sabbatical to write a book about the shift in how Christians talked about God at the beginning of the modern era (it became *The Domestication of Transcendence*). A student who interviewed me for the college paper reported that I planned to spend my leave "proving the existence of God." Well, I thought, there would be an accomplishment for a year's work! My project, though, might better have been described as "arguing that trying to prove the existence of God is a bad idea." Simply put, anything whose existence we can prove would not be God, but some sort of idol. Proof involves defining, and thus understanding, all the relevant terms, and, as Augustine said, "If you can grasp it, it isn't God."[3]

If we could prove the existence of God, moreover, then we would have this one God firmly established, and the claim that God is triune would be at most an afterthought, an added complexity to a basic belief in one God. If, however, as I believe, we can know God only as revealed in Christ through the Holy Spirit, then we *start* with three. What we know is that Jesus is God's self-revelation, and only the Holy Spirit enables us to believe this. The task of Trinitarian reflection is

1. Søren Kierkegaard, *Journals and Papers* #1334 (1844), trans. Howard V. Hong and Edna H. Hong (Bloomington: Indiana University Press, 1969), 2:93.
2. Jean-Luc Marion, *The Idol and Distance*, trans. Thomas A. Carlson (New York: Fordham University Press, 2001), 184–85.
3. Augustine, Sermon 117.5, trans. Edmund Hill, *The Works of Saint Augustine*, III/4 (Brooklyn: New City Press, 1992), 211.

then to show how these three are one, and it is a task central to Christian faith.

That task of showing the oneness of the triune God will not be undertaken here until chapter 4, after (in chapter 2) discussing God's self-revelation in Christ, and (in chapter 3) explaining how the Holy Spirit makes possible our faith in Christ *as* God's self-revelation. In this first chapter I argue that in these matters, apart from God's self-revelation, we can at best have unanswered questions we hardly know how to ask, mysteries, puzzles that point beyond anything we can experience or articulate. Keeping such puzzling questions alive can be important if it diverts us from a flattened secularity where nothing beyond the everyday things we can buy, sell, and use registers on our mental radar screens. But we should not try to form our own answers to these questions, much less prove that our answers are true—even if we could, we would end up with an idol rather than God.

Yet the student reporter captured a common attitude. What are theologians or philosophers supposed to do about God? Prove God's existence! (Or nonexistence!) This is an attitude often encouraged by introductions to philosophy, where the section on the philosophy of religion commonly contains a series of texts described as "arguments for the existence of God" from Anselm through Descartes, Kant, and some contemporary figures, often balanced by counterarguments, usually beginning with Hume.

Taking short passages out of context, such introductions impose a peculiarly modern project on texts from other eras. The categories "premodern," "modern," and especially "postmodern" are notoriously problematic, but many of the great European thinkers of the "modern" period (roughly from the mid-seventeenth century to the early twentieth) did try to make arguments for the existence of God in a way that would have seemed foreign to many of their intellectual predecessors, just as it seems foreign to us today. The project of arguing for God's existence thus might define one characteristic of the "modern." At any rate, thinking about what these modern thinkers did, and what sets their work apart from what came before and comes after, provides a useful starting point for thinking more generally about what we can know and say about God, and that in turn provides a necessary preliminary for understanding the importance of the doctrine of the Trinity.

CLEAR AND DISTINCT IDEAS

Descartes

"It is with Descartes that the philosophy of the modern period . . . properly begins," Hegel wrote in his *Lectures on the History of Philosophy*.[4] "Now we come for the first time to what is properly the philosophy of the modern world. . . . Here, we may say, we are at home and, like the sailor after a long voyage, we can at last shout, 'Land ho.'"[5] I suspect, however, that most intellectual voyagers today find themselves very little at home in Descartes' arguments—perhaps in itself a modest reason for taking talk of "postmodernism" seriously. Whatever era Descartes was in, we seem to be in a different one.

René Descartes lived in a time and place (1596–1650, France, Holland, and Sweden) in which tradition had been problematized. New discoveries had shown the outdatedness of Aristotelian science. Economic transformations had disrupted the social order. The people in the next country, or the next town, often had different religious beliefs, and wars between Protestant and Catholic forces bled Europe for a generation. A different kind of thinker might have tried to shore up a particular tradition with the beliefs and practices that could sustain it. John Calvin and Ignatius Loyola—both, as it happens, graduates of the same school Descartes attended—had tried something of the sort a century or so before. Descartes took another path.

We should begin, he said, by questioning everything we believe, and identify those ideas that are so "clear and distinct" that we cannot doubt them, using them as a foundation on which to construct an equally indubitable science. In ordinary affairs, he acknowledged, "no sane person" doubts that a world exists, that we have bodies, and so on.[6] Similarly, it would be impractical to begin with universal doubt in matters having to do with "faith and the conduct of life."[7] Indeed, he wrote at one point, "If God happens to reveal to us something about himself or others which is beyond the natural reach of our mind—such

4. G. W. F. Hegel, *Lectures on the History of Philosophy*, trans. R. F. Brown et al. (Berkeley: University of California Press, 1990), 3:108.

5. Ibid., 131.

6. René Descartes, "Replies to the Fifth Set of Objections," *Philosophical Writings*, trans. John Cottingham, Robert Stoothoff, and Dugald Murdoch (Cambridge: Cambridge University Press, 1984), 2:243.

7. Descartes, "Replies to the Fourth Set of Objections," *Philosophical Writings*, 2:172.

as the mystery of the Incarnation or of the Trinity—we will not refuse to believe it, despite the fact that we do not clearly understand it."[8]

A good many interpreters wonder if this bow to revelation, at least, was merely the cautious act of a man who did not want to follow Galileo to arrest by the Inquisition. Given the need for secrecy on such matters at the time and Descartes' introverted character, we lack the evidence to judge.[9] In any event, whatever role revelation might play, Descartes thought it could not give you *science*, and it was his project of setting science on secure foundations that dominated both his own interests and his influence. How could we find a starting point that would provide certainty for our conclusions?

He argued this way: I can doubt anything except my own existence as a thinking thing, but in that one case doubt leads to self-contradiction: if I doubt, nevertheless *I* doubt; if I am mistaken, still, *I* am mistaken—and therefore I exist. Since no rational doubt can challenge that proposition, it provides a place to start.

Having established his own existence as a thinking thing, he found himself with a variety of ideas, and the desire to know whether some external reality corresponded to any of those ideas. He took two things as "manifest by the natural light": First, "that there must be at least as much reality in the efficient and total cause as in the effect of that cause."[10] Second, even in the case of an idea, "in order for a given idea to contain such and such objective reality, it must surely derive it from some cause which contains at least as much formal reality as there is objective reality in the idea."[11] If *x* causes *y*, then *x* must have at least as much reality as *y*, and, further, if *x* causes *an idea of y*, then *x* must still have at least as much reality as *y*.[12] If I am thinking of a rock, then the cause of that idea must have at least as much reality as an actual rock.

So Descartes began to survey his ideas. What about that rock? Well, the rock is a finite being like me, he said. Therefore I contain at least as much reality as the rock and could be the cause of my idea of it. And so it went with his review of his various ideas, until he came to his idea of God:

> By the word "God" I understand a substance that is infinite, eternal, immutable, independent, supremely intelligent, supremely power-

8. Descartes, "Principles of Philosophy," *Philosophical Writings,* 1:201.

9. I have learned much about both Locke and Descartes from Nicholas Wolterstorff, *John Locke and the Ethics of Belief* (Cambridge: Cambridge University Press, 1996), and am puzzled that Wolterstorff never there considers the possibility that Descartes might be saying things simply to stay out of trouble.

10. Descartes, "Meditations on First Philosophy," *Philosophical Writings*, 2:28.

11. Ibid., 29.

12. I am simply following Descartes here, and leaving open the question of whether there can be degrees of reality.

> ful, and which created both myself and everything else (if anything else there be) that exists. All these attributes are such that, the more carefully I concentrate on them, the less possible it seems that they could have originated from me alone. So from what has been said it must be concluded that God necessarily exists.[13]

The only thing with enough reality to be the total and efficient cause of my idea of God is, it turns out, God. Therefore God exists. Since I contain an idea of infinite perfection, moreover, only God has enough reality to be the total and efficient cause of *me*. Therefore God made me.

God is perfect—a fact I can learn simply by reflecting on my idea of God—and therefore would not deceive, "for in every case of trickery or deception some imperfection is to be found; and although the ability to deceive appears to be an indication of cleverness and power, the will to deceive is undoubtedly evidence of malice or weakness, and so cannot apply to God."[14] Therefore, Descartes continued, if I use the faculties God gave me as they were designed to be used, I will not be deceived. If scientists use their senses and their reason with proper caution, their results can be trusted.

Everything in this argument depends on Descartes' analysis of his idea of God: "If I do not know this, it seems that I can never be quite certain about anything else."[15] Yet (as I can report after many years of experience) college freshmen in the first week of their first philosophy class can find any number of flaws in Descartes' argument for God's existence. For example, although his method explicitly involved rejecting any dependence on the categories of medieval metaphysics, he used terms like "more reality" or "the natural light" without definition or defense. His project depended on having "clear and distinct ideas"—being able to define his terms. But his argument about God employed the idea of "infinity," which he elsewhere admitted, "if it is to be a true idea, cannot be grasped at all, since the impossibility of being grasped is contained in the formal definition of the infinite."[16]

13. Descartes, "Meditations on First Philosophy," *Philosophical Writings*, 2:31.

14. Ibid., 37.

15. Ibid., 25.

16. Descartes, "Fifth Replies," *Philosophical Writings*, 2:253. For Descartes, "infinite" has to mean "unreachable through the method," "incomprehensible to objective science." Jean-Luc Marion, "The Idea of God," in *The Cambridge History of Seventeenth-Century Philosophy*, ed. Daniel Garber and Michael Ayers, 2 vols. (Cambridge: Cambridge University Press, 1997–98), 1:276. It is interesting that until the thirteenth century, theologians rarely used "infinite" as an attribute of God. They retained the Greek notion of infinity as potency and therefore imperfection. See Michael Hanby, *Augustine and Modernity* (London: Routledge, 2003), 153.

These flaws cause the contemporary Catholic phenomenologist Jean-Luc Marion to demand impatiently, "What do we really know of the infinite if it is interchangeable with the incomprehensible? What reality will its idea have if we absolutely cannot apprehend it as an object?"[17] Descartes actually developed a number of different arguments for God's existence, but, as Marion has shown, in the process he just got himself into deeper trouble, since each argument begins with a different definition of God, and Descartes could not show that the definitions are compatible.[18]

1. As already noted, in Meditation 3 he defined God as "infinite," an idea that he said cannot be grasped, though he had earlier insisted that all the ideas used in his arguments had to be clear and distinct.

2. "Most perfect" (his starting point in Meditation 5), on the other hand, is a relative term extrapolated from finite conceptions of relative perfection. It can be understood by measuring God on a scale of different levels of perfection.

3. "Cause of itself" (*causa sui*—his starting point in the replies to the first and fourth sets of objections) likewise presupposes that God lies in the realm of things that have causes. Since understanding things means figuring out their causes, this means God can be understood.

Definitions 2 and 3 thus place God in the realm of things whose character can be grasped, and therefore not in the realm of the ungraspable "infinite," where Descartes had first placed God, and where any religiously viable God would seem to belong. As Heidegger once devastatingly remarked, "Before the *causa sui*, man can neither fall to his knees in awe, nor can he play music and dance before this god."[19] Descartes' three definitions of God, Marion concludes, are "divergent," and the last two are inconsistent with the first.[20]

Most of Descartes' confusion seems to center around one point. As Jean-Marie Beyssade has written, "There is a paradox at the heart of Cartesian metaphysics. On the one hand, Descartes' whole system of scientific knowledge depends on our assured knowledge of God, but on

17. Jean-Luc Marion, *On Descartes' Metaphysical Prism*, trans. Jeffrey L. Kosky (Chicago: University of Chicago Press, 1999), 250.

18. Jean-Luc Marion, "The Essential Incoherence of Descartes' Definition of Divinity," in *Essays on Descartes' Meditations*, ed. Amelie Oksenberg Rorty (Berkeley: University of California Press, 1986), 317–30. See also Jean-Luc Marion, *Sur la théologie blanche de Descartes* (Paris: Quadriga and Presses Universitaires de France, 1991), 451; and Eberhard Jüngel, *God as the Mystery of the World*, trans. Darrell L. Guder (Grand Rapids: Eerdmans, 1983), 125.

19. Martin Heidegger, *Identity and Difference*, trans. Joan Stambaugh (New York: Harper & Row, 1969), 72. See also Jean-Luc Marion, *God without Being*, trans. Thomas A. Carlson (Chicago: University of Chicago Press, 1991), 35.

20. Marion, "Idea of God," 291–92; idem, "Essential Incoherence," 317, 325.

the other hand, the idea of God is explicitly stated by Descartes to be beyond our comprehension."[21] The problem is that Descartes wanted to establish an argument for the existence of God that would play a crucial role in the founding of his new science; he thought that good arguments have to involve clear and distinct ideas, and he also believed that God is incomprehensible. But those three claims are inconsistent.

Locke

One could provide political or psychological reasons for the weaknesses in Descartes' arguments, or just conclude he made a mistake, but almost the same problem emerged a generation later in a very different philosopher, John Locke. It starts to look as if we are dealing with something other than individual idiosyncrasy or error. Locke made the following argument for the existence of God:

1. "Man has a clear idea of his own being; he knows certainly he exists."
2. "Man knows, by an intuitive certainty," that "bare nothing" cannot produce a real being.
3. Since something (me!) now exists, and nothing can come from nothing, "from eternity there has been something."
4. Whatever exists must derive its power from its source of being, "and so this eternal Being must also be the most powerful."
5. Senseless matter could not "put into itself sense, perception, and knowledge," but we recognize these within ourselves. Therefore this eternal, most powerful being must also have knowledge, and this adds up to a being "which whether any one will please to call God, it matters not."[22]

A page later, with no relevant intervening argument, Locke declared, "From what has been said, it is plain to me we have more certain knowledge of the existence of a God, than of anything our senses have not immediately discovered."[23]

21. Jean-Marie Beyssade, "The Idea of God and the Proofs of His Existence," in *The Cambridge Companion to Descartes,* ed. John Cottingham (Cambridge: Cambridge University Press, 1992), 174. For Marion, Descartes' theology is "white" (i.e., God finally dissolves into incoherence) because his ontology is "gray" (i.e., he cannot finally decide whether to ground being in God or in the ego). Marion, *Théologie blanche,* 451.

22. John Locke, *An Essay concerning Human Understanding* 4.10.2–6; ed. Alexander Campbell Fraser (New York: Dover, 1959), 2:307–9.

23. Ibid., 4.10.6; 2:310.

Even if we accept Locke's argument, it gives us only some sort of powerful, eternal (and for Locke this meant existing in all time, but still existing in time) being with knowledge—but then he claimed to have proven the existence of God. Somehow, a big jump happened. A century later David Hume would note at least two flaws in all such arguments: (1) The evidence does not necessarily imply a conscious maker of the universe, as a clock implies a clockmaker. Maybe the universe is more like an animal or a plant than a clock, and it makes more sense to think of it as having a soul or having grown from a seed than having been produced by a maker. Who knows? Since we have only one case of a universe to go on, all the analogies on which such arguments depend break down.[24] (2) Given the apparent evil and chaos in the world, we cannot at any rate argue back to an *infinite* and *good* creator. Perhaps those who believe in God can come up with explanations of why God would allow evil, but, if we do not already believe and are trying to establish the existence of God from the evidence of the world around us, it just is not good enough.[25] Locke might get us to a not terribly competent creator, but not to a perfect God.

Before the modern age, theologians might well have argued, further, that the very structure of Locke's arguments placed God into the realm of comprehensible rules of causation, so that whatever he might prove the existence of, it could not be God anyway. As with Descartes, many of Locke's arguments reflect a discrepancy between a theory of argument that required carefully defined ideas and a theology that insisted that God lies beyond our understanding. Locke talked puzzlingly of the "idea we have of the incomprehensible Supreme Being."[26] If it is incomprehensible, how can it correspond to an idea?

Locke tried to explain how we could come up with the ideas he thought we have of God, but at crucial points he made moves that his philosophical principles, as stated elsewhere, ruled out. We derive from ourselves, he said, ideas of existence, duration, knowledge, and power, and then we "enlarge them" to the level of infinity, "and so putting them together, make our complex idea of God."[27] Thus what distinguishes our complex idea of God from any other idea is that it includes the idea of infinity: "There is no idea we attribute to God, barring infinity, which is not also a part of our complex idea of other spirits."[28]

24. David Hume, *Dialogues concerning Natural Religion in Focus,* ed. Stanley Tweyman (London: Routledge, 1991), part 7, 138.
25. Ibid., 10; 160.
26. Locke, *Essay* 2.23.33; 1:418.
27. Ibid.
28. Ibid., 2.23.36; 1:421. The text has "bating" rather than "barring."

Yet earlier in the *Essay concerning Human Understanding* Locke had written that God is "incomprehensibly infinite." Can we then have a clear idea of infinity at all? Locke tried to break "infinity" into component elements and thereby achieve at least some understanding of it. With respect to "duration and ubiquity" he proposed that we can simply keep adding to our finite ideas of spatial and temporal extension to get an idea of the infinite—though elsewhere he said that we cannot form an idea of duration without end.[29] Even if he could explain ubiquity and infinite duration, he admitted that infinity with respect to power, wisdom, and goodness is "more figurative" and can only mean some quantity that will always "surmount and exceed" any ideas we have of such qualities.[30]

Elsewhere Locke maintained that the "figurative application of words" serves "for nothing else but to insinuate wrong ideas, move the passions and thereby mislead the judgment."[31] Thus, from a very different philosophical position, Locke arrived at the same problem Descartes faced: although God is by definition beyond our comprehension, we have to have clear ideas about God in order for God's existence to be the conclusion of an argument.

Similarly for Kant (and one could make similar arguments in the case of Leibniz or Hegel), as Nicholas Wolterstorff notes, God cannot be an object of experience and one cannot form a definite description of God, since such a description would involve concepts. Thus Kant rejected not only the traditional arguments for God's existence but *any* talk of God in the realm of theoretical philosophy. He did, however, famously argue for a moral duty to believe in God, since without God morality would dissolve into incoherence.

Employment of the "categories" (in his philosophy, the basic concepts of the understanding—like substance, existence, and causation), Kant insisted, can never extend further than to objects of experience.[32] If one tries to extend such principles of understanding beyond objects of experience, "there arise *sophistical* theorems [*vernünftelade Lehrsätze*] which can neither hope for confirmation in experience nor fear refutation by it."[33] And God is not an object of experience. Yet Kant also argued that every moral agent has a moral duty to believe in God—a God with specifiable properties (like goodness) and relations (like regulating the world).

29. Ibid., 2.19.15; 1:294.
30. Ibid., 2.17.1; 1:276.
31. Ibid., 3.10.34; 2:146.
32. Immanuel Kant, *Critique of Pure Reason* A353/B309; trans. Paul Guyer and Allen W. Wood (Cambridge: Cambridge University Press, 1998), 349–50.
33. Ibid., A421/B449; 467.

Therefore, he had to assert that "we can somehow get God in mind well enough for our convictions to be convictions about God rather than about something else or nothing at all."[34] But his own philosophy did not give him permission to do that. How can one have, then, for Kant above all philosophers, a moral duty to believe nonsense?

A good many skeptical historians of modern philosophy have concluded that this is simply the sort of mess otherwise sensible people get themselves into when they keep trying to talk about God. But suppose, instead, the error lies in the *way* these modern philosophers went about trying to talk about God.

FAITH SEEKING UNDERSTANDING

When philosophy textbooks gather under the same heading a range of texts from the Middle Ages to today, from Anselm and Aquinas through Descartes, Locke, Leibniz, and Kant to contemporary writers, as if all these folks were doing the same thing—offering "proofs for the existence of God"—they mislead the students who read them. In fact, the medieval texts so cited were usually doing something like the opposite—giving an account of God that would render anything like a "proof" altogether inappropriate. Those who seek to reduce Christian faith to the arena of rational proof—whether liberal Deists trying to eliminate Christianity's "irrational" elements or conservative advocates of "intelligent design" trying to make religion fit their own version of the "scientific"—are not preserving traditional Christianity but engaging in a particular and characteristically modern project that has diverged from the Christian tradition.[35]

Medieval authors lived in a biblically shaped world, and the God made known in the Bible is not the subject of rational proofs. Indeed, this God cannot be represented by any image; the divine name cannot even be pronounced. When the Roman general Pompey conquered Jerusalem, he horrified the Jews by pushing into the Holy of Holies, the sacred space only the high priest could enter once a year. The story goes that Pompey was puzzled when, at the center of the Holy of Holies, where he expected to see the most valuable and sacred religious artifact, there was only empty space. As Jacques Derrida wrote:

34. Nicholas Wolterstorff, "Can Theologians Recover from Kant?" *Modern Theology* 14 (1998): 12.
35. Hans W. Frei, *Types of Christian Theology* (New Haven: Yale University Press, 1992), 3.

> This place and this figure have a singular structure: the structure encloses its void within itself, shelters only its own proper interiorized desert, opens onto nothing, confines nothing, contains as its treasure only nothingness: a hole, an empty spacing. . . . Nothing behind the curtains. Hence the ingenuous surprise of a non-Jew when he opens, is allowed to open or violates the tabernacle, when he enters the dwelling or the temple, and after so many ritual detours to gain access to the secret center, he discovers nothing—only nothingness.
>
> No center, no heart, an empty space, nothing.[36]

The closer you get to seeing God, Gregory of Nyssa said, the more you realize that God is invisible.[37]

Anselm

What would it mean to "argue for the existence" of a God so represented and understood (that is, not represented and not understood)? Consider Anselm and Aquinas, the two best-known sources of premodern Christian "arguments for the existence of God." Of Anselm, Karl Barth noted,

> That Anselm's Proof of the Existence of God has repeatedly been called the "Ontological" Proof of God ["ontological" means "having to do with being"; it is a kind of argument for God's existence developed by Descartes and Leibniz and critiqued by Kant], that commentators have refused to see that it is in a different book altogether from the well-known teaching of Descartes and Leibniz, that anyone could seriously think that it is even remotely affected by what Kant put forward against these doctrines—all that is so much nonsense on which no more words ought to be wasted.[38]

But let me waste a few words.

Chapter 2 of Anselm's *Proslogium* ("Discourse") presents the famous version of what is generally called "the ontological argument for the existence of God." To summarize:

36. Jacques Derrida, *Glas*, trans. John P. Leavey Jr. and Richard Rand (Lincoln: University of Nebraska Press, 1986), 49.
37. Gregory of Nyssa, *The Life of Moses* 163, trans. Abraham J. Malherbe and Everett Ferguson (New York: Paulist Press, 1978), 95.
38. Karl Barth, *Anselm: Fides Quaerens Intellectum*, trans. Ian W. Robertson (London: SCM, 1960), 171.

1. God is "a being than which nothing greater can be conceived." (This is at least part of what we mean by "God.")
2. Such a being exists in the understanding. (When I read the words, "a being than which nothing greater can be conceived," I understand what they mean.)
3. Things that exist in reality as well as in the understanding are greater than things that exist only in the understanding. (It is pleasant to imagine your lovely house on the lake, but even better if your house on the lake really exists.)
4. Therefore, if "a being than which nothing greater can be conceived" exists only in the understanding, it would be possible to conceive something greater—an otherwise identical being that also existed in reality.
5. But this is a contradiction: it is not possible to conceive something greater than "a being than which nothing greater can be conceived."
6. Since the hypothesis that "a being than which nothing greater can be conceived" exists only in the understanding leads to a contradiction, it is false. Therefore "a being than which nothing greater can be conceived" does not exist only in the understanding.
7. Thus "a being than which nothing greater can be conceived" exists in reality too.
8. But "a being than which nothing greater can be conceived" is God. Therefore God exists in reality.[39]

When the proof if presented like this, Anselm might seem here to have offered an argument for the existence of God like those of Descartes and Locke, starting from neutral premises and reaching a supposedly clearly defined conclusion. But did he?

Descartes began with methodological skepticism: in order to establish a secure foundation for the sciences, he started by doubting everything. Anselm, by contrast, started and ended with prayer. The whole of the *Proslogium,* in which Anselm's "argument" appears, is, as Benedicta Ward remarks, "the longest and most subtle of Anselm's prayers."[40] Chapter 1 begins by addressing the reader: "Up now, slight man! flee, for a little while, thy occupations. . . . Enter the inner cham-

39. Anselm, *Proslogium* 2, in *Basic Writings*, trans. S. N. Deane, 2nd ed. (repr. LaSalle, Ill.: Open Court, 1966), 7–8.

40. Benedicta Ward, "Anselm of Canterbury and His Influence," in *Christian Spirituality: Origins to the Twelfth Century*, ed. Bernard McGinn et al. (New York: Crossroad, 1985), 199.

ber of thy mind; shut out all thoughts save that of God, and such as can aid thee in seeking him."[41] But almost immediately the form shifts to prayer to God—passionate and full of allusions to Augustine's vision of faith, nowhere more so than at the end of chapter 1:

> I do not endeavor, O Lord, to penetrate thy sublimity, for in no wise do I compare my understanding with that; but I long to understand in some degree thy truth, which my heart believes and loves. For I do not seek to understand that I may believe, but I believe in order to understand. For this also I believe—that unless I believed, I should not understand.[42]

And then Anselm turned to chapter 2 and the "argument."

In contrast to Descartes' claim to specify at least one of God's properties, Anselm rejected the attempt to "penetrate" to an understanding of God. Throughout the *Proslogium*, Anselm never described his goal as "proving" (*probare*) but always as "understanding" (*intelligere*), and chapter 1 declared that understanding *presupposes belief*. His famous definition of God as "that than which nothing greater can be conceived" does *not* say that we can conceive God; it only specifies that we can conceive nothing *greater* than God (and thus maybe cannot conceive God either!). Indeed, later in the discourse Anselm stated explicitly that God lies beyond our conceptual capacity: "O Lord, thou art not only that than which a greater cannot be conceived, but thou art a being greater than can be conceived."[43] Our intellectual capacities fall far short of God: "Truly, O Lord, this is the unapproachable light in which thou dwellest. . . . My understanding cannot reach that light, for it shines too bright. It does not comprehend it."[44]

Unaided reason cannot get us to God. Understanding, like belief, comes by grace, and the appropriate response to it is gratitude. So, Anselm concluded, "I thank thee, gracious Lord, I thank thee; because what I formerly believed by thy bounty, I now so understand by thine illumination."[45] The *Proslogium* is a meditation on the meaning of "God" from within faith. It is hard to imagine something less like an argument from neutral premises.

41. Anselm, *Proslogium* 1; *Basic Writings,* 3.
42. Ibid., *Basic Writings,* 7.
43. Ibid., 15; *Basic Writings,* 22.
44. Ibid., 16; *Basic Writings,* 22.
45. Ibid., 4; *Basic Writings,* 10.

Still, how could he seek to move toward understanding something he kept describing as *beyond* his understanding? In fact, for Anselm what we understand about God is principally how little we can understand.[46] Understanding is possible, as already noted, only "in some degree" and only of that which the heart already "believes and loves."[47] If we take Anselm at his word, he was arguing for a kind of incommensurability between believers' and unbelievers' talk of God. Here is his conclusion: "So, then, no one who understands what God is can conceive that God does not exist, although he says these words in his heart, either without any, or with some foreign, signification."[48] The unbeliever who says that God does not exist, as Barth put it, "will have no meaning in his mouth or in his heart or will have an alien meaning which has nothing at all to do with God himself. . . . He will not know what he is denying. He will be denying an idol."[49] Those who understand God aright recognize that God necessarily exists, but for Anselm this is an account of the internal logic of faith, not an argument from skepticism to belief. Syllogisms cannot lead from unbelief to belief, since the unbeliever cannot state premises that properly capture what the believer means by God. Anselm's whole project would be misunderstood, Barth wrote, "were the fact to be ignored that Anselm speaks about God while speaking to him." The knowledge he sought can only come as gift, which is "why it has to be sought in prayer."[50]

Aquinas

Aquinas was likewise not engaged in "proofs" in the modern sense. Famously, he offered five arguments that God exists. From (1) the fact of motion, (2) the series of efficient causes, (3) the contrast between contingent and necessary things, (4) the gradations found in things, and (5) the series of final causes, he reasoned back to a first mover, a first efficient cause, a necessary being, the possessor of the highest gradation, and the ultimate final cause. But none of the five arguments concludes, "And

46. See Anselm, *Monologium* 15; *Basic Writings*, 61; *Monologium* 36; *Basic Writings*, 99.

47. Ibid., 28; *Basic Writings*, 87. The theme of God's necessary existence becomes more explicit in *Proslogium* 3. On the meditative character of the exercise, see Benedicta Ward, "Introduction," in *The Prayers and Meditations of Saint Anselm* (New York: Penguin, 1979), 77–78.

48. Anselm, *Proslogium* 4; *Basic Writings*, 10.

49. Barth, *Anselm*, 168.

50. Ibid., 101–2. For an argument similar to Barth's from a very different standpoint see Jean-Luc Marion, *Cartesian Questions*, trans. Jeffrey L. Kosky (Chicago: University of Chicago Press, 1999), 145–56.

therefore God exists." Rather, they end with puzzlingly indirect phrases: "to which everyone gives the name 'God'" or "and this we call God."

Aquinas knew that if these arguments prove anything, it is not the existence of the God of Christian faith. If he could have read Hume's critique, for instance, he would have conceded that it certainly applies to the last of them: given the mixture of order and disorder we see around us, an argument from the orderedness of the world to a cosmic orderer would *at best* give us evidence of some not particularly competent semi-deity. Aquinas's arguments, moreover, are philosophically inconsistent. The first follows Aristotle in tracing the series of causes of motion back to an "unmoved mover," but Aristotle believed that any involvement in the world would get God caught up in change and thus be inconsistent with the divine unmovedness.[51] By contrast, Aquinas's fifth way implies a God who watches over and directs all things. And the fourth way seems grounded in a Platonism of unclear relation to the Aristotelianism behind the others. And so on. But not to worry, Victor Preller explains:

> For Aquinas to say, "There are five ways in which the existence of God may be demonstrated," is not for him to say, "There are five ways in which *I* can demonstrate, on the basis of *my* philosophy, that God exists." It is merely to say that there are five ways in which philosophers have traditionally proved the existence of God. It happens to be the case that the *rationes* [reasons] on which the five *viae* [ways] are based are mutually inconsistent. . . . It happens further to be the case that none of the five ways as they now stand is compatible with Aquinas' understanding of the logic of "God." Such an observation would not disturb Aquinas in the least.[52]

The "five ways" were not Aquinas's way. "Our way," he had said in the preface to the discussion, is Christ.[53] Only through Christ can our minds come to God.

Anselm had claimed that Christian and skeptical talk of God were incommensurable; we do not mean the same things by "God," and what the Christian means cannot be translated into the atheist's language. Aquinas, however, found people around him at the University of Paris believing in God but understanding God in ways based at least

51. Aristotle, *Metaphysics* 12.9; trans. W. D. Ross, in *The Basic Works of Aristotle*, ed. Richard McKeon (New York: Random House, 1941), 885.

52. Victor Preller, *Divine Science and the Science of God* (Princeton: Princeton University Press, 1967), 24–25.

53. Aquinas, *Summa Theologica* 1a.2 pref.; trans. Fathers of the English Dominican Province (Westminster, Md.: Christian Classics, 1981), 11. See also 3a. pref.; 2019.

primarily on Aristotle's philosophy rather than Christian faith. Was their talk of God utterly incommensurable with that of Christians? Aquinas wanted to say no; he wanted to show *some* common ground, some relation between the God to which their philosophical works referred and the God of Christian faith in order to foster ongoing conversation. In context, this was at least the primary function of the "five ways—to take arguments his conversation partners would have accepted and acknowledge that they at least roughly grow out of questions to which the God of Christian faith is an answer."[54]

But, if the conclusions of the "five ways" do not correspond to his own Christian idea of "God," what did Aquinas himself mean when he talked about God? He seems to identify a standard list of divine attributes: God is simple, perfect, good, infinite, immutable, eternal, one. But, examined more closely, his discussions do not lay out properties of God, but rather specify ways in which we cannot talk about God. "Immutability," for instance, is not a quality God possesses, but a rule that says we cannot think about God in ways that would involve change. In his preface to question 3 of the *Summa Theologiae*, Aquinas made quite clear what he was doing: "Now, because we cannot know what God is, but rather what He is not, we have no means for considering how God is, but rather how He is not."[55]

If that did not make matters clear enough, Aquinas began his account of God's attributes with "simplicity," surely not the first quality that would come to mind if one were trying to define or describe God. But "simplicity" provides a category for beginning to specify how impossible it is to think or talk about God. It therefore turns out to be very complicated to say just how simple God is—or, to put it another way, to begin laying out the sorts of things we cannot say about God.

Contrast God with the sort of thing about which we *can* talk. A book sits on my desk—a copy of volume 1 of Aquinas's *Summa Theologiae,* as it happens. I can describe its color, shape, size, and location. But God is not a body, so none of those terms can apply to God. If you did not know what a book was, I could make a start by explaining that it was made of paper, glue, and ink—its *matter*—put together in the *form* of a book. But God, who is pure act, has neither matter nor parts. I cannot talk about what God is "made of." I might talk about what I could do to the book—put it back on the shelf, tear out pages to start a

54. Lubor Velecky, *Aquinas' Five Arguments in the Summa Theologiae 1a.2.3* (Kampen: Kok Pharos, 1994), 60.
55. Aquinas, *Summa Theologica* 1a.3 pref.; 14.

fire. But God has no potential; we cannot talk about what could be done to God. In talking about the object on my desk as a "book," I have already specified its genus, the kind of thing it is. But for Christians God is not a kind of thing—there is not a class of things we can name "Gods" of which God is one instance.

Conversely, I can distinguish this book from others—it is rather large, it has small print, it is the book that is now on my desk. But God has no "accidents," no properties that distinguish the way God happens to be from alternative ways of being God. There *are* no alternative ways of being God. And so on. We cannot know, understand, think about, speak about, or grasp God. As Aquinas put it, "God as an unknown is said to be the terminus of our knowledge in the following respect: that the mind is found to be most perfectly in possession of the knowledge of God when it is recognized that His essence is above everything that the mind is capable of apprehending in this life."[56]

The purpose of Aquinas's talk about God's attributes was to keep ruling out ways we are tempted to talk about God without dismissing such talk altogether. As the philosopher Ludwig Wittgenstein would remark centuries later, "Man feels the urge to run up against the limits of language. . . . But the inclination, the running up against something, *indicates something.*"[57]

We *can* talk about God correctly, Aquinas acknowledged, but when we do we literally do not understand what we are saying. In his terminology, when we talk about a property like God's "wisdom," the "thing signified" belongs properly to God, and belongs "more properly" than it belongs to creatures, but the "mode of signification" does not.[58] If we were in a position to understand God, we would recognize that God is indeed wise, and that wisdom as it appears in creatures is but a pale reflection of divine wisdom—but what it means for God to be wise would turn out to be something utterly beyond our current imagining. We trust in the appropriateness of language whose meaning we cannot understand: "Though our lips can only stammer, we yet chant the high things of God."[59]

56. Thomas Aquinas, *Commentary on Boethius' "De Trinitate"* 1.2 ad 1, in *The Trinity and the Unicity of the Intellect*, trans. Rose Emmanuella Brennan (St. Louis: B. Herder, 1946), 29.

57. Ludwig Wittgenstein, December 30, 1929, in Friedrich Waismann, *Wittgenstein and the Vienna Circle*, trans. Joachim Schulte and Brian McGuinness (New York: Barnes and Noble Books, 1979), 68–69.

58. Aquinas, *Summa Theologica* 1a.13.3; 62; see Preller, *Divine Science and the Science of God*, 173; George A. Lindbeck, *The Nature of Doctrine* (Philadelphia: Westminster, 1984), 66–67; Gregory P. Rocca, *Speaking the Incomprehensible God* (Washington, D.C.: Catholic University of America Press, 2004), 334–52.

59. Ibid., 1a.4.1 ad 1; 21, quoting Gregory the Great.

Eckhart

There is such a long history of misunderstanding Aquinas that one has to conclude that, at least to modern readers, in spite of his remarkable clarity, he somehow invited the confusion. The very limpidity of his prose, particularly when now combined with centuries of authoritative status, makes it hard not to think of him as setting forth a set of true propositions about God, not a series of reminders about how little we can know or say about God. The writings of his follower, the great German mystical writer Meister Eckhart, who piled paradox on paradox and used rhetorical strategies of exaggeration and indirection, may cast Aquinas's views in ways that bring out more clearly the features to which I want to call attention. I think most of the points are in fact the same. Eckhart and Aquinas studied with the same teacher, Albert the Great. Eckhart was only the second occupant of the Dominican "chair" at the University of Paris invited to fill a second term there—Aquinas had been the first.[60] And Eckhart appealed to Aquinas when under attack concerning his orthodoxy.[61]

"Eckhart was obviously fascinated by the question of what we think we are doing when we attempt to speak about God," the greatest Eckhart scholar today, Bernard McGinn, notes. "In one sense, his whole surviving corpus is an exploration of this issue."[62] What *are* we doing? Certainly not stating true propositions about God. Propositions involve making distinctions, and, in Eckhart's words, "No distinction can exist or be understood in God."[63] (Aquinas's account of divine simplicity said the same.) We must somehow know God, if at all, "without means, without images, and without likeness."[64] "God is nameless, because no one can say anything or understand anything about him. . . . So be silent, and do not chatter about God; for when you do chatter about him, you are telling lies and

60. Bernard McGinn, *The Harvest of Mysticism in Medieval Germany* (New York: Herder & Herder, 2005), 95, 99.

61. See, for instance, Meister Eckhart, "The Defense," *Meister Eckhart*, trans. Raymond Blakney (New York: Harper & Brothers, 1957), 305. "Eckhart seems perpetually afflicted with a theological neurosis lest he get God idolatrously wrong, so he watches his theological language with a vigilance so anxious—violent even—as to arouse a suspicion: that he writes as if striving for that which he also knows to be impossible, as if there were some superior ideal theological syntax reserved for addressing God in correctly. . . . Thomas, knowing that you will never get God finally right anyway, seems less anxious." Denys Turner, *Faith, Reason and the Existence of God* (Cambridge: Cambridge University Press, 2004), 103.

62. Bernard McGinn, *The Mystical Thought of Meister Eckhart* (New York: Herder & Herder, 2001), 90.

63. Meister Eckhart, *Commentary on Exodus* 60, trans. Bernard McGinn, in *Meister Eckhart: Teacher and Preacher*, ed. Bernard McGinn (New York: Paulist Press, 1986), 64.

64. Eckhart, Sermon 70, ibid., 318.

sinning."[65] God is "a non-God, a nonspirit, a nonperson, a nonimage,"[66] "nothing at all."[67]

We tend today to think about "mysticism" as the effort to express certain "mystical experiences." The great contemporary theologian Jürgen Moltmann begins his discussion of the topic by saying, "Mystical theology aims at being a wisdom drawn from experience. . . . It is mystical only because it tries to put mystical experience into words."[68] In terms of Eckhart, and indeed nearly all Christian mystics before the early modern period, however, it would be hard to be more wrong. Many of them did not mention special experiences at all, and those who did downplayed their significance. Instead, they used a dialectic full of paradoxes to show that we *cannot* capture God in human experience.[69] Eckhart himself condemned the efforts of some to have visions of God as manifesting a "merchant mentality"—what Marxists would now call "commodification," like those who look at a cow and see only milk and cheese.[70] As Mark McIntosh elegantly puts it, whereas modern "mystical" writers attempt to describe *experiences of negation*, earlier mystics developed a theology of the *negation of experience*.[71] Denys Turner states the problem:

> The revenge of the possessive self, the self of "imagination," threatened by the vacuum of detachment, is to rush to fill the vacuum in by means of a perverted "spirituality," designed to reproduce the vacuum in a specialized set of "spiritual" experiences of it: as if the vacuum itself could be made an *object of experience*. But the cultivation of such pseudo-experiences, of inwardness and detachment, can serve only to displace the vacuum by this attempt to reproduce it experientially.[72]

In the face of an unknowable mystery, one seeks to keep mastery by asserting that at least one is thinking about *one's own experience* of

65. Meister Eckhart, Sermon 83, *Meister Eckhart: The Essential Sermons, Commentaries, Treatises, and Defense,* trans. Edmund Colledge and Bernard McGinn (New York: Paulist Press, 1981), 206–7.

66. Ibid., 208.

67. "Er ist nihtes niht." Sermon 23, quoted in McGinn, *Mystical Thought*, 99.

68. Jürgen Moltmann, *The Spirit of Life*, trans. Margaret Kohl (Minneapolis: Fortress, 1992), 198.

69. Denys Turner, *The Darkness of God* (Cambridge: Cambridge University Press, 1995), 267. "Detachment and interiority are, for Eckhart, not so much the names of experiences as *practices for the transformation of experience*" (ibid., 179). These conclusions about mysticism parallel George Lindbeck's critique of "experiential-expressivism" in theology generally. See Lindbeck, *Nature of Doctrine*, 31–32.

70. Françoise Meltzer, *For Fear of the Fire* (Chicago: University of Chicago Press, 2001), 141.

71. Mark A. McIntosh, *Mystical Theology* (Oxford: Blackwell, 1998), 67–68.

72. Turner, *Darkness of God*, 209–10.

unknowable mystery, and thus keeping things at least in some measure under one's own control. In doing that, however, one fails to exercise the humble surrender characteristic of premodern mystical writers. They understood the need to surrender themselves to God in order to know God. Too many modern and postmodern folks "interested in mysticism" want to keep themselves at the center of the world of their experience while finding a place for God somewhere in that world. As a result, one ends up with something so different that Turner wonders if there is any but a purely verbal relation between medieval and modern "mysticism."[73]

In *The Mystic Fable* Michel de Certeau looks at texts from the transition time, in the sixteenth and seventeenth centuries, and traces a shift from the "mystical theology" of the Middle Ages to the modern science of *mystics*.[74] He argues that at that point mysticism moved away from the task of reminding theologians how little they could say of God—a task central to theology—and became an empirical account of mystical experiences, marginalized from the main business of theology.[75]

In sum, premodern thinkers like Anselm and Aquinas, and the mystical tradition before the early modern age, were not trying to prove God's existence, define God's essence, or describe their own experiences of God. They were trying, instead, to show that such enterprises are impossible and that God lies beyond all our proofs and definitions and imaginations. But the world changed,[76] and after the Reformation, in a divided Christian world, each party wanted to be able to argue for its own correctness, which meant drawing matters of faith into a realm where decisive argument was supposedly possible.[77] Protestant orthodoxy, for example, took the doctrine of Scripture—in the hands of Luther and Calvin a way of *challenging* tradition—and turned it into a theory of propositional authority. The Westminster Confession of 1647, which unlike previous Protestant statements of faith began with the authority of Scripture rather than with God, provides one mark of the change. Catholics countered with new definitions of the authority of the church.

73. Ibid., 267.

74. Michel de Certeau, *The Mystic Fable*, trans. Michael B. Smith (Chicago: University of Chicago Press, 1992), 107, 122–23, 179.

75. See also Louis Dupré, *Passage to Modernity* (New Haven: Yale University Press, 1993), 222–23.

76. John Milbank seems to think that all the relevant changes took place when Scotus said that existence could be attributed univocally to God and creatures; I think the story is a bit more complicated than that. See for instance John Milbank, *Theology and Social Theory* (Oxford: Basil Blackwell,1990), 302–3; John Milbank, *Being Reconciled* (London: Routledge, 2003), 74–78.

77. See Ephraim Radner, *The End of the Church* (Grand Rapids: Eerdmans, 1998).

Further, the triumphs of science in the seventeenth century gave its methods of empiricism and proof new authority. Puritans and Pietists turned from writing biblical commentaries to writing diaries—accounts of their own experience that thus began with their own world rather than the world of Scripture. Even mystics turned empirical. Religious language, which had been, in Michel de Certeau's phrase, "never anything but the unstable metaphor for what is inaccessible,"[78] came to be systematized. As Jean-Luc Marion has observed, "By excessively appropriating 'God' to itself through proof, thought separates itself from separation, misses distance, and finds itself one morning surrounded by idols, by concepts, and by proofs, but abandoned by the divine."[79] And we are back to Descartes and Locke.

RUNNING AGAINST THE BOUNDARIES OF LANGUAGE

If European modernity took a wrong turn in thinking about God, the solution does not lie in returning to the Middle Ages, even if we could. We cannot go home again, and in any event the medieval world is not our home. For one thing, medieval Europe was a world in which pretty much everyone took talk about God for granted. Theologians could nurture reflection on God's mystery by showing the paradoxes of God-talk and encouraging what Denys Turner calls "that silence which is found only on the other side of a general linguistic embarrassment"[80] with the confidence that talk of God would continue.

We live today, by contrast, in a time when many people, at least in Europe and North America, are all too willing to be silent about God. Life is busy, and we have so many choices to make between one product and another that ultimate questions easily get lost in the shuffle. Politics and even religion become yet additional commodities offered for our delectation. If Christian theologians today say that it is very hard to talk about matters that point beyond our ordinary lives of getting and spending, many of our contemporaries are not inclined to argue but are more than willing simply to abandon such questions altogether.

So the theological task becomes more difficult. If we try to talk about God in a way that fits God into human categories and systems, we end up not with God but with an idol (and our arguments for the

78. De Certeau, *Mystic Fable*, 77.
79. Marion, *Idol and Distance*, 12.
80. Turner, *Darkness of God*, 23.

existence of the idol do not work very well anyway). Idols are things we can control. In Isaiah the prophet appropriately ridicules those who take some wood, use part of it to roast meat and warm themselves, and make the rest into a god (Isa. 44:16–17)—as if we could make gods for ourselves as and when we needed them. But if we too quickly simply acknowledge the meaninglessness of all talk about God, we run the risk that our secular contemporaries will rest content in their unqualified secularity, have a beer, and go bowling—whether alone or not.

A theology appropriate to our postmodern time, therefore, might ask whether there are permanently unanswerable questions that point beyond the realm of our experience and to which Christian revelation could provide a totally unexpected answer. A line of philosophers has been exploring such possibilities at least since Kant,[81] but the task is tricky. On the one side lies the risk of falling back into the modern project and coming up with some answer we can understand to "ultimate questions"—an answer that inevitably describes an idol. On the other side is the danger of pointing toward an answer so amorphous that it collapses into a vaguely poetic way of talking about what turns out in the end to be just ordinary experience.

It is intriguing how many philosophers of the twentieth century—from phenomenologists to critical theorists to British linguistic philosophers to feminists—implicitly or explicitly, successfully or unsuccessfully, search for a path between what I am describing as idolatry and pure secularity.[82] Those who write most tentatively about God are more interesting conversation partners for Christian theology than those who march confidently forward in proofs of God's existence. As John Milbank has written, "The 'bad' philosophers of modernity have always been more truly theological than the 'sound' ones. For they have refused to conclude to God from uninflected objective reason, and thereby have inadvertently, and in some measure, avoided idolatry."[83] The final section of this chapter will look at three of the greatest of such complex and tentative writers about God—Søren Kierkegaard, Emmanuel Levinas, and Ludwig Wittgenstein—to measure their successes and failures. Before considering them, however, I need to say something about a real or apparent

81. Kant, *Critique of Pure Reason*, A296/B352–53, 385–86.

82. For instance, Martin Heidegger, "Letter on Humanism," trans. Frank A. Capuzzi, in *Basic Writings from Being in Time (1927) to the Task of Thinking (1964)*, ed. David Farrell Krell (New York: Harper & Row, 1977), 218; Theodor W. Adorno, *Negative Dialectics*, trans. E. B. Ashton (New York: Seabury, 1975), 399–405; John Wisdom, "Gods," *Philosophy and Psycho-Analysis* (repr. Berkeley: University of California Press, 1969), 149–68; Luce Irigaray, "Divine Women," quoted in Elizabeth Grosz, *Sexual Subversions* (Sydney: Allen & Unwin, 1989), 159.

83. John Milbank, *Being Reconciled* (London: Routledge, 2003), 117.

theological challenge to even considering such approaches to reflection on God.

The greatest theologian of the twentieth century, Karl Barth, is often presented as arguing that any reference to such philosophical arguments inevitably builds a Procrustean bed into which theology is then bent and trimmed in order to fit. Barth, after all, proposed that Christian theologians should simply stand inside the world of Christian faith and seek to describe it with a detail and all-inclusiveness that may begin to have a compelling power—the best apologetics is a good dogmatics. He rejected every claim to stand in some "neutral" position from which one could make an argument for Christianity from an objective, outside point of view. We always stand somewhere in particular, Barth insisted, and standing outside Christian faith, with its central commitment to the triune God, can claim no privileged objectivity—it is just another perspective, and in fact an un-Christian one. As an admirer of Barth, then, what am I doing starting this book with a chapter on how philosophers have kept questions about God alive?

What often gets missed in interpretations of Barth is how much he believed that *from* a Christian perspective one can engage in conversation with anybody about anything—from Mozart to Nietzsche to Pure Land Buddhism, to cite the topics of a few of the lengthy excurses in the *Church Dogmatics.*[84] Close to the end of the *Church Dogmatics*, he wrote at some length about "parables of the kingdom":

> We may think of the mystery of God, which we Christians so easily talk away in a proper concern for our own cause. We may think of the peace of creation, or its very puzzling nature, and the consequent summons to gratitude. We may think of the radicalness of the need of redemption or the fullness of what is meant by redemption if it is to meet this need. . . . Are not all these phenomena which with striking frequency are found *extra muros ecclesicae* [outside the walls of the church], in circles where little or nothing is obviously known of the Bible and Church proclamation except perhaps by very devious ways and in very attenuated forms? Is there nothing to be learned from these phenomena? However alien their forms, is not their language that of true words, the language of "parables of the kingdom of heaven"?[85]

84. If Barth had less to say in relation to natural science than to other topics, this was a matter of the limits of his own education rather than any principle.

85. Karl Barth, *Church Dogmatics,* IV/3/1, trans. G. W. Bromiley (Edinburgh: T. & T. Clark, 1961), 125.

Such "parables" offer an honest way of challenging the flattened secularity of parts of our society, and Barth was not afraid of them. Writing of Barth's method, Hans Frei explained that he always began with the world rendered by the biblical narratives, insisting that it is the world in which we live and move and have our being. Nevertheless, within the context of that world

> he will do ethics to indicate that this narrated, narratable world is at the same time the ordinary world in which we are responsible for our actions; and he will do *ad hoc* apologetics, in order to throw into relief particular features of this world by distancing them from or approximating them to other descriptions of the same or other linguistic worlds. . . . But none of these other descriptions or, for that matter, argument with them can serve as a "pre-description" for the world of Christian discourse which is also this common world, for to claim that it can would mean stepping out of that encompassing world; and that by definition is impossible.[86]

What matters is that such strategies remain ad hoc. Those (like me!) who pursue them are conscious that no one set of questions defines the starting point of theology, very much aware that our initial questions may be altogether misguided, resistant to all claims of a neutral starting point.[87] Ad hoc apologetics will not lead us to God. If we are to know God, God has to come to us. By showing us how thought breaks down, ad hoc apologetics can at most give us an intellectual advantage equivalent to the advantage the Gospels assign to the poor and sinful. Those not wealthy or virtuous will be less inclined to think they can construct their own security, and thus perhaps more open to hearing the good news of grace. So, analogously, those whose efforts to understand their world and their lives by their own reason and experience have at some point encountered collapse or roadblock may be more open to hearing the good news of revelation. God has "made foolish the wisdom of the world" (Rom. 1:20); those conscious of their own foolishness may find it a bit easier to hear God's wisdom, though it must always be emphasized that foolishness in itself is not the voice of God but, like any other human condition, can only provide a place to wait until, and if, God speaks.[88]

86. Hans W. Frei, "Eberhard Busch's Biography of Karl Barth," in *Types of Christian Theology* (New Haven: Yale University Press, 1992), 161. See 3–4, 38–46, for a description of Frei's "Type 4" theology.

87. See Turner, *Faith, Reason,* 12.

88. See Paul Ricoeur, "Religion, Atheism, and Faith," trans. Charles Freilich, *The Conflict of Interpretations*, ed. Dan Ihde (Evanston, Ill.: Northwestern University Press, 1974), 448, on the difference between the philosopher and the prophetic preacher.

I should acknowledge that this argument flies in the face of the conclusions a very great theologian, Dietrich Bonhoeffer, reached near the end of his life. In his *Letters and Papers from Prison* he warned against using "God as a stop-gap for the incompleteness of our knowledge. . . . We are to find God in what we know, not in unsolved problems but in those that are solved. That is true of the relationship between God and scientific knowledge, but it is also true of the wider human problems of death, suffering, and guilt."[89] Theological strategies that start with human failures of whatever sort, Bonhoeffer said, turn Christianity into a rearguard action, always hoping for some corner of things human reason has not yet explained, so that we will still have room for God. Moreover, they end up celebrating human failures and limitations in a way that is "in the first place pointless, in the second place ignoble, and in the third place unchristian."[90]

I agree that appealing to God in the face of less-than-ultimate questions risks facing the news tomorrow that human reason can handle them after all. Further, as I have argued all along, the "God" who answers such questions turns out to be an idol anyway. Still, I think there are some questions whose very formulation we find extraordinarily difficult, whose character we would misunderstand if we thought of them as the sort of thing that science or any other human enterprise could "answer." I am not concerned, for example, about picking up the newspaper to discover that some researcher has figured out the truth about what Wittgenstein called "the meaning of life." Thinking about the relation such issues might have to belief in God does not seem to me an exercise in demeaning human nature but a matter of simple honesty about our limitations and the mysteries that surround us. Does that mean resisting secularity? That depends, I suppose, on how flattened into everydayness one's world has to be in order to be "secular."

The appropriate strategies in our time, however, when making ad hoc connections between Christian faith and matters that even many non-Christians may find intrinsically mysterious, must be more like the premodern examples I have discussed than the modern ones. Talk of "proof" is inappropriate, for proof involves defining one's terms, and an entity so defined is inevitably an idol rather than God. Neither human reason nor human religious experience can lead us to God. At most they leave us usefully puzzled, aware of the inadequacies of our human

89. Dietrich Bonhoeffer, to Eberhard Bethge, 29 May 1944, *Letters and Papers from Prison*, trans. Reginald Fuller et al. (New York: Macmillian, 1972), 311.

90. Bonhoeffer to Bethge, 8 June 1944, ibid., 327.

modes of understanding and not quite sure where to turn next. One could pursue many such puzzles, from the question of the origin of all things to pressing issues of how to define justice in an intellectually pluralistic world. In what follows I consider three not quite random examples: from the nineteenth century Søren Kierkegaard, and from the twentieth Emmanuel Levinas of the continental tradition of philosophy and Ludwig Wittgenstein of the analytic tradition. I hope these examples will at least show how puzzles that might leave one open to encountering God can emerge in a variety of contexts. As already noted, finding a general set of principles or a classificatory scheme for the relevant questions would move us away from ad hoc conversation to a supposed systematic starting point outside Christianity, and that, I am arguing, takes us down a path than can lead only to idols.

Kierkegaard

No one has ever been more systematically unsystematic about such matters than Søren Kierkegaard. Kierkegaard faced the odd problem, he said, of how to introduce Christianity into Christendom. A missionary to a non-Christian land could straightforwardly present the strange, demanding call to follow the crucified Jesus, but comfortable Danes would only say, "Yes, yes, we know all about that. We are all already Christians." If Christianity were a matter of objective information, one could communicate it directly, like the proof of the Pythagorean theorem, or the outcome of last night's Cubs-Mets game, presenting "something to the attention of one who knows, that he may judge it, or to the attention of one who does not know, that he may learn something."[91]

Christianity, however, is not a matter of memorizing the right answers, and teaching it as if one "translates everything into results and helps all mankind to cheat by copying these off and reciting them by rote" gives people only an illusion of faith.[92] Rather, Christian faith involves a personal process Kierkegaard called "appropriation" or "inwardness." Faith has to impassion Christians, transform them and the way they live their lives. But "inwardness cannot be directly communicated."[93] You cannot give me faith by whispering the right answer so that I can properly repeat it to the Teacher.

91. Søren Kierkegaard, *Concluding Unscientific Postscript*, trans. David F. Swenson and Walter Lowrie (Princeton: Princeton University Press, 1941), 247.
92. Ibid., 68.
93. Ibid., 232.

So Kierkegaard had to try an "indirect method."[94] He identified three not really Christian ways of life he called "the aesthetic," "the ethical," and "religiousness A," the religious life that does not include belief in the paradox that God became human. Rather than criticizing any of them from the outside, in pseudonymous works he immersed himself in each of them and showed, from within, how each breaks down—not by proving logical inconsistencies but by showing the puzzles inherent in such a life.[95] "If you can do that," he wrote, "if you can find exactly the place where the other is and begin there, you may perhaps have the luck to lead him to the place where you are."[96]

Writings from the aesthetic stage, therefore, capture the passion for the moment that is characteristic of every bright, romantic, ironic college sophomore. Aesthetic heroes cultivate their talents and satisfy their urges. The poet suffers to produce her beautiful poetry; Don Juan sleeps with yet one more woman. The indirect communicator does not condemn. Rather, "If you are capable of it, present the aesthetic with all of its fascinating magic."[97] Yet the aesthetic life sustains no ongoing commitment; one is lost always in the passion of the moment, for the aesthetic is like living your life according to the system of crop rotation, with a different crop always to be planted in the field next year.[98] Or living like Don Juan, whose pattern of seducing a different woman every night leaves us doubtful that he is really a "lover."[99] The human spirit presses to break out to some less transitory form of life.

Ethics offers more continuity than the momentary fulfillments of the aesthetic, and another set of Kierkegaard's pseudonyms explored from the inside the ethical life. Among other things, they showed how the ethical account of life breaks down in the face of the story of Abraham's setting off to kill Isaac at God's command. The only judgment that ethics can legitimately make of Abraham is that he was a man preparing to murder his son. Despite this, readers of the story find themselves somehow in awe of Abraham. If we are not either to make him a monster or to trivialize him (Isaac was a spoiled kid who needed a scare? Abraham knew in advance that God would not really make him

94. Søren Kierkegaard, *The Point of View for My Work as an Author,* in *A Kierkegaard Anthology*, ed. Robert Bretall (Princeton: Princeton University Press, 1947), 332.

95. "A pseudonym is excellent for accentuating a point, a stance, a position. It creates a poetic person." Søren Kierkegaard, *Armed Neutrality, and An Open Letter*, trans. Howard V. Hong and Edna H. Hong (Bloomington: Indiana University Press, 1968), 88.

96. Kierkegaard, *Point of View*, 335.

97. Ibid.

98. Søren Kierkegaard, "The Rotation Method," *Either/Or*, part 1, trans. Howard V. and Edna H. Hong (Princeton: Princeton University Press, 1987), 281–300.

99. Kierkegaard, "The Immediate Erotic Stages," *Either/Or*, part 1, 95.

do it?), it is necessary to find categories for describing Abraham's story that reach beyond the ethical.[100] That means that ethical categories cannot be the last word on human life.

At the level of religion, another pseudonym imagines "religiousness A," in which belief in God grows out of "an evolution within the total definition of human nature."[101] In "religiousness A" believers work their own way up to some kind of spirituality where they think about "God," and all that matters is that they relate to that God with sufficient passion and sincerity. (This is surely the sort of thing so many of our contemporaries mean when they describe themselves as "spiritual but not religious.") But such a "religiousness" shipwrecks on the shoals of human sin. Because human beings are sinful and selfish, even (especially?) when they seek to develop their spiritual sides, they invent spiritual goals that encourage them to do what they were going to do anyway to satisfy their own self-centered desires. They imagine a God in the image of the fulfillment of their own wishes (Marcus Borg's picture of Jesus, it seems to me, is attractive in just this way[102]). In Kierkegaard's terms, their subjectivity is in untruth. The "God" they are thinking about always turns out to be a creature of their own imagination, designed to support their sense of their own importance or virtue.

Imagine, in contrast, a "religiousness B" in which *God came to us*, in that God became a human being and accomplished our salvation (in part by demolishing all our comforting idolatries). Analysis of one's own wants or needs might leave one vaguely hungry for such a religiousness, however inchoately imagined, but it cannot get one there, for, if God has not taken the initiative, all human wishes cannot make God appear. (And if God does take the initiative, the results may have little to do with fulfilling our wishes.) Indeed, even if God did thus come, human experience and understanding could not see that revelation as God. God can appear to human beings only in humanly observable and comprehensible forms. In this case, then, not only is the *passion* of faith paradoxical, Kierkegaard said, believing with certainty that which cannot be proven, but also the *content* of what it believes is itself a paradox—that something as apparently unlike God as, say, a wandering Jewish teacher killed on a cross, actually *is* God among us.[103] Rather than trying to prove the probable

100. Søren Kierkegaard, *Fear and Trembling*, trans. Howard V. Hong and Edna H. Hong (Princeton: Princeton University Press, 1983), 55.

101. Kierkegaard, *Concluding Unscientific Postscript*, 496.

102. Marcus J. Borg, *Meeting Jesus Again for the First Time* (San Francisco: HarperSanFrancisco, 1995).

103. Søren Kierkegaard, *Philosophical Fragments*, trans. Howard V. Hong and Edna H. Hong (Princeton: Princeton University Press, 1985), 65.

truth of what Christianity teaches, Kierkegaard wanted to emphasize here its wild improbability so that we do not mistakenly seize on some easier, probable belief and think we have found Christian faith.

Kierkegaard, David Tracy writes, "will try any genre—diaries, music, exercises, dialogues, discourses, narratives. He will try anything except a system."[104] The problem with systems (Kierkegaard had Hegel preeminently in mind) is that their authors forget that people—even systematic philosophers—have to live. They forget, "in a sort of world-historical absent-mindedness, what it means to be a human being,"[105] imagining or pretending that they can live in the midst of the story as someone who already stands looking back from its conclusion.

I do not persuade you by showing you where *you* fit into *my* system. I can only connect with you by imagining your life from within itself. If you are not a Christian, I cannot simply start talking about God and faith. Describing Abraham's faith, I can only write, as one of Kierkegaard's pseudonyms does, as one who cannot understand Abraham. And it is the nature of Abraham's faith that he cannot speak of it.

A Kierkegaardian negative apologetics thus contents itself with noting the problems of life apart from faith and insisting on the mysterious greatness of faith in the face of those who would like to reduce it to something more commonplace (one of Kierkegaard's pseudonyms notes that, in a world full of people dedicated to making tasks simpler, his goal is to make the task of faith more difficult[106]). Faith might come—by grace—or not. That alternative indeed generates "fear and trembling": absent grace, Kierkegaard's project leads from manageable if perhaps ultimately unsatisfactory forms of life to a state of complete despair. Human talk can at most preserve a space grace might fill, in a society anxious to fill every corner with busyness and consumerism, but no human effort can provide more than empty space, and empty space is terrifying.[107]

Levinas

The twentieth-century philosopher Emmanuel Levinas, whose influence pervades much contemporary French philosophy and who is increasingly

104. David Tracy, "Fragments," in *God, the Gift, and Postmodernism*, ed. John D. Caputo and Michael J. Scanlon (Bloomington: Indiana University Press, 1999), 172.

105. Kierkegaard, *Concluding Unscientific Postscript*, 109.

106. Kierkegaard, *Philosophical Fragments,* 155.

107. Blaise Pascal, *Pensées* #206; trans. W. F. Trotter (New York: Dutton, 1958), 61.

influential in English-speaking countries, undertook a task somewhat analogous to Kierkegaard's.[108] A Lithuanian Jew, Levinas saw the world of his parents destroyed by Communist revolution and later spent much of World War II in a Nazi concentration camp. His was a life that would make one suspicious of those who offer grand synthetic systems to make sense of the world. Systems, Levinas argued, try to fit everything into one "totality," and this can be done only through violence of one form or another to the particular elements within the systems, by cutting off or squashing bits and pieces so that they will fit into the package. "Infinity," however, breaks out of the possibility of totality—it just will not fit inside any proposed totalizing system. After all, one cannot finish up adding a column of numbers and get a final answer if one of the numbers is "infinity." So one way to describe Levinas's philosophy (or at least one stage of it) is as a championing of infinity over against totality.

Levinas found infinity first and foremost in the immediate impact of a human face. If, he believed, one really looks into the face of a beloved parent, a beggar on the street, an enemy in the gunsight, a neighbor in pain, one recognizes an *infinite* ethical demand that needs no theory to justify itself:[109] "The encounter with the other is the great experience, the grand event."[110] The immediacy of ethics was the starting point of Levinas's philosophy, and it was ethics that for him set human beings apart from all other beings:

> The fundamental trait of being is the preoccupation that each particular being has with his being. Plants, animals, all living things, strive to exist. For each one it is the struggle for life. And is not matter, in its essential hardness, closure and shock? In the human, lo and behold, the possible apparition of an ontological absurdity. The concern for the other breaches concern for the self. This is what I call holiness. Our humanity consists in being able to recognize this priority of the other.[111]

Humanness, Levinas believed, consists in our capacity to recognize in the face of the other an obligation that puts to the side the primacy of self-preservation that characterizes every other being.

108. "Of all modern European thinkers, Levinas perhaps is closest to Kierkegaard." Michael Weston, *Kierkegaard and Modern Continental Philosophy* (London: Routledge, 1994), 156.

109. Emmanuel Levinas, *Ethics and Infinity*, trans. Richard A. Cohen (Pittsburgh: Duquesne University Press, 1985), 86.

110. Emmanuel Levinas, *Is It Righteous to Be?* trans. and ed. Jill Robbins (Stanford: Stanford University Press, 2001), 234.

111. Ibid., 235.

Levinas could carry this sense of obligation to the other to almost masochistic levels. He repeatedly quoted Dostoevsky's line that we are all guilty, "and I more than the others,"[112] and cited Pascal's observations that the I is detestable and that an individual's place in the sun is the image and beginning of the usurpation of the whole earth.[113] There are no limits, it would seem, to the call to sacrifice oneself for the other: "I would say to the very end: I owe him everything."[114] Asked by an alarmed interviewer, "The *I* as ethical subject is responsible to everyone for everything; his responsibility is infinite. Doesn't that mean that the situation is intolerable . . . ?" Levinas firmly replied, "I don't know if the situation is intolerable. It is not what you would call agreeable, surely; it is not pleasant, but it is the good."[115]

Such good does occur from time to time. People risk their lives to save a stranger. The best among them often find it hard to give a "reason." "'How often should I forgive?' . . . 'Not seven times, but, I tell you, seventy times seven'" (Matt. 18:21–22). How to account for individuals, amid the horrors of Nazi concentration camps, the Soviet Gulag, the killing fields of Cambodia, who risked everything to provide a moment of comfort for a stranger they would likely never see again? When Philip Hallie probed the French villagers of Le Chambon, who saved so many Jews from the Nazis, for their motivations, they could only say in a puzzled way that these were human beings in danger of death, and saving them seemed, after all, the right thing to do.[116]

In Levinas's understanding of the Jewish tradition the law is a blessing rather than a burden.[117] We should be grateful to know things we can do in obedience to God. Even so, given the limitless demands Levinas thinks are made on us, one might welcome a greater possibility of forgiveness than he seems to have on offer. Is ethics simply the activity of noting our inevitable failure? Moreover, the problem of justice raises hard questions about how to sort out the competing infinite demands of various others: how can one fulfill the demands of one's aged parents and one's own children, to say nothing of needy strangers, if each

112. For instance, Levinas, *Ethics and Infinity*, 98.

113. Levinas, *Is It Righteous to Be?* 225. For a similar critique, see Milbank, *Being Reconciled*, 144.

114. Emmanuel Levinas, *Of God Who Comes to Mind*, trans. Bettina Bergo (Stanford: Stanford University Press, 1998), 83. David Ford wishes that Levinas had learned something like Jüngel's concept of joy. David F. Ford, *Self and Salvation* (Cambridge: Cambridge University Press, 1999), 74.

115. Emmanuel Levinas, *Entre Nous: On Thinking-of-the-Other*, trans. Michael B. Smith and Barbara Harshav (New York: Columbia University Press, 1998), 203.

116. Philip Hallie, *Lest Innocent Blood Be Shed* (New York: Harper & Row, 1979). As Levinas insisted, "The vocation of holiness is recognized by every human being as a value" (Levinas, *Is It Righteous to Be?* 220).

117. Levinas, *Is It Righteous to Be?* 229.

demand is infinite?[118] It is not clear that Levinas had answers to such questions.

One sort of answer would appeal to divine forgiveness. That was not the path Levinas took, but he did talk about God. He wrote, "I am not afraid of the word God, which appears quite often in my essays."[119] But he resisted a God who would return thought to system, a God who would undercut the primordial appeal of the other's face by setting up rules or standing atop a hierarchy that explained *why* we should do good to the other.[120]

More than that, in the aftermath of Auschwitz, he searched for a way to continue to believe in God without believing in theodicy or trusting in a divine promise.[121] God as any sort of entity distinguishable from the ethical demands of the other therefore always made him nervous. His path lay in sticking firmly to the infinite call of the human face: "The dimension of the divine opens forth from the human face. . . . It is our relations with men . . . that give theological concepts their only signification."[122]

Is it possible, Levinas wondered, to think about God without fitting God into our lists of the things in the universe—and therefore speaking of something that is no longer God but an idol? Theology and philosophy (not least ontology, the part of philosophy dealing with "being"), he argued, have brought God

> into the course of being, while the God of the Bible signifies in an unlikely manner the beyond of being, or transcendence. That is, the God of the Bible signifies without analogy to an idea subject to *criteria*, without analogy to an idea exposed to the summons to show itself true or false. And it is not by accident that the history of Western philosophy has been a destruction of transcendence. Rational theology, fundamentally ontological, endeavors to accommodate transcendence within the domain of being by expressing it with adverbs of height applied to the verb "to be." God is said to exist eminently or *par excellence*. But does the height, or the height above all height, which is thus expressed, still depend on ontology?[123]

118. See Levinas, *Entre Nous*, 21, 103–4.
119. Levinas, *Ethics and Infinity*, 105.
120. Levinas, *Of God Who Comes to Mind*, 77.
121. See Levinas, *Entre Nous*, 100, 206.
122. Emmanuel Levinas, *Totality and Infinity*, trans. Alphonso Lingis (Pittsburgh: Duquesne University Press, 1969), 78–79.
123. Levinas, *Of God Who Comes to Mind*, 56.

If we start with "being" as a general category and seek to include God as specified by various adjectives or adverbs, we will inevitably fall short of God's radical otherness. Levinas therefore searched for another way, one in which

> God is pulled out of objectivity, out of presence and out of being. He is neither object nor interlocutor. His absolute remoteness, his transcendence, turns into my responsibility—the non-erotic *par excellence*—for the other. And it is from the analysis just carried out that God is not simply the "first other," or the "other *par excellence*," or the "absolutely other," but other than the other, other otherwise, and other with an alterity prior to the alterity of the other, prior to the ethical obligation to the other and different from every neighbor, transcendent to the point of absence, to the point of his possible confusion with the agitation of the *there is* [*il y a*]. This is the confusion wherein substitution for the neighbor gains in disinterestedness, that is, in nobility; wherein the transcendence of the Infinite thereby likewise arises in glory.[124]

As Jesus says in the Gospel, "In as much as you do it to the least of these, my brothers and sisters, you do it to me" (Matt. 25:40). "When I speak to a Christian," Levinas once remarked, "I always quote Matthew 25; the relation to God is presented there as a relation to another person. It is not a metaphor: in the other, there is a real presence of God."[125] The other is situated "in a dimension of height and of abasement—glorious abasement; he has the face of the poor, the stranger, the widow and the orphan, and, at the same time, of the master called to invest and justify my freedom."[126] The response to God is the ethical obligation to the neighbor.

Did the human other, for Levinas, thus simply *become* God? He wanted to preserve God's *radical* transcendence by refusing to say *anything* about anything that might lie behind the face of the other ("his transcendence *turns into* my responsibility . . . for the other"). But if we deny God "being" and insist that "theology begins in the face of the

124. Ibid., 69. The very common French expression *il y a*, usually translated "there is" (as in "There is a car blocking the driveway"), would literally mean "It (or he) has there." But the "it" has no referent, nothing that "has" this state of affairs. Levinas is thus exploring the possible meaning of this "it" that "has" so much of reality but is not itself an entity.

125. Levinas, *Entre Nous*, 110. Perhaps Derrida made him nervous about "presence." In other works, Levinas preferred to refer to the "trace" constituted in "the beyond from which a face comes." Emmanuel Levinas, "The Trace of the Other," in *Deconstruction in Context: Literature and Philosophy*, ed. Mark C. Taylor (Chicago: University of Chicago Press, 1986), 355.

126. Levinas, *Totality and Infinity*, 251.

neighbor" and "the divinity of God is played out in the human,"[127] if we see the numinous *only* "in the face of the neighbor,"[128] then do we have a radically transcendent God, or have we simply replaced God with other human beings?[129] It seems at this point, Jean-Luc Marion has written, "that Levinas has not only admitted an ambiguity but knowingly emphasized it. For the face which appeals can be assigned equally to the Other or to God."[130]

Thus from one side Merold Westphal worries that Levinas has produced a "theology without God. If God is only 'the *he* in the depth of the you,' does this mean that God is not a distinct personal being, but rather the depth dimension of the human person?"[131] From the other side, Jacques Derrida, who admired Levinas immensely, was nevertheless concerned that his whole project rested on a too-precarious "theological context,"[132] held up only "by means of the enigma, the ambiguity of uncertain and precarious epiphanies."[133] We are back to the twin dangers I mentioned at the beginning of this section: idolatry on the one hand, and pure secularism modified by a little poetry on the other.

I worry that Levinas sometimes too nearly simply identified God and the human other, and regret that he was so unwilling to consider any other context for talk of God *except* the ethical. Still, I admire his effort to find a middle ground between the idolatry that defines God as a particular object and the secularity that dismisses God-talk altogether. Levinas wrote, he said, "after the death of a certain god inhabiting the world behind the scenes"[134] (the Wizard of Oz!). He rejected a God who is one more thing in the world, never mind how important or unusual a thing. He therefore spoke of a God who cannot be the object of speech,[135] who in his "absolute remoteness" is "neither an object nor an interlocutor."[136] Yet the infinite ethical demand in the face of the

127. Levinas, *Is It Righteous to Be?* 236.

128. Levinas, *Of God Who Comes to Mind*, 73.

129. For a similar critique of Luce Irigaray on this point see Serene Jones, "This God Which Is Not One," in *Transfigurations*, ed. C. W. Maggie Kim, Susan M. St. Ville, and Susan M. Simonaitis (Minneapolis: Fortress, 1993), 125, 137–38.

130. Jean-Luc Marion, "The Voice without Name," in *The Face of the Other and the Trace of God*, ed. Jeffrey Bloechl (New York: Fordham University Press, 2000), 227.

131. Merold Westphal, "Commanded Love and Divine Transcendence in Levinas and Kierkegaard," in *Face of the Other*, ed. Bloechl, 216.

132. Jacques Derrida, *Writing and Difference*, trans. Alan Bass (Chicago: University of Chicago Press, 1978), 103.

133. Jacques Derrida, "At This Very Moment in This Work Here I Am," trans. Ruben Berezdivin, in *A Derrida Reader: Between the Blinds*, ed. Peggy Kamuf (New York: Columbia University Press, 1991), 436.

134. Emmanuel Levinas, *Otherwise than Being*, trans. Alphonso Lingis (The Hague: Martinus Nijhoff, 1981), 300.

135. Ibid., 12.

136. Emmanuel Levinas, "God and Philosophy," in *Collected Philosophical Papers*, trans. Alphonso Lingis (The Hague: Martinus Nijhoff, 1987), 165.

other raises the question of something other than the human other, albeit something beyond speech or objectification. Once we have said that the other human being poses an infinite question of ethical responsibility, and that this infinity, like all forms of infinity utterly resistant to totalizing systems, points somehow beyond the other human being without our being able to specify an object to which it points, is there any more to say? But is that enough?

Wittgenstein

In his *Tractatus Logico-Philosophicus* Ludwig Wittgenstein offered another approach to talk of God. Earlier, as an Austrian soldier fighting in World War I, Wittgenstein had brooded over the possibility of talking about God and the meaning of life:

> What do I know about God and the purpose of life?
> I know that this world exists. . . .
> That something about it is problematic, which we call its meaning.
>
> That this meaning does not lie in it but outside it. . . .
> The meaning of life, i.e. the meaning of the world, we can call God.[137]

Wittgenstein had become disillusioned with the artificiality and phoniness of Viennese talk about life and God—the pompous circumlocutions of imperial bureaucracy, the public moral face belied in private, the traditional language of religion repeated without apparent belief—talk that must have seemed all the more pointless to one who had seen combat and now anticipated the collapse of the dual monarchy.[138] Trained initially as an engineer, he looked for ways of getting rid of this fuzzy chatter. Language, he thought, could picture the world's states of affairs and display the laws of logic—and that was all it could do. *The world that language can describe* has no place for purpose, value, or God.

> 6.41 The sense [*Sinn*] of the world must lie outside the world. In the world everything is as it is, and everything happens as it does

137. Ludwig Wittgenstein, *Notebooks 1914–16*, trans. G. E. M. Anscombe (Oxford: Blackwell, 1961), 72e-73e, entry for 11.6.16.

138. See Alan Janik and Stephen Toulmin, *Wittgenstein's Vienna* (New York: Simon & Schuster, 1973).

> happen: *in* it no value exists—and if it did exist, it would have no value.
>
> If there is any value that does have value, it must lie outside the whole sphere of what happens and is the case. . . .
>
> It must lie outside the world.
>
> 6.42 And so it is impossible for there to be propositions of ethics.
>
> Propositions can express nothing that is higher.[139]

Many of Wittgenstein's interpreters, from Bertrand Russell to the logical positivists, took such comments as dismissive of everything beyond what could be said clearly.[140] The logical positivists, who believed that only definitions, logical laws, and statements of empirical fact were meaningful, saw Wittgenstein as one of their own, a philosopher interested only in the language of science who wrote some rather puzzling remarks at the end of his book that no one needed to take very seriously. Even the finest Wittgenstein scholars often dismiss the *Tractatus*'s admittedly cryptic concluding remarks as, in David Pears's phrase, "a baffling doctrine bafflingly presented":[141]

> 6.432 *How* things are in the world is a matter of complete indifference for what is higher. God does not reveal himself *in* the world. . . .
>
> 6.44 It is not *how* things are in the world that is mystical, but *that* it exists.
>
> 6.45 To view the world *sub specie aeterni* [under the category of eternity] is to view it as a whole—a limited whole.
>
> Feeling the world as a limited whole—it is this that is mystical.[142]

For Wittgenstein, though, his concluding remarks on what could not be said were precisely the most important. He had earlier written in his notebooks:

> To believe in a God means to understand the question about the meaning of life.

139. Ludwig Wittgenstein, *Tractatus Logico-Philosophicus*, trans. D. F. Pears and B. F. McGuinness (New York: Humanities Press, 1961), 145.

140. See Russell's introduction to the *Tractatus*, xxi; and Otto Neurath's comment, "One should indeed be silent, but not *about* anything." (In other words, for Neurath there is nothing beyond the realm of the things of which we can speak.) Otto Neurath, "Sociology and Pluralism," in *Logical Positivism*, ed. A. J. Ayer (Glencoe, Ill.: Free Press, 1959), 284.

141. David Pears, *The False Prison* (Oxford: Clarendon, 1987), 143.

142. Wittgenstein, *Tractatus Logico-Philosophicus*, 149.

> To believe in a God means to see that the facts of the world are not the end of the matter.
>
> To believe in God means to see that life has a meaning.[143]

But in the famous final words of the *Tractatus*:

> 7 What we cannot speak about we must pass over in silence.[144]

Life seriously led poses questions whose answers lie beyond language's reach, questions that can be answered only in the living. But Wittgenstein, like Kierkegaard and Levinas, recognized how impoverished life would be absent such questions. The *Tractatus*, he wrote to his friend Paul Engelmann, is a book about ethics.[145] That is, it was what cannot be said that was his real concern. As he wrote to the editor Ludwig von Ficker,

> My work consists of two parts: the one presented here plus all that I have *not* written. And it is precisely this second part that is the important one. My book draws limits to the sphere of the ethical from the inside as it were, and I am convinced that this is the ONLY *rigorous* way of drawing those limits. In short, I believe that where *many* others today are just *gassing*, I have managed in my book to put everything firmly into place by being silent about it.[146]

Why is there something rather than nothing? Why this world rather than a very different one? Is there a purpose to things? Is there a meaning to good and evil, right and wrong, beyond simply accepting the values of a particular culture? Human beings find themselves, puzzled, asking such questions about what Aquinas called "the beginning and end of all things."[147] Language provides no way of answering, or even of meaningfully defining, such questions, but they do not on that account dissolve.

143. Wittgenstein, *Notebooks 1914–16*, 74e, entry for 8.7.16.

144. Wittgenstein, *Tractatus Logico-Philosophicus*, 151. "I know nothing of religion, but there is surely something right in the concept of a God and of an afterlife—only something quite different from what we are capable of imagining." Wittgenstein to Heinrich Groag, sometime in 1916, quoted in Brian McGuinness, *Wittgenstein: A Life: Young Ludwig* (Berkeley: University of California Press, 1988), 255–56.

145. Paul Engelman, *Letters from Ludwig Wittgenstein, with a Memoir*, trans. L. Furtmüller (New York: Horizon, 1968), 97. "Positivism holds—and this is its essence—that what we can speak about is all that matters in life. Whereas Wittgenstein passionately believes that all that really matters in human life is precisely what, in his view, we must be silent about." Ibid.

146. Wittgenstein to Ludwig von Ficker, 22 November 1919, quoted in McGuinness, *Young Ludwig*, 288.

147. Aquinas, *Summa Theologica* 1a.2 pref.; 11.

Nothing Wittgenstein wrote later, I think, fundamentally changed his views on this. More than twenty years after writing the *Tractatus*, he could still say, "The results of philosophy are the uncovering of one or another piece of plain nonsense *and* of bumps that the understanding has got by running its head up against the limits of language."[148] But the bumps are significant. Speaking in late 1929 to the puzzled positivists of the Vienna Circle, Wittgenstein tried to explain: "Man feels the urge to run up against the limits of language. . . . Kierkegaard too saw that there is this running up against something and he referred to it in a fairly similar way (as running up against paradox). . . . But the inclination, the running up against something, *indicates something*."[149] In his later work, already emerging in 1929 but fully developed in the posthumously published *Philosophical Investigations*, Wittgenstein grew more tolerant of things he would have called "nonsense" in the *Tractatus*, less austere in his insistence on silence. He now argued that language can have many uses, to be understood in the contexts of the forms of life in which they occur. Still, the idea that something important lies beyond the limits of language remained.

In the lecture originally given in Cambridge that he was discussing with the Vienna Circle in the passage just quoted, he talked about experiences like that of wondering at the existence of the world ("how extraordinary that anything should exist"), that of feeling *absolutely* safe, or that of feeling guilty in a way that is sometimes "described by the phrase that God disapproves of our conduct."[150] Analyzed in terms of the ordinary meanings of words, he said, the descriptions we give of such expressions are nonsense. We are therefore tempted to try to find some more arcane analysis that would really explain them, but

> when this is urged against me I at once see clearly, as it were in a flash of light, not only that no description that I can think of would do to describe what I mean by absolute value, but that I would reject every significant description that anybody could possibly suggest, *ab initio* [from the start], on the ground of its significance. That is to say: I see now that these nonsensical expressions were not nonsensical because I had not yet found the correct expressions, but that their nonsensicality was their very essence. For all I wanted to

148. Ludwig Wittgenstein, *Philosophical Investigations* #119; trans. G. E. M. Anscombe, 2nd ed. (repr. Oxford: Blackwell, 1997), 48e, emphasis added.

149. Ludwig Wittgenstein, December 30, 1929, in Waismann, *Wittgenstein and the Vienna Circle*, 68–69.

150. Ludwig Wittgenstein, "A Lecture on Ethics," *Philosophical Occasions 1912–1951* (Indianapolis: Hackett, 1993), 41–42. Lecture originally given November 17, 1929.

> do with them was just *to go beyond* the world and that is to say beyond significant language. My whole tendency and I believe the tendency of all men who ever tried to write or talk Ethics or Religion was to run against the boundaries of language.[151]

But running up against the limits of language *indicates something.*

Between Idolatry and Secularity

I have argued that it was a characteristically modern project to try to come up with definitive answers, about God as well as everything else, as part of rationally defensible philosophical or scientific systems, and that that project fell into inevitable contradiction as it tried to make that which lies beyond all things one of the entities in our world. Our contemporary culture too often wants to dismiss such questions as silly or irrelevant and get on with the business of consumerism, a strategy, we are learning, that leads to empty despair. Some of the best postmodern thinkers rightly try to think about these questions and so keep the rumors of something beyond secularity alive, yet without allowing their thinking to fall into any system, without proposing answers that involve one more thing or set of things in the world we understand, and thus falling into the worship of an idol.

Levinas found in the face of another human being an infinite demand that deconstructed all totalities, though he then could not quite decide whether that infinite demand pointed beyond the other human being. Though he kept playing at hints of something more, he at least teetered on the edge of falling into a radical secularity in which there is nothing beyond human ethics. Wittgenstein found himself haunted by questions that by his own rules it made no sense to ask. Answering the questions in clear language would give us idols; abandoning them would leave us with flat secularity. Wittgenstein's interpreters continue to debate where he ended up.[152] Kierkegaard gets us further, I think, precisely because there is always a Christian author behind his various pseudonyms. He let his pseudonyms show from the inside the unsatisfactory character of various forms of life, without then claiming to offer any *argument* for a kind a religiousness that could

151. Ibid., 44.
152. For a more critical interpretation, see Marion, *Idol and Distance*, 193.

come only by revelation. He left us, one might say, with an empty space into which God's revelation might enter.

These philosophers do not offer us "arguments for the existence of God," but hints and guesses that could serve in our time as analogues to what the "five ways," properly understood, provided for Aquinas, posing humanly unanswerable questions that keep us away from a flattened secularity. Like the doorkeeper in Kafka's parable, they keep the door open so that we can see some sort of radiance within—but nothing more.[153]

In the modern age, epistemology, the theory of how we know, has generally taken center stage in philosophical discussion. In the ancient world metaphysics, the account of what exists, took that center place. Modern (and postmodern) thought therefore characteristically pushes its limits epistemologically: is there something so beyond what we can know that we cannot even clearly formulate questions about it? In the ancient world of the early church, the questions pushed to the limits had to do with what exists: is there an entity so transcendent as to dwell altogether beyond any possibility of connection with us? Many philosophies and theologies of that age, from Neoplatonism to Gnosticism, dealt with that issue by positing all sorts of intervening beings. The One, the Good, or whatever name one gave to that highest mystery, could only relate to something a bit less high, which in turn related to something else . . . and so on, until one came to a being so minimally transcendent that it could create a world or interact with human beings.

One of the great insights behind the doctrine of the Trinity was that such mediation does not work. No matter how many rungs are in the ladder, the topmost rung is still on the ladder, and therefore not an utterly transcendent mystery. The only way we can be connected with the utterly transcendent is if it/he/she reaches out to us in love, overcoming all the intervening levels in one act of condescension. That is what happens in Jesus Christ, and explaining the logic of how that can be led Christian theologians to the Trinity.[154]

The issues discussed in this chapter invite in our time an analogous move in an epistemological mode. The world of our experience keeps pushing uncomfortably against its borders, but any effort on our part to see beyond those borders gets us into epistemological trouble—either the questions melt away or we answer them in ways that leave us

153. Franz Kafka, *The Trial*, trans. Willa and Edwin Muir (New York: Modern Library, 1957), 267–76.
154. See Khaled Anatolios, *Athanasius* (London: Routledge, 1998), 113.

holding onto idols within our control. In the face of certain kinds of questions we do not know how to answer and indeed scarcely know how to pose, we can come to knowledge only if it is revealed to us. And the logic of such revelation leads us, likewise, to the Trinity—that will be the argument of the rest of this book.

Great religious texts from many traditions keep the questions alive while rejecting all our answers, in a dialectic that never comes to closure. Like Jacob at the Jabbok, we see God only in nights of wrestling with unknown strangers, and we go away limping.[155] Nothing to be captured in the clear light of day. No marching forward. No answer, really, to the puzzling question of why we thought the stranger was God and felt compelled to worship. Again and again in Upanishadic dialogues the teacher reminds the student, "Now therefore there is the teaching, not this, not this."[156] Apophatic texts from the *Tao Te Ching* to Plotinus offer similar remarks.

Biblical texts claim to tell us more. It is God's self-revelation, and that alone, that can get us beyond fumbling, unanswered questions, beyond, "Not this, not this."[157] "Every phenomenon of revelation," Marion has written, "would imply the radical anonymity of that which appeals."[158] The one with whom Jacob wrestles never gives a name. We take the first step to controlling someone if we know their name, and a "revelation" we can control comes from an idol of our own making. As Marion puts it, "Strictly speaking, an appeal which would say its name would no longer appeal, but instead presents the one who appeals, delivering it back to the simple visibility of an occupant of the world, stifling the world with the evidence of a spectacle."[159] If God appeared as a man six yards tall, or as "a very rare and tremendously large green bird, with a red beak, . . . perhaps even whistling in an unheard of manner," Kierkegaard wrote, this would render *faith* impossible.[160] We would simply have to account for one more object in the world.

155. I am paraphrasing a sermon of my late colleague Eric Dean.

156. *Bṛhad-āraṇyaka Upaniṣad* 2.3.6, in *The Principal Upaniṣads*, trans. S. Radhakrishnan (New York: Harper & Brothers, 1953), 194. See also 3.9.26 (243); 4.2.4 (254); 4.4.22 (279); 4.5.15 (286).

157. Eric Voegelin contrasts the Upanishads with the Abrahamic traditions, as represented by the "Apocalypse of Abraham," an Essene text probably from the first century. Like the Upanishads, the Apocalypse runs through a list of things that prove not to be the Ultimate. But, rather than ending there, it continues with the prayer "May God reveal Himself through Himself," in response to which, "The voice of a mighty-one fell from heaven in a cloudburst of fire and called: 'Abraham! Abraham! . . . You seek the God of gods, the Creator, in the mind of your heart. I am He!'" Eric Voegelin, *Order and History*, vol. 4: *The Ecumenic Age* (Baton Rouge: Louisiana State University Press, 1974), 323.

158. Jean-Luc Marion, "The Voice without Name," in *Face of the Other*, ed. Bloechl, 232.

159. Ibid., 235.

160. Kierkegaard, *Concluding Unscientific Postscript*, 219–20.

It is different when God comes among us as an ordinary human being, in the form of a servant. Nothing tempts us to say that we now understand God, yet God has been present among us. So, at the transfiguration, the apostles see a dazzling spectacle, but the voice from heaven calls them not to attend to the vision but to listen to the Son. Then all distinctive spectacle vanishes. "Suddenly when they looked around, they saw no one with them any more, but only Jesus" (Mark 9:8).

2

The Word Made Flesh

If belief is absolutely necessary, let it be in . . . a religion out of joint, fuming, subterranean, without an end. Like a novel, not like a theology.

—Umberto Eco[1]

Christ came to introduce a break with logic
That made all other outrage seem as child's play:
The Mercy on the Sin against the Sermon.
Strange no one ever thought of it before Him.
'Twas lovely and its origin was love.

—Robert Frost[2]

Variation on an old joke: asked for directions to somewhere, the local yokel starts and stops several times, gets more and more confused, and finally declares, "You can't get there from here." So with respect to God: no matter how impressive the argument, the religious experience, the tradition, you can't get there from here. Indeed, where you get, if you think you have gotten to God by your own efforts, is always an idol. But here is the good news of Christian faith: we do not need to try to find our way to God, for in Jesus Christ *God* has come to *us*. God, Calvin wrote, "is *invisible* and that not merely to the eyes of the body, but also to human understanding."[3] But "It is not necessary for us to mount up on high to inquire about what must be hidden from us at this moment. For God lowers himself to us. He shows us only in his Son—as though he says, 'Here I am. Contemplate me.'"[4] Luther makes much the same point: "Those who want to ascend advantageously to the love and knowledge of God should abandon the human metaphysical rules concerning knowledge of the divinity and apply themselves first to the humanity of Christ. For it is exceedingly godless temerity,

1. Umberto Eco, *Foucault's Pendulum*, trans. William Weaver (New York: Harcourt Brace Jovanovich, 1989), 528.

2. Robert Frost, "A Masque of Mercy," in *The Poetry of Robert Frost*, ed. Edward Connery Lathem (New York: Henry Holt, 1979), 511.

3. John Calvin, *Commentary on the Epistle to the Colossians* (on Col. 1:15), trans. William Pringle, *Calvin's Commentaries* 21 (repr. Grand Rapids: Baker, 1989), 149–50, translation altered.

4. John Calvin, *Congregation on Eternal Election*, in Philip C. Holtrop, *The Bolsec Controversy on Predestination, from 1551 to 1555* (Lewiston, N.Y.: Edwin Mellen, 1993), vol. 1, book 2, 717.

where God has humiliated Himself in order to become recognizable, to seek for oneself another way."[5]

Jesus Christ is "the image of the invisible God" (Col. 1:15), "the reflection of God's glory and the exact imprint of God's very being" (Heb. 1:3). Seeing him, we see God. Yet this self-revelation is a *hidden* revelation—hidden not to make things harder, but because we could not bear it otherwise.[6] Jesus' divinity was accessible only to the eyes of faith. God could, I suppose, have appeared among us as a seventy-foot high angel with glowing wings or Kierkegaard's "very rare and tremendously large green bird" rather than a wandering Jewish teacher. Such a vision would of course still not constitute seeing God; indeed it might lead us astray, tempting us to think that this quite remarkable phenomenon showed us what God looks like.

In Jesus of Nazareth, however, we encounter God *in human form*—no danger of thinking that, seeing him, we might think we could now describe God. According to orthodox christological doctrine, there is one *person*, Jesus Christ—one agent who does and suffers things. But that *person* has two *natures*, human and divine. No matter how closely we watch him, we can never see divinity. (What would it look like?!) But this one person, in addition to doing and suffering human things like being born, walking around, and dying, also does divine things like being God among us, being an appropriate object of worship, and accomplishing our salvation. In encountering him, we encounter God. Now if God's primary characteristic were almighty power, then this would be impossible: the crucified rabbi could not be the self-revelation of God. But if God is, first of all, love, then, odd as it might seem, God is *most* God in coming to us in the form of a servant for the sake of our salvation.[7] Starting with love, we can then even see what Gregory of Nyssa said about God's power: "God's transcendent power is not so much displayed in the vastness of the heavens or the luster of the stars or the orderly arrangement of the universe or his perpetual oversight of it, as in his condescension to our weak nature."[8] God is most powerful in being able even to become a servant.

5. Martin Luther, *Lectures on Hebrews* (on Heb. 1:2), trans. Walter A. Hanson, Luther's Works 29 (St. Louis: Concordia, 1968), 111, translation altered.

6. See Bonaventure, *The Soul's Journey into God* 7.1, in *Bonaventure*, trans. Ewert Cousins (Mahwah, N.J.: Paulist Press, 1978), 110–11.

7. Karl Barth, *Church Dogmatics*, IV/1, trans. G. W. Bromiley (Edinburgh: T. & T. Clark, 1956), 159.

8. Gregory of Nyssa, *An Address on Religious Instruction* 24, trans. Cyril C. Richardson, in *Christology of the Later Fathers*, ed. E. R. Hardy, Library of Christian Classics (Philadelphia: Westminster, 1954), 301.

We encounter this God-become-servant, however, only as mediated by the biblical texts. We have no photographs or other direct access, but only these stories. Yet, given the paradoxical character of the hidden revelation, this does not put us at a disadvantage over Jesus' contemporaries. Kierkegaard imagined a contemporary, even one who "had in his service a hundred secret agents who spied upon that teacher and with whom he conferred every night, so that he had a dossier on that teacher down to the slightest particular." Even so, he could say only, "I ate and drank in his presence; that teacher taught in our streets; I saw him many times; he was an unimpressive man of humble birth, and only a few individuals believed there was anything extraordinary about him, something I certainly was unable to discover, even though when it comes down to it I was just as contemporary with him as anyone."[9] God's presence remained a hidden presence.

But, one might protest, there were miracles, there was a resurrection. Whatever we make of healings and other such stories, however, Jesus' contemporaries would have seen them as the characteristic acts of wandering human wonder-workers. We even have references to several figures in Jesus' time who performed such wonders, and no one thought of them as God incarnate.[10] In the Gospels, he tells the witnesses of his miracles to remain silent, or the miracles themselves produce an ambiguous reaction. His parables are misunderstood. Jesus is poor, and at the end he seems abandoned by God—a strange sort of divine self-revelation.[11] Resurrection is a different matter, to which I will return in a few pages—for the moment it is enough to note how enigmatic are the Gospel accounts of it.

Starting from the conviction that we know God through God's hidden revelation in Jesus Christ, as known through the Bible, this chapter looks at three sorts of questions. First, focusing particularly on the Gospels, what sort of text are they, and how do they convey what they have to tell us about who Jesus was and is? Second, why should we confine ourselves to the texts of the Bible, and what do the Gospels and Paul's Letters particularly have to tell us about Jesus? Third, what is the idea of Christ that we get from these texts, both absolutely one with God and yet the Son separated from the Father?

9. Søren Kierkegaard, *Philosophical Fragments*, trans. Howard V. Hong and Edna H. Hong (Princeton: Princeton University Press, 1985), 60, 67.

10. See, for instance, the stories of Honi the Circle Drawer and Hanina ben Dosa in John Dominic Crossan, *The Historical Jesus* (San Francisco: HarperSanFrancisco, 1991), 142–56.

11. See Hans Urs von Balthasar, *The Glory of the Lord*, vol. 7: *Theology: The New Covenant*, ed. John Riches, trans. Brian McNeil (San Francisco: Ignatius, 1991), 202, 348.

STORIES OF JESUS, TELL THEM TO ME

In sum, Christians say, if you want to know about God, you need to know about Jesus, and, if you want to know about Jesus, you need to read some Bible stories: first stories about Jesus himself, then stories about God's covenant history with Israel and about the early church.[12] The stories about Jesus provide a kind of center around which we can interpret the other stories we find in the Bible,[13] and the whole collection of biblical stories helps us understand all the other stories in the world. They are, H. Richard Niebuhr once wrote, like those moments in the life of a family or group of friends when a particular remark or action reveals an individual's character and opens up a new understanding of the past and new expectations for the future.[14] Such disclosures occur in two ways—biblical stories provide exemplary models for thinking about other stories, and they provide the framework of one big story within which we can locate all the other stories we tell.[15]

Of course, the Bible contains more than stories—hymns, sermons, theological essays, laments, laws, and prophecies—and the stories themselves are diverse enough that thinking of them as in any sense a single whole is no easy task. It is a complex collection of books, and no one category can do it justice.[16] Nevertheless, the category of "story" or "narrative" does seem to have a certain priority: it seems more important to say, of each of the other biblical genres, that they derive part of their meaning from their relation to an overarching story than the other way round.[17] Likewise, many of the individual biblical stories resist efforts to fit them too neatly into overarching wholes, but they are gen-

12. Our talk about God must begin, Jüngel argues, with the humanity of God because it is there that God is revealed. But humanity means existence in time and history, and time and history can be spoken about in narration. Therefore, "If thinking wants to think God, then it must endeavor to tell stories." Eberhard Jüngel, *God as the Mystery of the World*, trans. Darrell L. Guder (Grand Rapids: Eerdmans, 1983), 303.

13. "The entire revelation concerning salvation is ordered to this manifestation of the Word, as to a central point—in a forward direction in the apostles and in the whole history of the Church to the end of time, in a backward direction in the Old Testament revelation in word and history, backward to the law and the prophets and even to the creation; for God upholds all things by the word of his power (Heb. 1:3), creates all things through, for and by his Word." Hans Urs von Balthasar, *Explorations in Theology*, vol. 1: *The Word Made Flesh*, trans. A. V. Littledale (San Francisco: Ignatius, 1989), 11.

14. H. Richard Niebuhr, *The Meaning of Revelation* (New York: Macmillan, 1960), 94.

15. George A. Lindbeck, *The Nature of Doctrine* (Philadelphia: Westminster, 1984), 117.

16. Paul Ricoeur, *Figuring the Sacred*, trans. David Pellauer (Minneapolis: Fortress, 1995), 224.

17. "The gospel is and should be nothing other than a chronicle, a story, a narrative about Christ." Martin Luther, "A Brief Instruction on What to Look for and Expect in the Gospels," trans. E. Theodore Bachmann, in *Word and Sacrament*, vol. 1, ed. E. Theodore Bachmann, Luther's Works 35 (Philadelphia: Muhlenberg, 1960), 117. "Christians learn the identity of God by learning the identity of Jesus as the Christ. This identity Christians learn principally through the history-like, realistic passion narratives of the four gospels." David Tracy, *On Naming the Present* (Maryknoll, N.Y.: Orbis, 1994), 37.

erally connected in a kind of chronology that runs from creation to eschaton and invites their readers to think about how they fit together.

In the case of most of Scripture, there is no way for us to get behind these stories. From nonbiblical sources (other writings, archeological remains, etc.) we can learn a good bit about Jesus' historical and cultural context, for instance, but virtually nothing about *him*. The things we might most want to know about Jesus—his motivations, his sense of the central purpose of his life—are among the hardest things for historians to determine. If the Gospels are fundamentally misleading about his identity, then he turns out to be one of many historical figures about whom we just do not know very much.

What could provide better evidence of this than the radically different conclusions provided by scholars engaged in the "quest of the historical Jesus"? John Dominic Crossan describes Jesus as a combination of radical peasant and Cynic philosopher. Marcus Borg sees him as a "Spirit person," who experienced visions that gave him a special intimacy with God. For John Meier, he was a "marginal Jew," Jewish in cultural context but challenging the power structure of his society from its edges. E. P. Sanders believes he was an eschatological prophet, announcing the imminent end of the world. N. T. Wright thinks that the important imminent event that Jesus was anticipating was the destruction of the temple in Jerusalem, which actually happened within a generation of his death.[18] The confidence of each in his conclusions seems oddly unshaken by the conclusions of the others, but, given their diversity and the passion and intelligence of every author, it is hard for an objective reader to be convinced that any one historical reconstruction is clearly correct.

We learn all sorts of valuable information about Jesus and his time through historical research, but precisely when we want to learn about who Jesus was, the enterprise of penetrating behind the New Testament to find some more "historical" Jesus seems least successful. From a Christian perspective, part of the problem is that a person's relation to God (not how they understand their relation, but the relation itself) is something about which historians' research can in principle tell us nothing. If it should be the case, therefore, that his relation with God was central to Jesus' identity, historical research cannot at the core of things help us understand him.[19] So we come back to four stories called

18. Crossan, *Historical Jesus*; Marcus Borg, *Jesus: A New Vision* (San Francisco: Harper & Row, 1987); John Meier, *A Marginal Jew*, 3 vols. (New York: Doubleday, 1991–2001); N. T. Wright, *Jesus and the Victory of God* (Minneapolis: Fortress, 1996).

19. David H. Kelsey, *Imagining Redemption* (Louisville: Westminster John Knox, 2005), 46.

the Gospels, which narrate the identity of Jesus as determined by his relation to the one he calls his Father. Do they tell us the truth about Jesus? Before we can answer that, we have to understand what kind of truth telling they have to offer.

Suppose I start to tell you a story: "A dog walked into a bar, sat down, and ordered a gin and tonic. . . ." If you rush out eagerly and dead serious to tell others that I have found a dog who not only talks but orders mixed drinks, you are not faithfully reporting me. You have misunderstood me—I meant to be telling a joke. Conversely, if I see a car crash and rush into the room yelling, "Call an ambulance; there's been an accident," you misunderstand me if you say, "Not bad," and assume I was trying out a dramatic sketch.

Before we can even ask about the truth or falsity of stories people tell, in other words, we need to understand what they mean, and that involves, among other things, understanding the *kind* of story they are telling. The beginnings and endings of stories often help particularly in this regard. Most contemporary Americans would recognize my dog story as an intended joke from the first few words. When John Bunyan ends part 1 of *Pilgrim's Progress* with "So I awoke, and behold it was a dream,"[20] we understand differently what has gone before.

I propose that the four canonical Gospels (the ones in the New Testament) are *history-like witnesses to truths both historical and transcendent.* This section and the next attempt to explain the meaning of that cumbersome phrase, drawing primarily from the Gospels' beginnings and endings to do so. It seems helpful to begin by contrasting with some things the Gospels are not: they are not works of fiction, not myths, and not the usual form of modern history.

Not works of fiction. A novel, for example, operates in its own secondary world, usually designed to seem plausible in the events it narrates, perhaps connected to our world by the insights it offers into human character, but not consistently recounting events that have happened in the same real world in which we live. A historical novel may use some characters and events from our world, but at some point it deliberately veers off in a "fictional" direction—that is the point of the exercise.

The Gospels are different. They refer to characters on the grand stage of history well known to many of their first readers: Herod, Pontius Pilate, Quirinius the governor of Syria. But so might a historical

20. John Bunyan, *The Pilgrim's Progress* (London: Penguin, 1965), 142.

novel. Something more, however, happens in the Gospels. Particularly in their endings, they reach out to include their readers in their world.[21] John is the clearest case. At the end of John 20 (some think the original end of the Gospel), the narrator steps out of the narrative frame and declares that "these things are written . . . so that you may come to believe that Jesus is the Messiah, the Son of God, and that through believing you may have life in his name" (John 20:31). Readers become figures in the world of the story, invited to belief.

Even more dramatically, the end of chapter 21 announces that the beloved disciple "is the disciple who is testifying to these things and has written them, and we know that his testimony is true" (John 21:24)—here not only an author who testifies to the truth of the narrative but that "we," a community that knows his testimony is true. The great Johannine scholar Raymond Brown notes how, until this point, the world of the Gospel has been self-contained, as if we were in a darkened auditorium watching a play. "But now, as the curtain is about to fall on the stage drama, the lights in the theater are suddenly turned on. Jesus shifts his attention from the disciples on the stage to the audience that has become visible and makes clear that his ultimate concern is for them—those who have come to believe in him through the word of his disciples."[22]

Mark's narrative strategy is almost exactly the opposite of John's, and yet he invites a similar relation between reading and text. Where the Fourth Gospel steps out of the frame of the narrated world to address its readers, Mark's enigmatic ending leaves its readers in a closed narrated world. Mary Magdalene, Mary the mother of James, and Salome have found the tomb empty of Jesus' body and encountered a mysterious young man. "And they went out and fled from the tomb; for trembling and astonishment had come upon them; and they said nothing to anyone, for they were afraid" (Mark 16:8). The only witnesses remain in fearful silence, with even an awkward and abrupt grammatical ending (the book ends with a preposition) to add to the sheer strangeness of the final sentence. As Robert Fowler puts it, "The story in Mark's Gospel seems to preclude the telling of Mark's Gospel."[23] Except that

21. It is perhaps worth noting that most of the Gospels' first "readers" would have been *listening* to texts read aloud.

22. Raymond E. Brown, *The Gospel according to John*, 2 vols., Anchor Bible (Garden City, N.Y.: Doubleday, 1970), 2:1049. "We can say in this regard that the Gospel is not a simple account of the life, teaching, work, death, and resurrection of Jesus, but the communicating of an act of confession, a communication by means of which the reader in turn is rendered capable of performing the same recognition that occurs in the text." Ricoeur, *Figuring the Sacred*, 162.

23. Robert M. Fowler, "Reading Matthew Reading Mark," *SBL 1986 Seminar Papers*, ed. Kent Harold Richards (Atlanta: Scholars Press, 1986), 14.

here, somehow, is this text. We are addressed from a community of faith, although no such community appears within the story itself. "The key to understanding Mark," Fowler concludes, "is not to understand the women or men *in* the story, but to understand what is happening in the women or men *reading* the story."[24] We as readers become part of the story we are reading, and thus enter into its world.

Something similar happens at the end of Luke and of Matthew. Consider, for instance, just how odd is Luke's introduction of the good news of Jesus' resurrection. On the first day of the week, a group of women goes to Jesus' tomb, only to find the stone rolled away and the tomb empty. They are perplexed (Luke 24:4). Then two men in dazzling clothes appear to them, and they are terrified (24:5). In the end they tell the news to the apostles, to whom the words seem "an idle tale, and they did not believe them" (24:11). Peter goes to the tomb himself, and he is amazed, astonished. The whole first section of resurrection accounts has passed by without a single unambiguously positive verb to describe a response. Even later, when Jesus appears to the eleven, the only description of their reaction is that "they were startled and terrified and thought they were seeing a ghost" (24:37).

Likewise, at the very end of Matthew, as the eleven disciples come to the mountaintop for their final commissioning, "They saw him, they worshiped him, but some doubted" (Matt. 28:17). References to doubt appear in a number of later resurrection traditions, but there, as in the story of doubting Thomas, they have an apologetic function. Doubts provide the occasion for decisive evidence.[25] Here, however, no such demonstration follows, and the only role of the doubt seems to be to leave the response within the narrated world ambiguous and thus thrust readers into the story as people called to make a decision. Again, the Gospels do not present themselves as self-contained worlds separate from ours.

The literary critic Erich Auerbach rightly insisted on the "tyrannical" character of these texts. Reading the *Iliad* or the *Odyssey,* Auerbach noted, we can escape to Homer's imagined world for a time, and even learn lessons about the meaning of heroism or the call of home. But "the Scripture stories do not, like Homer's, court our favor, they do not flatter us that they may please us and enchant us—they seek to subject

24. Robert M. Fowler, "Reader-Response Criticism: Figuring Mark's Reader," in *Mark and Method: New Approaches in Biblical Studies*, ed. Janice Capel Anderson and Stephen D. Moore (Minneapolis: Fortress, 1992), 80, emphasis added.

25. See Luke 24; John 20:25; Mark 16:11–14; and *Epistula Apostolorum* 1–10.

us."[26] These stories claim to offer a framework—a beginning, an end, a center—for all of history, and propose that our lives and all other events have meaning only to the extent that they fit into that framework. Their stories purport to *define* reality.

Now of course this is the *claim* they make. It may be false. Their authors may have been misled, confused, or lying. But a novel cannot, in that sense, be "false." It is not even making the sort of claim that raises such issues of truth and falsity.[27] Since the Gospels do raise such questions, whatever they are, they are not any ordinary sort of fiction.

My teacher Hans Frei contended that trying to *argue* that the Gospels are true has regularly led interpreters for the last two hundred years or so to misinterpret them.[28] Modern folk have assumed that the world of our ordinary experience, newspaper headlines, and the state of the economy is the real world. If something is to be true, *it* has to fit into *that* framework. Confronted with these odd Gospel texts, this assumption leads to two alternatives. *Either* we treat the Gospels as the raw material for history, and try to sort out from them what bits and pieces can be established by critical historical methods, *or* we derive from them moral lessons that we can apply to our lives. Either way, we start with our world and then argue that historians can show that the Gospel narratives belong to it or moralists can indicate that their lessons apply to it.

But either of these strategies, Frei argued, distorts the Gospels' meaning. Whether we end up with some historically established facts or abstract moral lessons, we have lost the *narrative* character that is central to what the Gospels are. The only way to preserve that character is to take them as an even odder sort of texts: stories that, as Auerbach (and Karl Barth) saw, propose that *they* define "the one common world in which we all live and move and have our being."[29] *Our* world makes sense only if we can fit it into *their* framework. If they are false, they are a weird kind of hyperfiction, novel-like works that claim to define the truth about our world. (I suppose those of us who are not Mormons think of Joseph Smith's works as roughly like this.) But if

26. Erich Auerbach, *Mimesis: The Representation of Reality in Western Literature*, trans. Willard R. Trask (Princeton: Princeton University Press, 1968), 15. See, almost identically, Bonhoeffer's account of the "complete reversal" that takes place when Christians read Scripture. Dietrich Bonhoeffer, *Life Together*, trans. John W. Doberstein (New York: Harper & Row, 1954), 54.

27. In other senses, a novel might be false—if the author, for instance, deliberately manipulated characters down paths foreign to their identities in order to make an ideological point.

28. Hans W. Frei, *The Eclipsed Biblical Narrative* (New Haven: Yale University Press, 1974), 133.

29. Hans W. Frei, "Eberhard Busch's Biography of Karl Barth," in *Types of Christian Theology* (New Haven: Yale University Press, 1992), 161.

they are true, they are a different, if perhaps equally strange, sort of text, providing a narrative such that only within it can we understand the world aright.

Not myths. The Gospels are also not, in at least one sense of a word with many senses, myths. I use "myth" here to mean a story about events occurring in a primordial time that is also, in Mircea Eliade's words, "a sort of eternal mythical present that is periodically reintegrated by means of rites."[30] The Babylonian creation myth, *Enuma Elish*, for instance, tells how Marduk, the deity of Babylon, defeated the goddess Tiamat and made the physical world out of her dead body. The story was recited each New Year's Day in a ritual that established order (an order that included the king's rule) for the coming year.

One could say of such a myth what Auerbach says of Scripture: it claims to define the framework for reality, a framework within which our own lives need to be lived. But in other ways such myths differ from the Gospel stories. The myth does not take place "when Quirinius was governor of Syria." It would not make sense to ask how many years had elapsed between Marduk's victory and this New Year; mythical time is not like that. It is related to our time not by chronological distance but by its eternal availability for ritual repetition.[31]

The Gospels, in contrast, narrate datable events. Here their beginnings effectively make the point. Matthew begins with a genealogy, locating Jesus in a line of well-known characters in Israel's history. Indeed, the fourteen generations each from Abraham to David, David to the deportation to Babylon, and the deportation to Jesus (Matt. 1:17), however symbolic their significance, could hardly, in their specificity, be more unlike the "once upon a time, long ago" characteristic of myths' temporal location. As soon as the story narrates Jesus' birth—in the very next phrase—it mentions Herod, a political figure known to the story's first readers, whether Roman, Greek, or Hebrew, as their near contemporary.

Luke adopts the beginning characteristic of the work of a Greek historian, acknowledging previous writers and making reference to eyewitnesses before announcing his intention, as someone who has "followed all things closely for some time past, to write an orderly account for you" (Luke 1:3). In terms of the conventions of Greek

30. Mircea Eliade, *The Sacred and the Profane*, trans. Willard R. Trask (New York: Harper & Row, 1961), 70.

31. See Paul Ricoeur, "Myth and History," *The Encyclopedia of Religion*, ed. Mircea Eliade (New York: Macmillan, 1987), 10:273.

writing, he could not make clearer that what follows is not myth. Mark's characteristic abuptness, by contrast, makes his genre initially less clear. He simply starts telling his story. But the very ordinariness of his scenes and characters draws us away from the world of myth. These are not Hesiod's gods or Homer's heroes but fisherfolk from a small village, in a time and place familiar to the story's first readers.

John's Gospel offers the most complicated case. How would one define the genre of its prologue? That "beginning" when the Word was with God might well be a kind of mythical time. But even in the prologue, the story quickly shifts to a different kind of time: "There was a man sent from God, whose name was John" (John 1:6)—not, the Gospel's original readers or hearers would soon have learned, long ago and far away, but fairly recently and in known territory. And the Word made flesh occupied the same time and place as this John. Here too, the story emerges as one not far from its first readers' own time and place.

Not the history of a modern historian. So are the Gospels history? That depends, of course, on what we mean by "history." Reading Shelby Foote's magisterial account of the Civil War, I trust that, when he says that the road was muddy, he has established by evidence from the time that the road *was* muddy. If he reports that first the general died and then the line of troops broke and fled, I believe that this is the order in which the events occurred.[32] (I actually do trust these things, even though Foote's three very long volumes contain not a single footnote. Foote had his critics and knew the rules of the game of history writing today; he would not have risked bluffing.) In contrast, as John Calvin noted long ago, "We know that the Evangelists were not very exact as to the order of dates, or even in detailing minutely everything that Christ said or did."[33] Details are inconsistent; chronology varies from one Gospel to another; events are reported (like Jesus' prayers in the Garden of Gethsemane) that it seems unlikely any observer could have known. Either the Gospel writers did not have the same goals as most modern historians, or else they did a really bad job of it. If we try to understand them as attempts at modern-style history, then, as Wittgenstein used to say, for a mistake this is too big.[34]

32. Shelby Foote, *The Civil War: A Narrative*, 3 vols. (New York: Random House, 1958–74).

33. John Calvin, *Commentary on a Harmony of the Evangelists, Matthew, Mark and Luke,* trans. William Pringle, vol. 1, Calvin's Commentaries 16 (repr. Grand Rapids: Baker, 1989), 216.

34. If someone said: "'Now, I'm going to add,' and then said: '2 and 21 is 13,'" I'd respond, "'For a blunder, that's too big.'" Ludwig Wittgenstein, *Lectures and Conversations on Aesthetics, Psychology, and Religious Belief*, ed. Cyril Barrett (Berkeley: University of California Press, 1967), 62.

But ancient historians *in general* had different methods than their modern equivalents. Thucydides, in many ways the most "modern" of them, assures us near the beginning of his *History of the Peloponnesian War*, "Either I was present myself at the events which I have described or else I heard of them from eye-witnesses whose reports I have checked with as much thoroughness as possible."[35] So far so good. But his history includes many speeches given on key occasions, and in this case, he admits, "I have found it difficult to remember the precise words used in the speeches which I listened to myself and my various informants have experienced the same difficulty; so my method has been, while keeping as closely as possible to the general sense of the words that were actually used, to make the speakers say what, in my opinion, was called for by each situation."[36] He was following conventions different from those accepted by historians today; he differed from other ancient historians only in the clarity with which he explained himself.

The Gospels likewise provide "history" in the minimal sense of stories about an actual human being who lived at a particular time and place not all that far distant from the time of their authors. That they are not "accurate" in many of the ways a modern historian would try to be is not a recent discovery. Calvin took it for granted that their authors rearranged details—the Sermon on the Mount, for instance, combined sayings originally delivered at different times.[37] His doctrine of "accommodation" allowed that God speaks to human beings in ways we can understand,[38] and that might mean expressing a spiritual truth in terms of the worldview that would make sense to a scientifically primitive people: "He who would learn astronomy, and other recondite arts, let him go elsewhere."[39] Luther, famously, believed that the gospel of salvation by grace through faith was the central message of Scripture and viewed with considerable suspicion biblical texts, like the Letter of James, that "epistle of straw," that seemed to deviate from it. He could casually talk about "errors" in Scripture and state forthrightly that the Gospel of John was far superior to the other three.[40] Both Reformers

35. Thucydides, *History of the Peloponnesian War* 1.22; trans. Rex Warner (London: Penguin, 1972), 48.

36. Ibid. 1.22; 47. I am not sure how to reconcile "keeping as closely as possible to the general sense of the words that were actually used" and making the speakers say "what, in my opinion, was called for."

37. "Pious and modest readers ought to be satisfied with having a brief summary of the doctrine of Christ placed before their eyes, collected out of his many and various discourses." Calvin, *Harmony of the Evangelists*, 1:259.

38. John Calvin, *Institutes of the Christian Religion* 2.11.13; ed. John T. McNeill, trans. Ford Lewis Battles, 2 vols., Library of Christian Classics (Philadelphia: Westminster, 1960), 1:462–63.

39. John Calvin, *Commentaries on the First Book of Moses Called Genesis*, trans. John King, Calvin's Commentaries 1 (repr. Grand Rapids: Baker, 1989), 79.

40. Martin Luther, "Preface to the New Testament," trans. Charles M. Jacobs, rev. E. Theodore Bachmann, in *Word and Sacrament*, 1, Luther's Works, 35:362.

understood that the authors of Scripture could move things around and change details to make their points clearer. Likely, the Gospel writers adapted and even made up some stories themselves. They would have been dramatically different from other historical writers of their time had they done otherwise.

One reason the Reformers and their successors recognized such freedom with detail is that they knew the Bible so much better than we do and were therefore aware of the smallest discrepancies. Genesis 46:27 declares than "seventy Israelites" went down into Egypt, while in Acts 7:14 Stephen says that there were seventy-five. Matthew's genealogy of Jesus makes Joram the father of Uzziah, while 1 Kings 8:24 and 1 Chronicles 3:11–12 indicate that Joram was the father of Ahaziah, and Uzziah came several generations later. The "Protestant scholastic" theologians in the generations following the Reformation proposed various explanations, including scribal errors in copying the manuscripts.[41] Indeed, by the nineteenth century the great defenders of Princeton orthodoxy, Charles Hodge and B. B. Warfield, used that argument as a general device: they proposed that the "original autograph" of Scripture had been inerrant, but errors had crept in as time went on. Unfortunately, this approach had the odd effect of saving the "inerrancy of Scripture" by assigning it to an unknowable text, while admitting errors in every text available to us.[42]

Hodge was on safer ground, I think, when he distinguished the authority of what the sacred writers "teach" from what they "themselves may have thought or believed."[43] We should trust the message they are being used by God to communicate to us, but "As to all matters of science, philosophy and history, they stood on the same level as their contemporaries."[44] And, I have tried to argue, an accurate account of the details of Jesus' life and ministry was not what they were "teaching."

We therefore misread the stories if, following the example of the Jesus Seminar, we evaluate their truth in terms of the percentage of things they report that Jesus actually said or did (assuming some method permitted us to do this reliably). That is not faithful to the character of these narratives. Rather, we should think about them as David Kelsey says Karl Barth did: "as a source of anecdotes about what Jesus said or did which one would tell to show 'what he was like.' The

41. Richard A. Muller, *Post-Reformation Reformed Dogmatics* (Grand Rapids: Baker, 2003), 2:308–9.
42. Ibid., 414.
43. Charles Hodge, *Systematic Theology* (repr. Grand Rapids: Eerdmans, 1992), 1:170.
44. Ibid., 165.

anecdotes that fall together into a given group are interchangeable. Barth is not interested in them for themselves but for the *patterns* that recur in a number of them. The incidents the anecdotes recite serve to *illustrate* Jesus' personhood, not to constitute it."[45] The stories concern who Jesus was—someone who healed others, someone who called God "Father," someone who hung out with outsiders, and so on—rather than the chronology of his ministry or the accuracy of every saying or deed they report.

The New Testament scholar Dale Allison rightly argues that in ordinary human experience we are usually more inclined to remember general characteristics than individual events:

> I may, for instance, not remember exactly what you said to me last year, but I may recall approximately what you said, or retain what we call a general impression. It is like vaguely recollecting the approximate shape, size, and contents of a room one was in many years ago—a room which has, in the mind's eye, lost all color and detail. After our short-term memories have become long-term memories, they suffer progressive abbreviation. I am not sure that I remember a single sentence that either of my beloved grandparents on my father's side ever said to me. I nonetheless know and cherish the *sorts* of things they said to me.[46]

An approach like that of the Jesus Seminar builds its picture of Jesus' identity out of *some* stories established as particularly certain on historical grounds and ignores the characteristics of Jesus manifested in a wider range of stories that show patterns of his behavior but are individually less historically reliable. That flies in the face of common sense. My memory of Grandfather's one wildly out-of-character moment may be the single incident I remember about him with greatest certainty; that does not make it the key to understanding his character. Rather, I trust my general memories of what he was usually like, even if each of them individually is a bit fuzzy. So, as Hans Frei wrote,

> In the instance of Jesus, it may well be that certain of his sayings or specific, isolated episodes recounted from his brief ministry, which are quite enigmatic in character and tell little about him, such as his condemning a fig tree because it would not yield fruit out of season

45. David H. Kelsey, *The Uses of Scripture in Recent Theology* (Philadelphia: Fortress, 1975), 43.

46. Dale Allison, "The Historical Jesus and the Church," unpublished paper for the Center of Theological Inquiry's Seminar on the Identity of Jesus, 6–7, emphasis added.

> (Mark 11:12–14), are much more nearly reliable historical reports than those in which his over-all personal intention is more clearly depicted.[47]

This is not a reason to try to base our understanding of him on a collection of such enigmatic stories.

An emphasis on general characteristics does not dodge the question of truth. A character portrait of Adolf Hitler that makes him out to be a nice guy is false—even if every report within it of kindness to dogs and small children is true. So the Gospels would be false, not if some of their details were inaccurate, but if they did not convey the person Jesus was.

Many of their episodes we can take to be illustrative anecdotes, moreover, but in some cases a story narrates an event so central to the picture of Jesus a Gospel presents that, in Frei's words, it "allows and even forces us to ask the question, 'Did this actually take place?'"[48] He could have healed one person rather than another, spoken of love in one set of words rather than another, and still have been the same person. But not, for instance, if he lived to a ripe old age rather than dying on a cross.

Where do we get these rules for deciding what matters and what doesn't? We have to get them first and foremost from the stories themselves. There are, to be sure, endless borderline cases, but that does not mean that we cannot identify some matters as clearly on one side or another of a line. Is Matthew 14 an attempt to show how Jesus was always mysterious to his disciples, even when in their midst, or is it telling us that one of Jesus' characteristics was that he could walk on water? I myself would vote for the first interpretation, but I concede the need for an argument. On the other hand, how could we read any of the Gospels and think that the crucifixion is simply an illustrative anecdote showing Jesus' compassion? Or how could we notice how John dates the crucifixion differently from the other three Gospels and think that chronological accuracy is central to their understanding of the truth of the matter?

The fourfold character of the Gospels reminds us that the church has not characteristically taken them as history in the modern sense. Each story is different; there are inconsistencies. The church down the centuries has consistently resisted combining them into a single narrative;

47. Hans W. Frei, *The Identity of Jesus Christ* (Philadelphia: Fortress, 1975), 141.

48. Ibid., 140. This seems to me so clear that I am always puzzled at the number of Frei's readers who ignore it.

perhaps we should pause in surprise at this fact more than we do. What would have been more natural, it might seem, than conflating disparate accounts into a single consistent story? But Christians have apparently realized that doing so would distort the kind of material the Gospels represent. Indeed, each Gospel has its own narrative logic. The way it begins and ends, its ordering of incidents, the manner in which its picture of Jesus emerges—these and other factors are part of the way in which the particular Gospel renders Jesus' identity, and they would be lost if we conflated all the Gospels into a single narrative.[49] We have to accept that if the identity of Jesus is accessible to us at all, it is accessible as mediated through this fourfold text.

WITNESSES

The Gospels, then, to return to my thesis, are history-like witnesses to truths both historical and transcendent. They are, first of all, *witnesses.* Their authors give *testimony* to events that have transformed their lives. Paul Ricoeur's analysis of testimony draws out at least three relevant features. First, witnesses relate what they have seen or heard.[50] "You are witnesses of these things," the risen Christ tells disciples in Luke 24:48—meaning that they should now narrate to others what they have themselves encountered. The Gospel writers, as near as we can figure the chronology, are themselves witnesses at second or third hand, narrating what they have heard from their predecessors.

Second, "witness" evokes the setting of the courtroom, where, in Ricoeur's phrasing, "The solemnity of testimony is eventually enhanced and sanctified by a special ritual of swearing or of promising which qualifies as testimony the declaration of the witness."[51] Thus, for instance, in Acts 5:32 Peter and the apostles "are witnesses" before the Sanhedrin of things related to Jesus. Witnessing is not idle storytelling. In a trial, something important is at stake. As a witness, one commits oneself to the truth of that to which one witnesses. Indeed, third, witnessing involves risk on the witness's part. As Aristotle says, witnesses "share the

49. "If it were possible to produce 'a harmony of the Gospels' and, correspondingly, a harmony of all the New Testament theologies in the sense of a system, then gnosis would have won the victory over agape." Hans Urs von Balthasar, *The Glory of the Lord,* vol. 7: *Theology: The New Covenant,* ed. John Riches, trans. Brian McNeil (San Francisco: Ignatius, 1989), 103–4. See also Irenaeus, *Against Heresies* 3.11.8, trans. A. Cleveland Coxe, Ante-Nicene Fathers 1 (repr. Grand Rapids: Eerdmans, 1973), 428–29.

50. Paul Ricoeur, "The Hermeneutics of Testimony," *Essays on Biblical Interpretation,* ed. Lewis S. Mudge (Philadelphia: Fortress, 1980), 123.

51. Ibid., 124.

risk of punishment if their evidence is pronounced false."[52] Witnessing on behalf of an unpopular person or cause risks punishment even when speaking the truth. Thus in the early church, "witness" (*martyr* in Greek) came to mean one who died for the faith.

The Gospels are, more specifically, *history-like* witnesses. They do not primarily witness to scientific truths or poetic insights or myths but to events in time and place near to that of their authors and first readers. They are thus like history. As already noted, they are not like the kind of narrative most historians today would write—far more casual, for instance, about details and chronology, far more willing to include their understanding of the events' ultimate meaning in the telling of their stories. In this, they resemble other ancient biographies (often in the Greek world of philosophers), which sought to capture the core of their subject's identity and teaching rather than the details of a life. Nevertheless, they are *witnesses*. Once we understand the points of the stories, we can be confident of the authors' commitment to their truth. They are asserting that this is the person Jesus was: the *sort* of person he was as anecdotally illustrated by characteristic sayings and actions, and the particular person he was as manifested in the events of his life that most defined his identity. This is the event that happened in Jesus: the way things have changed in the world because of him, the difference that makes to the Gospels' authors, the difference it can make to the Gospels' readers. On such matters, their authors commit themselves.

The Gospels witness to *truths both historical and transcendent*. Some of what they witness is as ordinary as dirt. There was a man named John, who baptized Jesus. Jesus ate with tax collectors, taught that we should forgive our enemies, helped those who were sick and outcast, and died on a cross. The words have their most literal and everyday meaning. Other cases are different. Jesus declares, in Mark's Gospel, "And then they will see the Son of Man coming in clouds with great power and glory. Then he will send out the angels, and gather his elect from the four winds, from the ends of the earth to the ends of heaven" (Mark 13:26–27). In John he describes himself as "the light of the world" (John 8:12) and says, "The Father judges no one, but has given all judgment to the Son" (John 5:22). The Gospel writers clearly mean

52. Aristotle, *Rhetoric* 1.15.12, §1376a, in *The Basic Works of Aristotle*, ed. Richard McKeon (New York: Random House, 1941), 1376. Even more strongly: "If the witness is a false witness, having testified falsely against another, then you shall do to the false witness just as the false witness had meant to do to the other. So you shall pursue the evil from your midst. The rest shall hear and be afraid, and a crime such as this shall never again be committed among you. Show no pity: life for life, eye for eye, tooth for tooth, hand for hand, foot for foot" (Deut. 19:18b–21).

to witness to the truth of these sayings. I use "transcendent" as a convenient if vague way of saying that such claims reach beyond ordinary history, toward either an eschatological future or a realm different from that of events in this world.

The Gospels, to be sure, often make the relation of historical and transcendent claims complicated. It is a historical event that a Jewish woman named Mary or Miriam had a baby, and that a particular Jewish teacher was crucified outside Jerusalem by the Roman authorities. But the Gospels claim that these are *also* transcendent events: the incarnation of God's Son, and his redemptive death for the salvation of the world.[53]

This complexity reaches its peak in the accounts of Jesus' resurrection. Some women went to Jesus' tomb and found it empty; the disciples had not stolen the body—such claims are true or false in a quite ordinary sense. On the other hand, the Gospels' narrations of the events after his resurrection shift from the relatively parallel and clear accounts of Jesus' last hours to a jumble of very different stories—different in location, in character, in how they seem to picture how Jesus "appeared." As Rowan Williams puts it, "The stories themselves are about difficulty, unexpected outcomes, silences, errors, about what is not readily accessible or easily understood. . . . In short, it is not a straightforward matter to say what the gospels understand by the resurrection of Jesus; but this seems to have something to do with the fact that the Christian communities of the last quarter of the first Christian century didn't find it all that straightforward either."[54] Nor should this be surprising. If these witnesses are truthful, then Jesus' resurrection was not an ordinary historical event but one that transformed the whole of history.

Even temporal issues become complicated. On the one hand, if Jesus was raised from the dead, that must have happened between the time he died and the time his disciples began to preach that they had seen him alive, and this is a datable and specific period. On the other hand, if Karl Barth is right to talk about Jesus' resurrection as an "eternal" event contemporary with every believer, then it can no longer simply be

53. "An identity description of Jesus arrived at only through historical research cannot include God's relation to Jesus as essential to his identity, for the evidence and argument proper to historical research do not claim relevance or competence regarding questions about God and God's relation to anything, including Jesus." David H. Kelsey, *Imagining Redemption* (Louisville: Westminster John Knox, 2005), 46. But the Christian claim is of course precisely that his relation to God *is* central to Jesus' identity.

54. Rowan Williams, *On Christian Theology* (Oxford: Blackwell, 2000), 187.

assigned a particular temporal location,[55] and how we talk about it has to be more complicated.

Indeed, whenever we deal with transcendent events—whether they transcend history in the direction of the eternal or the eschatological future—such complexities arise. We are using words to point toward realities we cannot understand. To use categories from Thomas Aquinas mentioned in the previous chapter, in such cases our words refer truly to the "thing signified" but not to the "mode of signification."[56] To use the kind of example that Aquinas had in mind, if it is true that God is wise, then, confronted with God and looking back at my earthly life, I would see that, yes, "wise" was an appropriate term to apply to God (the "thing signified"), but the *way* "wise" applies to God (the "mode of signification") turned out to be beyond anything I could have imagined. Analogously, one who fully understood, as we never will in this life, what it means to say that Jesus was raised from the dead would recognize the appropriateness of the language of "raised" and "now lives" but find the way in which these terms are true unexpected and astonishing.

So how do the Gospels mean? They are history-like witnesses to truths both historical and transcendent. Neither fiction nor myth nor historical works in the modern sense, they narrate events that convey who Jesus was and is—some as illustrative anecdotes, some as claims about specific events that define his identity. Their narration involves historical elements, where they use words in quite ordinary senses, and transcendent elements, where they use words the manner of whose truth we cannot now imagine. If we believe them, then this combination of historical and transcendent claims should be the complex object of our belief.

Why *should* we believe them? Answering that question leads to the Holy Spirit, and to the next chapter. "No one can say 'Jesus is Lord,' except by the Holy Spirit" (1 Cor. 12:3). "They who strive to build up firm faith in the Scripture through disputation are doing things backwards," Calvin insisted.[57] "The same Spirit . . . who has spoken through the mouths of the prophets must penetrate into our hearts to persuade us that they faithfully proclaimed what had been divinely commanded."[58] When that happens, we find ourselves persuaded of

55. Barth, *Church Dogmatics*, IV/1: 291, 318.

56. Thomas Aquinas, *Summa Theologica* 1a.13.3; trans. Fathers of the English Dominican Province (Westminster, Md.: Christian Classics, 1981), 62; *Summa Contra Gentiles* 1.30.2; trans. Anton C. Pegis (Notre Dame: University of Notre Dame Press, 1975), 140. See Victor Preller, *Divine Science and the Science of God* (Princeton: Princeton University Press, 1967), 173; Lindbeck, *Nature of Doctrine*, 66–67.

57. Calvin, *Institutes* 1.7.4; 1:79.

58. Ibid.

the complex truths they propose, and of a way of seeing the world that has those truths at its center.

CANON

But why just these particular texts? In discussing the witness of biblical narratives, I have disagreed with some of the proposals made by the Jesus Seminar to whittle down our source material concerning Jesus to specific sayings and stories that can be established by their methods as historically reliable. Another way of thinking about Jesus has received at least as much attention recently—not cutting back source material but adding to it from noncanonical sources, early Christian texts that did not end up in the New Testament.

Whether described in historical works, cited by religious writers, or lying in the background of Dan Brown's *Da Vinci Code*, various noncanonical texts have drawn remarkable popular interest. Even some scholars who know better, I have to say, hint at secret truths about Jesus hidden by ecclesial conspiracies. For Christian theologians, the good news in all this is the continuing fascination so many people have with the figure of Jesus; the bad news is the extent even of churchgoers' suspicions of the churches and their scholars.

In such a context, a few simple facts need to be stated at the outset:

—The canonical Gospels are almost certainly our earliest extended accounts of Jesus. Relatively cautious scholars date Mark 64–70, Matthew and Luke in the 80s, and John in the 80s or 90s. Our only earlier sources are Paul's Letters, the earliest of them written within twenty years of Jesus' death. No noncanonical Christian materials can be clearly dated before the second century.

—Some noncanonical materials may contain a few authentic sayings of Jesus—I find some of the sayings in the *Gospel of Thomas* particularly attractive in this respect. But this material is highly fragmentary, and scholarly arguments for its authenticity appeal mostly to the way such sayings "sound like" the Jesus we encounter in the canonical Gospels. We cannot piece together a historically convincing picture of Jesus on the basis on nonbiblical sources. If we do not accept the rough reliability of the picture of Jesus we get in the Bible, then we just cannot know who he was.

—Many noncanonical materials reflect the perspective of Gnosticism, the label for those within early Christianity who believed in multiple levels of spiritual reality and secret revelations through which alone those multiple levels could become known. According to gnostics, ordinary faith penetrated only one level of heavenly truth; it was only secret revelation that led to higher truths. The gnostic views characteristic of many noncanonical texts do not represent the voices of socially marginalized outsiders in contrast to the "establishment" voices of canonical texts. On the contrary, according to Gnosticism only a spiritual elite knows the secret truths that lead to salvation. It is the New Testament that offers an openly proclaimed gospel available to ordinary folk.

—Recently discovered texts like those found at Nag Hammadi in Egypt and the *Gospel of Judas* certainly add to our knowledge of the diversity within early Christianity, but they do not radically transform the picture already available. Hans Jonas's brilliant *Gnostic Religion*, written before most of this material was available, remains one of the best books on Gnosticism.[59] It turns out that the early church fathers were honest enough in reporting their opponents' beliefs to provide us with a fairly trustworthy picture.

All the headlines about the fundamental challenges facing Christian faith because of this or that manuscript discovery are thus wildly exaggerated or simply untrue. But that still does not explain why we should draw a line so sharply around the biblical canon when we seek guidance about Jesus' identity. To understand that, we need to reflect further on what it means to have a canon of Scripture.

Scriptures are books that a religious community uses as fundamental guides to its faith and practice. This is simply what it means to call something "Scripture." What should we believe? How should we live? Christians may ordinarily derive their answers from what their Sunday school teacher taught them, or what their pastor preached, or what they recite in a creed, or what they read in a book by some widely admired Christian author. But if someone else, or their own conscience, asks, "Are you sure that's the Christian answer?" they will generally try to see

59. Hans Jonas, *The Gnostic Religion* (Boston: Beacon, 1958).

if this particular belief is faithful to the Bible (Catholics would add, "and/or to the traditions of the Church"[60]). For instance, when the brave opponents of the Nazi effort to take over the Protestant churches declared their principles in the Barmen Declaration of 1934, they also insisted, "If you find that we are speaking contrary to Scripture, then do not listen to us!"[61] Scriptures provide a measuring stick against which a religious community gauges its beliefs and practices.

To identify a particular set of scriptural texts as the "canon," David Kelsey has written, "is to say that *just these* writings are *sufficient* for the ends to which they ought to be used in the church. . . . That is, in declaring just these writings 'canon' the church was giving part of a self-description of her identity: we are a community such that certain uses of scripture are *necessary* for nurturing and shaping our self-identity, and the use of 'just these,' i.e., 'canonical,' writings is *sufficient* for that purpose."[62] A Christian community thus affirms, in the words of the Scots Confession of 1560, "We believe and confess the Scriptures of God sufficient to instruct and make perfect the man of God."[63] We do not need anything else to guide us in knowing what to believe and how to act.

The early church shaped its canon gradually, over a period of several hundred years, and the historian can sometimes find the process a puzzling one. Though the New Testament had taken roughly its present form by the end of the second century, the first list exactly corresponding to our New Testament did not appear until Athanasius's Easter Letter of 367. Reading many of the texts that did not make it into the canon, I find myself generally admiring, if only on aesthetic grounds, the church's wisdom. Imagine a Bible including the *Infancy Gospel of Thomas*, where the child Jesus causes a neighborhood boy who accidentally bumped him on the shoulder to fall down and die, or the *Second Treatise of the Great Seth*, with its lengthy discussions of many layers of heavenly aeons and the "archons belonging to the place of Yaldabaoth."[64]

Still, if the canon had included, say, the *Gospel of Thomas* or left out the Letter of Jude, the Christian community would not be radically different. What is hard to imagine is how we could now get there from

60. *Dogmatic Decrees of the Council of Trent*, 8 April 1546, *First Decree: Acceptance of the Sacred Books and Apostolic Traditions*, in *Creeds and Confessions of Faith in the Christian Tradition*, ed. Jaroslav Pelikan and Valerie Hotchkiss, 4 vols. (New Haven: Yale University Press, 2003), 2:822.

61. German Evangelical Church, *Barmen Declaration*, in ibid., 3:505.

62. Kelsey, *Uses of Scripture*, 105.

63. *Scots Confession*, article 19, in *Creeds and Confessions*, ed. Pelikan and Hotchkiss, 2:399.

64. *Infancy Gospel of Thomas* 4, *Second Treatise of the Great Seth*, in Bart D. Ehrman, *Lost Scriptures* (Oxford: Oxford University Press, 2003), 58, 83.

here. That is, given that Christian communities have in effect had a "closed canon" for almost nine-tenths of our history now, opening again the question of what should count as Scripture would fundamentally change the sort of community we are, leaving us much less connected with much of our tradition and much more open to shifts of fashion. Just to start: if we started editing, what principles would we follow? To be sure, it can be tempting to drop some apparently anti-Semitic or misogynistic scriptural texts, but, again, one would thereby open the door for others to begin their own editing, and where would it stop? In a world full of crackpots and villains, opening biblical texts for adjustment seems a very dangerous proposition. The Christian community has been and is a community that treats this set of texts as its canon.

Does this particular set of texts as we now have them provide us with what is necessary and sufficient for shaping and nurturing our Christian identity? I will return to such questions in the next chapter; for the moment, it is enough to point out how great the difficulties that would follow if we said no.

ALTERNATIVE PORTRAITS

So we come back to the canon. I will say something about our earliest sources concerning Jesus, the Letters of Paul, later in this chapter. First, however, while the Gospels point us backward to the Hebrew Scriptures and forward to the rest of the New Testament (more of that later), they also provide us with our richest stories about Jesus. The four of them present the stories in different ways, and we must not ignore the differences if we want to understand what they have to tell us about Jesus. I have already noted some of the characteristics of their beginnings and endings. Mark is the starkest and most jagged, the shortest, awkward in its Greek, driven forward by its repeated "immediately . . . and then immediately. . . ." *Euthys*, the Greek word for "immediately," occurs forty-two times in Mark, eleven times already in the page and a half of the first chapter.[65] This Gospel is oddly postmodern in style, full of strange juxtapositions, a "book of secret epiphanies" in which Jesus keeps calling for silence from those who discern his identity, the disciples

65. Mark Allan Powell, *Fortress Introduction to the Gospels* (Minneapolis: Fortress, 1998), 41. I am indebted to Powell's helpful summary for many of the specific points in this section.

consistently misunderstand, and the whole story ends oddly, with an emptiness where the dead Jesus had lain and women running away in fear, telling no one what they had seen.

This Jesus keeps transgressing boundaries: he touches lepers, demoniacs, unclean women, and corpses; heals and approves of plucking grain on the Sabbath. His relatives think he is mad; the scribes attribute his powers to demonic possession. If so radical a challenger of the status quo is not crazy or possessed, then there must be something wrong with the status quo. As a great recent scholar of Mark, Donald Juel, put it, "No guarantees are available that he will not bring the whole social and religious structure crashing down about him."[66] Most scholars seem to agree that Mark, writing to an audience of outsiders facing hard times, pictures an isolated Jesus, most divine in his most human moments of suffering. His central message concerns the kingdom of God, but it is a kingdom unlike any other, and the only road to it lies through suffering. The text proclaims him "Son of God" in the very first verse, but no human recognizes him as such until, right at the end, a Roman centurion sees him hanging on the cross—recognition of divinity at what might seem the least likely place, the moment of apparently complete powerlessness.

Matthew gives us Jesus as the second Moses, a teacher whose five great discourses (chaps. 5–7, 10, 13, 18, and 24–25) correspond to the five books of Moses' law,[67] and the events of whose life again and again recall the fulfillment of Jewish prophecy.[68] Communities matter in this Gospel—Matthew not only looks back often to the community of Israel but is the only Gospel in which Jesus talks explicitly about the church. He replaces Mark's abrupt beginning with a genealogy locating Jesus as the descendant of Abraham and David, and he ends, not with women running away in fear from an empty tomb, but with the risen Jesus commissioning his disciples from a mountaintop to "make disciples of all nations" (Matt. 28:19). Like Mark, Matthew talks about the kingdom (perhaps from the traditional Jewish reluctance to pronounce the divine name, he usually says "kingdom of heaven" rather than "kingdom of God"), but in even more dramatically contrasting ways. On the one hand, Matthew is the most apocalyptic of the Gospels, see-

66. Donald H. Juel, *A Master of Surprise* (Mifflintown, Pa.: Sigler, 2002), 40–41, 67.

67. A point already noted in the second century. See the anonymous second-century fragment quoted in Peter F. Ellis, *Matthew: His Mind and His Message* (Collegeville, Minn.: Liturgical Press, 1974), 10.

68. In fact, Matthew offers twelve fulfillment citations—the number traditionally symbolic of Israel, which was made up of twelve tribes. Powell, *Fortress Introduction to the Gospels*, 66.

ing the world as a cosmic conflict between God and Satan, and anticipating that God will soon triumph. On the other hand, he talks regularly of God's *presence* in Jesus, so that we may be left puzzled as to whether the triumph is yet to come or already here. On nine occasions, always with approval, he speaks of people "worshiping" Jesus.

As noted earlier, Luke follows most nearly the pattern of a Greek historian, "setting down an orderly account" for most excellent Theophilus "after investigating everything carefully from the very first" (Luke 1:3). His genealogy traces Jesus back to Adam, the ancestor not just of Jews but of all humankind. He locates his story in the world of Herod the king, the emperor Tiberius, and Quirinius, governor of Syria, and he ends (taking Acts as part of his work), not with the death and resurrection of Jesus, but, after an account of the growth of the early church, with Paul preaching the gospel in Rome, the good news arrived at the center of empire. In contrast to the apocalyptic urgency of other New Testament texts, he assumes that history will continue for a while, giving opportunity for the growth of the Christian community.

Jesus prays more in this Gospel than in the others, and he seems to be constantly eating symbolically significant meals. Many of those meals are at the tables of "sinners," and Luke's Gospel is particularly concerned about society's outsiders. The rich are "fools" (12:20), who will be "sent away empty" (1:53); "woe to you who are rich" (6:24). Jesus even summarizes the goal of his ministry as "to bring good news to the poor" (4:18). Where Matthew has Jesus declare, "Blessed are the poor in Spirit" (Matt. 5:3), Luke has a more blunt "Blessed are you who are poor" (Luke 6:20).

Yet this Jesus does not simply draw in economic terms the line defining the "outsiders" he seeks to embrace. He has come "to proclaim release to the captives" and "to let the oppressed go free" (Luke 4:18). He eats with tax collectors (5:29–30), despised collaborators with the Roman government and notoriously corrupt but apt to be wealthy, and praises Samaritans (9:51–56; 10:33; 17:11–19), the ethnic group Jews in his time regarded with greatest contempt. Repeatedly, Luke emphasizes that the good news is not just for Israel but for all people (2:31–32; 3:5–6; 4:24–30; 13:29; 14:21; 24:47). Writing in a patriarchal culture, he gives women prominent and honored roles in his story. Admirable women appear at the beginning and end of the story, and women are often cited as moral examples along the way. Nor are their virtues always those of passive obedience. Luke practically begins his story with Mary's radical words:

> He [God] has scattered the proud in the thoughts of their hearts.
> He has brought down the powerful from their thrones,
> and lifted up the lowly;
> he has filled the hungry with good things,
> and sent the rich away empty.
>
> (1:51–53)

It is hard to imagine a more forceful protest against injustice.

John of course offers the greatest contrasts: long discourses rather than short parables, no exorcisms, no secrets here, but a Christ fully revealed from the start, God's Word made flesh in the prologue, identified by both John the Baptist and Nathanael as "Son of God" before even the first chapter has concluded. He puts love at the center of his ethics and presents God as one not to be feared but only to be loved. He speaks of the Holy Spirit as the "Paraclete"—the "helper," "comforter," or "advocate." While John's Jesus also talks about future hopes, his emphasis falls on an "eternal life" available even now, a transformed existence in the midst of our current life. He works signs to show his identity and proclaims, "I am . . ." in a way that identifies him with the "I am" in the sacred name of the God of Israel told to Moses from the burning bush: "*I am who I am*. . . . Thus you shall say to the Israelites, '*I am* has sent me to you'" (Exod. 3:14). In Mark Powell's words, "In John . . . not only does Jesus tell what God is like and show what God is like, but in a fundamental sense, Jesus *is* what God is like. He not only reveals the truth; he *is* the truth (John 14:6)."[69] Repeatedly, the story puts Jesus himself in the place law and temple would have filled in Jewish rituals. In John, Jesus' cross is already a triumph.

Starting with these diverse Gospels, one could move out to encompass the even greater diversity of the rest of Scripture (though I do not mean to be dogmatic about the connections that follow). Matthew points back to Moses and the Exodus narrative and forward to Hebrews' reinterpretation of Jewish sacrificial ritual. Mark points back to the prophets, whose high points in the tragedy of Jeremiah and Second Isaiah's picture of the Suffering Servant so anticipate Mark's picture of Jesus, and forward to the dark comfort offered a suffering Christian community in 1 Peter (both Mark and 1 Peter are identified in tradition with Peter). Luke's genealogy beginning with Adam points back to the primal narratives in Genesis and forward to Paul's discussion of

69. Powell, *Fortress Introduction to the Gospels*, 131–32.

Jesus as second Adam, but Luke also particularly identifies Jesus as the son of David, thus recalling the tragedy of King David and presenting Jesus as monarch, in however radically new a sense. John's Logos Christology points back to wisdom texts and forward to the cosmic Christology of the deutero-Pauline letters and to the victorious Lamb of Revelation.[70] Christian worship that, through use of the lectionary or otherwise, employs rich and diverse scriptural readings can capture the ways in which the whole of the Bible reveals to us the identity of the God made most fully known in Jesus Christ.

Starting with the Gospels, though, raises the question of the coherence of the portraits they give us of Jesus. We have several pictures; yet if it is to be true that we know God through the Jesus whose doings and sufferings are rendered by these narratives, their variety must somehow function to provide a single Jesus. The solution here does not lie in combining the stories in a way that papers over their differences; to be faithful to Scripture as we have it, we must honor its diversity, but look for ways in which the Gospels capture recognizably the same person in diverse but powerful portraits, as several great artists might.

So what can we say? Though the stories themselves are far richer than any list of characteristics to be drawn from them, and interpreters must always come back to the stories, some common features certainly manifest themselves:[71]

—Jesus is *obedient* to the will of the one he calls his "Father." In contrast to this obedience, the Gospels have oddly little to say, for instance, about his faith.[72] But from the start, when the child Jesus must be about his Father's affairs (Luke 2:49), to the agonized "not my will but yours be done" in Gethsemane (Luke 22:42), he accomplishes his salvific work, as Calvin said, "by the whole course of his obedience."[73] In the passion narratives, where the pattern of his obedience comes most to the fore and he seems most fully himself, the varied narratives have most in common.

—His teaching has the *love* of God and neighbor at the core of its content. Not only does he identify love of God and neighbor as

70. I developed some of the ways the Hebrew Scriptures can contribute to Christology in William C. Placher, *Jesus the Savior* (Louisville: Westminster John Knox, 2001), chaps. 2, 7, 16, and 25.

71. For a somewhat different list, see H. Richard Niebuhr, *Christ and Culture* (New York: Harper & Row, 1951), 11–29.

72. Frei, *Identity of Jesus Christ*, 105–6.

73. Calvin, *Institutes* 2.16.5; 1:507.

the sum of the law, but in both his teaching and his activity they keep emerging close to the center of things.

—He particularly associates himself with society's outsiders, outcasts, rejected ones, whether touching the terrifyingly unclean flesh of lepers or sitting down to dinner with tax collectors and sinners. But his welcome does not buy into any single demarcation of good from bad—he will help tax collectors and Roman centurions, despised parts of the system of oppression, as quickly as he helps those despised because of their poverty.

—He is often in conflict with Pharisees and others, who are presented as preoccupied with details of the law. Whether such a picture accurately represents all, some, a few, or no historical Pharisees (a matter much debated), the contrast in the stories serves to fill out the Gospels' picture of Jesus. He does not divide the world into those who have managed to keep the law and those who have failed. We all fail, and therefore we are all in need of God's forgiveness.

—The form of his teaching, whether in brief Synoptic parables or longer Johannine discourses, involves paradoxes and unexpected juxtapositions that challenge our normal ways of seeing the world. He imagines a world in which people love their enemies, masters pay those who worked only the last hour as much as those who labored all the day, and forgiving fathers run forth to greet returning prodigals.

—He anticipates the approaching end of the current order of things, a transformation leading to the "kingdom of God," in which the reversals his parables present will come to be real. Though it is hard to fit all his remarks into a consistent picture, he seems to think of this transformation as already tentatively present in his own activity and people's response to it, but to be made full and public still in the future.

—The Gospels focus not just on the message but on the messenger. Who Jesus is becomes a central question within the story. The titles given him vary from one Gospel to another, and their meaning is not always clear. (Does "Son of Man," for instance, refer to the apocalyptic figure described in Daniel 7, is it just a synonym for "human being," or does it have some other meaning?) But people worship him in Luke; in John he says that whoever has seen the Son has seen the Father; Matthew assigns more authority to Jesus than to God's law; Mark calls his story that of "the Messiah, the Son of God"; and in all the Gospels people's relation to Jesus determines their relation to God's kingdom. The Gospels say of Jesus all sorts of things Jews would normally say only of God.

—All the Gospels have a turning point somewhere in the middle, with Peter's confession and the transfiguration. After a ministry primarily in Galilee, Jesus now begins to teach his disciples that he must suffer, and he turns his face toward Jerusalem.

—His brutal end was, in John Howard Yoder's words, "not a difficult family situation, not a frustration of visions of personal fulfillment, a crushing debt, or a nagging in-law; it was the political logically-to-be-expected result of a moral clash with the powers ruling his society."[74] This person who associated with outsiders dies as a radical outsider; condemned by the authorities and abandoned by his friends, he dies in a way both excruciating and humiliating and, according to some of our texts, identified with being cursed by God.[75]

—After his death, his friends—through whatever combination of the discovery of his empty tomb or experiences with him whose descriptions stretch the limits of language—encounter him as one who yet lives.

—The story is one in which, as Hans Urs von Balthasar has written, the Word becomes steadily more flesh and the flesh steadily more Word.[76] The Word becomes flesh: that which had manifested itself in creation, law, and prophecy becomes ever more specific in the life of this human being—discussed somewhat in abstractions in the birth stories, a specific person during his ministry, and then a particular human *body* as he suffers and faces death. And the flesh becomes steadily more Word: as Hans Frei put it, "Jesus' individual identity comes to focus directly in the passion-resurrection narrative rather than in the account of his person and teaching in his earlier ministry. It is in this final and climactic sequence that the storied Jesus is most of all himself, and there—unlike those earlier points at which we can get to his individual identity only ambiguously—we are confronted with him directly

74. John Howard Yoder, *The Politics of Jesus* (Grand Rapids: Eerdmans, 1972), 129.

75. Deuteronomy 21:22–23 directs that anyone executed by being hanged on a tree must be removed before nightfall lest he defile the land, for those hung on a tree are cursed. In Gal. 3:13 Paul understands Jesus' crucifixion as a dying on a tree and thus as a way in which Christ becomes cursed for us.

76. Balthasar, *Explorations in Theology*, 1:13.

as the unsubstitutable individual who is what he does and undergoes and is manifested directly as who he is."[77] It is at the end of his life that what he does and suffers most clearly communicates, indeed becomes, God's Word.

Here also it is most clear that he is God in that he is the one enacting God's redeeming love. In his passion and death, Frei wrote, "the initiative of Jesus disappears more and more into that of God; but in the resurrection, where the initiative of God is finally and decisively climaxed and he alone is and can be active, the sole identity to mark the presence of that activity is Jesus. God remains hidden, and even reference to him is almost altogether lacking. Jesus of Nazareth, he and none other, marks the presence of the action of God."[78] Jesus had taught that one has to lose one's life to find it, and now he loses his life in radical obedience to God's will only to find his own identity decisively in being God's presence. After Jesus' death, the only way God is present is in the crucified Jesus, who still bears the marks of his manner of dying. But that is enough for us to see how much God loves us, and that is the most important thing to know about God.

WHO DO YOU SAY THAT I AM?

As just noted, the titles the Gospels apply to Jesus ("Christ," "Son of Man," "Son of God," and so on) are varied, and their meanings, in their original historical context, are often far from clear. The doctrine of the Trinity, with its affirmation that the Son is fully the equal and of one substance with the Father, did not fully develop until the fourth century. Therefore it is tempting to say that all this business about Jesus being God was a relatively late development in the thought of the early church. But the story is at least more complicated than that.

I have already discussed the rich ways in which the Gospels render Jesus' identity. But I earlier promised something further: going back behind the Gospels to our earliest sources of information about Jesus, the Letters of Paul. Paul was converted to following Jesus in 34 or 35, two to five years after Jesus' death. Two or three years after his conversion, he visited Jerusalem and talked with some of Jesus' original disciples. His earliest known letter, 1 Thessalonians, was written in 49 or 50, still within

77. Frei, *Identity of Jesus Christ*, 142–43.
78. Ibid., 121.

twenty years of Jesus' death, and the seven letters even skeptical scholars attribute to him[79] were all written in the ten years after that. As historical evidence from the ancient world goes, this is, in terms of closeness to the event, quite astonishingly good (much better, for instance, than any sources about someone as famous as Alexander the Great).

Yet Paul already had what theologians call a "high Christology"; he did not picture Jesus as simply a very holy human being, but as divine and worthy of worship. "At an astonishingly early point," Larry Hurtado has written, "in at least some Christian groups there is a clear and programmatic inclusion of Jesus in their devotional life, both in honorific *claims* and in devotional *practices*."[80] Martin Hengel calls the speed with which this happened, particularly given the monotheistic context of the earliest church and the lack of any real analogy in the culture of the time, "amazing," "an explosion."[81]

Consider three terms Paul used: Christ, Lord, and Son of God. Two hundred seventy times in those seven letters of undisputed Pauline authorship he referred to Jesus as "Christ," the Greek translation of the Hebrew term "Messiah," or "anointed one." Jews had long hoped-for one or more great leaders sent from God to save Israel; different Jewish thinkers pictured this hoped-for Messiah in different ways. Paul did not use the term to refer just to a great political or military leader of Israel but expanded its significance to the broadest cosmic, eschatological framework. For him, to call Jesus "Messiah" or "Christ" meant, as Hurtado writes, at least "to assert his significance as the divinely approved figure who acts as the eschatological agent of God."[82] God has put everything in subjection under Christ (1 Cor. 15:27) until "the end, when he hands over the kingdom to God the Father, after he has destroyed every ruler and every authority and power" (1 Cor. 15:24). Jesus of Nazareth is the Christ, and this whole world is now under Christ's subjection, until he hands it over to God the Father. And these ideas do not seem to be Paul's invention: he was particularly apt to refer to Jesus as "Christ" in reference to his death and resurrection,[83] in passages that seem to be formulas he was quoting, so the usage likely goes back even earlier than Paul's own writing.[84]

79. Romans, 1 and 2 Corinthians, Galatians, Philippians, 1 Thessalonians, Philemon.

80. Larry W. Hurtado, *Lord Jesus Christ* (Grand Rapids: Eerdmans, 2003), 4.

81. Martin Hengel, *Between Jesus and Paul*, trans. John Bowden (Philadelphia: Fortress, 1983), 31; Martin Hengel and Anna Maria Schwemer, *Paul between Damascus and Antioch*, trans. John Bowden (Louisville: Westminster John Knox, 1997), 283–84.

82. Hurtado, *Lord Jesus Christ*, 100.

83. For instance, Rom. 5:6; 14:9, 15; 1 Cor. 5:7; 8:11; 15:20; Gal. 2:21; 3:13.

84. Hurtado, *Lord Jesus Christ*, 100.

"Lord," which the undisputed Pauline letters use of Jesus one hundred and eighty times, is an even more complicated term. Like its English translation, the Greek word *kyrios* can refer either to God or to a human superior. So to say "Jesus is Lord" need not have meant any more than "Jesus is the leader I am following." But it could have meant much more. Jews reluctant to say the sacred name of God, YHWH, would often substitute *adonai*, meaning "Lord," for God's name, and, if they spoke Greek, *kyrios* would be the natural translation. When Paul regularly (about a hundred times) called Jesus "*the* Lord," that definite article points to his unique status, and when he said that "God also highly exalted him and gave him the name that is above every name, so that at the name of Jesus every knee should bend, in heaven and on earth and under the earth, and every tongue should confess that Jesus Christ is Lord" (Phil. 2:9–11a), we have left human lords far behind.

In 1 Corinthans 16:22 Paul transliterated into Greek the Aramaic prayer *Marana tha*, meaning "Our Lord, come!" That the formula is Aramaic points to a pre-Pauline Palestinian use among Christians, and that Paul did not think he needed to translate it into Greek or explain it implies that it was widely used in the Christian community. This prayer, affirming Jesus as Lord and praying for his return, is as early as any evidence we have about what Christians did and believed, and it already presents him as God's eschatological representative, to whom it is appropriate to pray. Jews had not said such things about Moses, David, the Maccabean heroes, or anyone else.

"Son of God" is a much less common term in Paul's writings. In the ancient Middle East, kings were regularly identified as "sons of God." Israel was more cautious of the term, but in 2 Samuel the prophet Nathan, speaking in God's name, promised David concerning his son Solomon, "I will be a father to him, and he shall be a son to me" (2 Sam. 7:14). In Psalm 2 (perhaps used in the ritual when a new king was enthroned), the king declares, "I will tell of the decree of the LORD: He said to me, 'You are my son; today I have begotten you' (Ps. 2:7). In Psalm 89 God proclaims of the king, "He shall cry to me, 'You are my Father, my God, and the Rock of my salvation!' I will make him the firstborn, the highest of the kings of the earth" (Ps. 89:26–27). The whole people of Israel (Exod. 4:22–23; Jer. 31:9; 31:20; Hos. 11:1) or the hosts of angels (Ps. 89:6–7) could also be called "sons of God." Jewish writings from after the Old Testament period applied the term to the Messiah, especially righteous or charismatic individuals, or particular angels.[85]

Paul's undisputed letters refer to Jesus as God's Son only fifteen times, and in a variety of different formulas. Sometimes, however, his references to "sending" the Son seem to assume that the Son preexists (Gal. 4:4; Rom. 8:3–4).[86] Some scholars challenge this interpretation, but I share the majority view that someone who does not yet exist is not available to be sent.[87] Similarly, passages like Philippians 2 and 2 Corinthians 8:9, which talk of Jesus' self-impoverishment, *might* refer to starting out a carpenter's son and ending up on a cross, but the more natural reading seems to propose a glorified preexistence from which he took human form. The same can be said of Romans 8:32, where Paul says that God "did not withhold his own Son, but gave him up for all of us"—this seems to mean not just giving up Jesus to the cross but giving up the Son to human incarnation. As soon as we have any information about Christians, in short, they were already calling Jesus the Son of God in ways that seem to imply his preexistence with the Father.

The relevant evidence, moreover, involves not just what early Christians *said* about Jesus but what they *did* with respect to him. They counted on him for their salvation. They prayed to him—the openings and benedictions of Paul's letters regularly invoke God and Christ together, and in 2 Corinthians 12:8–9 Paul speaks of his repeated appeals to "the Lord" to remove some affliction from which he suffers.[88] They baptized in his name and sang hymns to him. Jews simply did not worship anyone but God (even Jews who compromised with Hellenism on many issues never bent on monotheism[89]), and yet Paul, who made the points where he faced controversy clear, never suggested any controversy here. Christians apparently took worship of and prayer to Jesus for granted within twenty years of his death.

85. Jarl Fossum, "Son of God," *Anchor Bible Dictionary*, ed. David Noel Freedman, 6 vols. (New York: Doubleday, 1992), 6:128–37.

86. Ibid., 135.

87. See, for instance, James D. G. Dunn, *The Theology of Paul the Apostle* (Grand Rapids: Eerdmans, 1998), 266–93. In response see Hurtado, *Lord Jesus Christ*, 118–26.

88. Hurtado, *Lord Jesus Christ*, 139–40. Richard Bauckham complains of the scholars who underestimate the clear New Testament evidence for personal prayer to Jesus. Richard J. Bauckham, "Jesus, Worship of," *Anchor Bible Dictionary*, 3:813.

89. Even angels never received worship. See Richard J. Bauckham, "The Worship of Jesus in Apocalyptic Christianity," *New Testament Studies* 27 (1981): 322–41; Hurtado, *Lord Jesus Christ*, 30–31.

Could those earliest Christians have formulated their faith in the language of the Nicene Creed? No.[90] Presented with that language and no explanation of it, would they have at once accepted it? Probably not. Can one make the case that that language, properly understood, captures what they were trying to say, worked out through debates about issues that had not even occurred to them? I think the answer is yes, for reasons I have tried to indicate here and will return to in chapter 4.

THE SON'S JOURNEY INTO A FAR COUNTRY

The starting point for the early Christian reflection that led to the doctrine of the Trinity was this: Christians believed that there is one God; their beliefs and practices implied that Jesus Christ is God, and yet they recognized distinction and even separation between Jesus and the one he called his Father. Consider the point of starkest drama in Jesus' story. In the Gospel according to Mark, Jesus, the rabbi from Nazareth, has been betrayed by Judas, denied by Peter, abandoned by the rest of his disciples, arrested and condemned to death, mocked by soldiers, taunted even by one of those crucified with him. Dying on a cross, he cries, "My God, my God, why have you forsaken me?" (it is the first time he does not call on God as "Father"), gives a loud cry, and breathes his last. A Roman centurion, standing to the side, says, "Truly this man was God's Son."

Two of today's greatest theologians properly point to the dramatic way in which the story here presents Jesus as both God and not God. Jürgen Moltmann writes, "On the cross the Father and the Son are so deeply separated that their relationship breaks off. Jesus died 'without God'—godlessly. Yet on the cross the Father and the Son are at the same time so much at one that they represent a single surrendering moment."[91] Eberhard Jüngel puts it this way: "The God who identifies himself with the dead Jesus encounters himself in the death of Jesus in such a way that he participates in Jesus' God-forsakenness. But this is a meaningful assertion only if it is possible to make a *real* differentiation

90. It would seem to me, indeed, a denial of Jesus' temporal locatedness, and thus of his humanity, to claim that he himself could have used this later terminology to express the sense he nevertheless clearly had implicitly of his relation to the one he called Father. See N. T. Wright, "Jesus and the Identity of God," *Ex Auditu* 14 (1998): 3; Karl Rahner, "Dogmatic Reflections on the Knowledge and Self-Consciousness of Christ," *Later Writings*, trans. Karl-H. Kruger Theological Investigations 5 (Baltimore: Helicon, 1966), 193–215.

91. Jürgen Moltmann, *The Trinity and the Kingdom*, trans. Margaret Kohl (San Francisco: Harper & Row, 1981), 82.

between God and God. . . . But in the fatal encounter, God remains one God. For he remains as Father and Son in the Spirit the one 'event God.'"[92] God's own Child is the Godforsaken One. How can this be, if God is love? The logic of the Gospel narratives is that this is not only possible, but it is in this particular moment that we *most* see God as loving. Christ comes to be in solidarity with us in our separation from God, in an act of the triune God in which the Son goes off willingly even as the Father mourns. How can this *not* be, if God is love? The picture eventually needs to include the Holy Spirit as well, but, at the start, what is clear is that Christians have to find a way to say that Christ who is God died on the cross feeling himself abandoned by God—and yet there is one God. Trinitarian theology is the exercise in figuring out what needs to be the case in order for it to be possible to say that.

For the moment, suffice it to say that Christian talk of God involves one God—a God made known in the Word or Son who was made flesh in Jesus, in the one Jesus called his Father, and in the Holy Spirit, the Paraclete. The church would come to define these as the three persons of the Trinity. But among those persons, who does what? Christian theologians have rather consistently taught that all the works of God are the common work of all the three persons. At the beginning of Genesis, for instance, "a wind from God" or "the Spirit of God" (the Hebrew word for "wind" and "spirit" is the same) sweeps over the face of the waters, and God speaks, so that Spirit and Word and the one whose word the Word is are all active in creation. Still, theologians have traditionally assigned or "appropriated" different parts of God's work to different persons, associating creation with the Father, redemption with the Son, and sanctification and consummation with the Spirit.[93] Even the Apostles' Creed at least suggests as much, for there we affirm our faith in the Father, "who made heaven and earth," and speak of church and resurrection after (and following from?) the clause on the Holy Spirit. It is therefore with some nervousness that I question this practice of "appropriation."

Many theologians have complained about the recent practice of speaking of the Trinity as "Creator, Redeemer, Sustainer" in order to

92. Eberhard Jüngel, *God as the Mystery of the World*, trans. Darrell L. Guder (Grand Rapids: Eerdmans, 1983), 368.

93. Heinrich Heppe, *Reformed Dogmatics*, trans. G. T. Thomson (London: Allen & Unwin, 1950), 118; Karl Barth, *Church Dogmatics* I/1, trans. G. T. Thomson (Edinburgh: T. & T. Clark, 1936), 455. Beginning with Augustine, most theologians assumed that the Old Testament appearances of God were not necessarily of the Son but of any of the three persons, or of the Trinity as a whole. Peter Lombard then further claimed that any of the three persons of the Trinity could have been incarnated. See John Behr, *The Nicene Faith* 2/1 (Crestwood, N.Y.: St. Vladimir's Seminary Press, 2004), 3.

avoid using male language ("Father," "Son") for any of the persons. These terms, the critics say, imply that each of the persons of the Trinity only does one kind of work, whereas in fact all the activities of the triune God are the work of all three persons. I think the criticism is on target, but the problem to which it points goes far deeper than debates about contemporary feminist concerns.

Whenever God is revealed, it is the Word, the second person of the Trinity, the one who became incarnate in Jesus, who is God's self-revelation. "The God who of old appeared to the patriarchs was no other than Christ," Calvin says,[94] and indeed whenever and however God is made known to us, it is the Word or Son—the same Word who was made flesh in Jesus—through which God is made known. In Irenaeus's words, "For he is it who sailed along with Noah, and who guided Abraham; who was bound along with Isaac, and was a Wanderer with Jacob . . . God of God, Son of the Father, Jesus Christ."[95]

Keeping clear on this principle avoids a host of misleading debates on whether a "christocentric" theology minimizes the importance of the doctrine of creation or the role of the history of Israel in salvation. What we know of God we know through God's self-revelation, the Word—whether it is the Word whose speaking creates or the Word spoken by the prophets or the Word made flesh or the Word heard preached in the life of the church—just as our belief in God's self-revelation comes always through the Spirit (as we will see in the next chapter). The Word becomes flesh, and the Spirit enters within us to give us faith; the "Father" is not made known to us except through the Son and Spirit—those Irenaeus in the second century already called the Father's two hands.[96] The Father is the one who raised Jesus from the dead—yet, as already noted, at the resurrection no one is visible but Jesus.

So what does God reveal in this Word concerning who God is? Jesus' name for the one who sent him was often "Father."[97] This has become a problematic term. Particularly in a culture with a long history of patriarchy, calling God "Father" risks implying that all fathers are at least a bit like God. As we seek more equality in marriages, and particularly for

94. Calvin, *Institutes* 1.13.27; 1:156.

95. Irenaeus, fragment 53, Ante-Nicene Fathers 1:577. See also Justin Martyr, *Dialogue with Trypho* 127, Ante-Nicene Fathers 1:263.

96. Irenaeus, *Against Heresies* 4.pref.4, trans. W. H. Rambaut, Ante-Nicene Fathers 1:463.

97. I am less sure either that the usage "*Abba*" can be confidently traced back to Jesus himself or that it indicates a particular level of intimacy. See Mary Rose D'Angelo, "*Abba* and 'Father': Imperial Theology and the Jesus Traditions," *Journal of Biblical Literature* 111 (1992): 611–30; James Barr, "'*Abba* Isn't 'Daddy,'" *Journal of Theological Studies* 39 (1988): 28–47.

those whose experience of their human fathers was one of being abused, such connotations seem unhelpful at the least. If only "parent" could be used in the vocative case, that would at least avoid the gender issue, but "parent" is impersonal in its usage. We never call someone by crying, "Parent!" the way we say "Mother!" or "Father!" It may be merely a cultural accident that Jesus called the one he was revealing "Father" rather than "Mother," but in fact he did, and one diverges from his consistent usage only very cautiously. Jesus pictures himself as like a hen who would gather her brood under her wings (Matt. 23:37), and Julian of Norwich's image of "God almighty . . . our loving Father, and God all wisdom . . . our loving Mother," Jesus "our Mother, brother and saviour,"[98] has considerable rhetorical power without, so far as I can see, in any way endangering orthodoxy. Such examples from Scripture and the tradition encourage us to adopt a wider range of images for God. I also see no insurmountable objections to the formula (used in New York's Riverside Church among other places) "Father, Son, and Holy Spirit, One God, Mother of us all." Indeed, a certain amount of paradoxical juxtaposition may not be a bad thing when speaking of that before which all our words fail. Thus even as early as the seventh century the Council of Toledo spoke of the Son as begotten "from the womb of the Father,"[99] a paradox bolder than most of those proposed by contemporary theologians.

But I would not want to lose "Father" altogether. Apart from God's Word, God would be unknowable, somehow the beginning and end of all things in unfathomable ways. But Jesus, who is God's self-revelation, "the image of the invisible God" (Col. 1:15), authorizes us to speak of and to this Unknowable One as "Father" and teaches us what "Father" ought to mean. In dark times, he can throw his cares on the one he calls "Father." Obedience to his "Father" is joy and liberation, not burden, for in that obedience Jesus becomes most himself. And so it can be for us. We can have the most intimate of relations with this Unknowable God. As Hilary of Poitiers put it, "The Lord does not labor for this purpose, to teach you that God can create all things, but to inform you that God is the Father of the Son who is speaking."[100]

98. Julian of Norwich, *Showings* (long text) 58; trans. Edmund Colledge and James Walsh (New York: Paulist Press, 1978), 293.

99. Council of Toledo (675), Creed of Faith, in Heinrich Denzinger, *The Sources of Catholic Dogma* 276; trans. Roy J. Deferrari (St. Louis: B. Herder, 1957), 107. See also Thomas Aquinas, *Summa Contra Gentiles* 4.11.19; trans. Charles J. O'Neal (Garden City, N.Y.: Doubleday, 1957), 90.

100. Hilary, *The Trinity* 3.22; trans. Stephen McKenna (New York: Fathers of the Church, 1954), 83. See also Athanasius, *Defense of the Nicene Definition* 7.31, in *St. Athanasius: Select Works and Letters*, ed. Archibald Robertson, Nicene and Post-Nicene Fathers, 2nd ser., 4 (repr. Grand Rapids: Eerdmans, 1991), 17.

The greatest mystery here is how the Father who loves the Son can allow the Son to go off to suffering and death. The only answer lies in how much Father and Son love the sinners who need saving. There, I think, we need to stop. If we knew God's love, we could see what poor reflections of it all human forms of love are. But we literally cannot imagine it.

What it means that Jesus has a divine Father, and that we are allowed to call this one our "Father," transcends every human case of fatherhood ("Call no one your father on earth, for you have one Father—the one in heaven," Matt. 23:9). As Barth wrote, "No human father, but God alone, is properly, truly and primarily Father. No human father is the creator of his child, the controller of its destiny, or its savior from sin, guilt and death. No human father is by his word the source of its temporal and eternal life. In this proper, true and primary sense, God—and He alone—is Father. He is so as the Father of mercy, as the Father of His Son, of the Lord Jesus Christ."[101] If we ask what Jesus' story tells us in particular about the first person of the Trinity, it comes to this: this is one whom Jesus calls "Father," even as he invites us to do the same, with the meaning of "Father" that we glimpse only in the relation between this one and the Word made flesh in Jesus. Since the Son is the self-revelation of the Father, all that we can say uniquely about the Father is that the Father is the Father of the Son.

All this comes into clearest and most difficult focus at the cross. Christ has prayed that he might not have to taste this cup: "Nevertheless not my will, but thine, be done" (Luke 22:42). Then he dies on a cross, crying, "My God, my God, why have you forsaken me?" It would be "a foul evasion," Calvin said,[102] to deny that the one hanging on the cross did not feel a radical sense of abandonment. Yet in that moment he was enacting God's salvific love for the world: to use the traditional terms, the abandoned Son is utterly at one with the Father in accomplishing our salvation. Even a jaded Roman centurion can see that this was God's Son. In the resurrection, theologians have learned to say, Christ did not "rise"; he "was raised." He was dead; he could not do anything until someone else brought him back to life. Yet the abandoned one enacting God's will, the dead one raised, is here the only sign of God's presence. In this climax of the story, we keep encountering separation and oneness.

101. Karl Barth, *Church Dogmatics*, III/4, trans. A. T. MacKay et al. (Edinburgh: T. & T. Clark, 1961), 245. See also Diane Tennis's unjustly neglected book, *Is God the Only Reliable Father?* (Philadelphia: Westminster, 1985).

102. Calvin, *Institutes* 2.16.12; 1:518.

Before any of the Gospels was written Paul already quoted a hymn that predated even his citation of it, identifying Christ Jesus as one

> who, though he was in the form of God,
>   did not regard equality with God
>   as something to be exploited,
> but emptied himself,
>   taking the form of a slave,
>   being born in human likeness.
> And being found in human form,
>   he humbled himself
>   and became obedient to the point of death—
>   even death on a cross.
>
> Therefore God also highly exalted him
>   and gave him the name
>   that is above every name,
> so that at the name of Jesus
>   every knee should bend,
>   in heaven and on earth and under the earth,
> and every tongue should confess
>   that Jesus Christ is Lord,
>   to the glory of God the Father.
>
> (Phil. 2:6–11)

To be a Christian is to recognize that this Jesus, the crucified One known even when risen by the marks on his hands, feet, and side, is indeed Lord and that through him we know who God is. One might think that the glory of God the Father would be best served by denying worship to any other—but no, the paradox is that it is the bending of knees at the name of Jesus and the confessing that Jesus Christ is Lord that serves the Father's glory.[103] We learn who this Jesus is first and foremost through the Gospel stories, which narrate his identity. We believe that they tell us the truth about Jesus, and that Jesus is the self-revelation of God, only through the work of the Holy Spirit.

103. David S. Yeago, "The New Testament and the Nicene Dogma," *Pro Ecclesia* 3 (1994): 154.

3
The Epistemology of the Spirit

And though the last lights off the black West went
Oh, morning, at the brown brink eastward, springs—
Because the Holy Ghost over the bent
World broods with warm breast and with ah! bright wings.
—Gerard Manley Hopkins[1]

Earth's crammed with heaven
And every common bush alive with God:
But only he who sees, takes off his shoes,
The rest sit round it, and pluck blackberries.
—Elizabeth Barrett Browning[2]

The doctrine of the Holy Spirit affirms that not only the Word through whom God is revealed to us, but the Spirit through whom we come to believe, is God. "Epistemology" is the part of philosophy having to do with knowing and believing; hence the title of this chapter indicates that, for Christians, such matters are the province of the Spirit. At least by the end of the fourth century, Christian theologians had generally agreed that the claims for divinity they had come to apply to the Son ought to apply to the Holy Spirit as well. The Holy Spirit, after all, came upon Mary that she might give birth to Jesus, and the Spirit enters Christians that we might be saved. Wherever they turned in their theology, there was the Holy Spirit, acting as God just as clearly as did the Word incarnate. Gregory of Nazianzus put it forcefully:

> For if He is not to be worshipped, how can He deify me by Baptism? but if He is to be worshipped, surely He is an Object of adoration, and if an Object of adoration He must be God. . . . Look at these facts: Christ is born; the Spirit is His forerunner. He is baptized; the Spirit bears witness. He is tempted; the Spirit leads Him up. He works miracles; the Spirit accompanies them. He ascends;

1. Gerard Manley Hopkins, "God's Grandeur," *Poems and Prose* (London: Penguin, 1985), 27.
2. Elizabeth Barrett Browning, *Aurora Leigh* (New York: Universal, n.d.), 253.

> the Spirit takes His place. What great things are there in the idea of God which are not in His power?[3]

If the powers of the Holy Spirit include all the great things in the idea of God, so the argument went, then the Spirit too must *be* God.[4] Since God's self-revelation is *self*-revelation, moreover, the triune character of the way the one God is revealed to us, and even more specifically the way in which the Word reveals and the Spirit enables our belief in that revelation, mirror truth about how God is, though the truth they mirror is beyond our imagining.

"As long as Christ remains outside of us," Calvin wrote at the beginning of book 3 of the *Institutes*, "all that he has suffered and done for the salvation of the human race remains useless and of no value for us."[5] But, just as human efforts to understand God necessarily fall short apart from Christ, so human efforts cannot manage to believe in Christ apart from the Holy Spirit. Jesus' first disciples saw a young teacher walking around the Galilean countryside, soon in trouble with the authorities. Twenty centuries later, we encounter a historical figure presented to us in ambiguous evidence. In either case, neither careful observation nor historical research can establish Jesus' divinity.[6] It is the Holy Spirit that brings Christ within us; the Spirit is, Calvin declared, "the inner teacher by whose effort the promise of salvation penetrates into our minds, a promise that would otherwise only strike the air or beat upon our ears."[7] "The Holy Spirit is the bond by which Christ effectually unites us to himself."[8] Not merely God's self-revelation but our acceptance and appropriation of it are God's doing. As Balthasar explained, "while the sacred mystery is publicly proclaimed, it does not cease to be a mystery; we always need consecration, the gift of the Spirit, the 'eyes of faith,' if we are to discern the unveiled mystery."[9]

3. Gregory of Nazianzus, Oration 31:28–29; trans. Charles Gordon Browne and James Edward Swallow, in *S. Cyril of Jerusalem, S. Gregory Nazianzen*, Nicene and Post-Nicene Fathers, 2nd ser., 7 (repr. Grand Rapids: Eerdmans, 1955), 327.

4. "What then? Is the Spirit God? Most certainly." Ibid., 10; 7:321.

5. John Calvin, *Institutes of the Christian Religion* 3.1.1, ed. John T. McNeill, 2 vols., Library of Christian Classics, trans. Ford Lewis Battles (Philadelphia: Westminster, 1960), 1:537.

6. See Søren Kierkegaard, *Philosophical Fragments*, trans. Howard V. Hong and Edna H. Hong (Princeton: Princeton University Press, 1985), 58–62.

7. Calvin, *Institutes* 3.1.4; 1:541. "It is not possible to behold the person of the Father otherwise than by fixing the sight upon it through His image, the Only-begotten, and to Him again no man can draw near whose mind has not been illumined by the Holy Spirit." Gregory of Nyssa, "On the Holy Trinity, and of the Godhead of the Holy Spirit: To Eustathius," in *Gregory of Nyssa*, trans. William Moore and Henry Austin Wilson, Nicene and Post-Nicene Fathers, 2nd ser., 5 (repr. Grand Rapids: Eerdmans, 1954), 329.

8. Calvin, *Institutes*, 3.1.1.; 538.

9. Hans Urs von Balthasar, *Theo-Drama*, vol. 3; *Dramatis Personae: The Person in Christ*, ed. John Riches, trans. Graham Harrison (San Francisco: Ignatius, 1992), 507.

And the one Jesus called Father, that one's self-revelation in the Word, and the Spirit by whose "secret energy . . . we come to enjoy Christ and all his benefits"[10] are all one God.

The conviction that only the Holy Spirit can lead us to faith has the most practical of pastoral implications. "In actual fact," Calvin bluntly acknowledged, "the covenant of life is not preached equally among all people, and among those to whom it is preached, it does not gain the same acceptance either constantly or in equal degree."[11] But faith, when it occurs, is God's doing. Rejoicing that God will sometimes make use of even our poor efforts to the good of our sisters and brothers, we should put forth our best efforts of Christian witness—preaching, teaching, living out the Christian life. But we should do so with the cheerful freedom that comes from knowing that no one's salvation ultimately depends on us. Everyone is in God's hands. Therefore it is not appropriate to grow impatient or angry with those who do not believe, or urge them to try harder. Rather, we should pray for them. And we should dwell with them as fellow pilgrims, knowing that, to whatever degree we believe and they do not, it is no fault of theirs nor accomplishment of ours.

The doctrine of the Holy Spirit is a notoriously neglected theological topic, a fact for which one might offer many explanations (not least that some theologians, addressing theological topics in the traditional order, die before they get to it). One plausible element in the explanation is that the Spirit especially curbs our pride. Of those great intellectual figures who have removed us from the center of our world, Freud, with his theories of the unconscious mind, threatens us more than Copernicus or Darwin: bad enough that we are not at the center of the planetary system or the peak of the world of living things; much worse if we are not even lords of our own minds. Similarly, bad enough that we cannot figure out God without God's self-revelation; much worse that we cannot accept God's self-revelation except God work within us.[12]

SPIRIT IN SCRIPTURE

Ruach, the Hebrew word for "Spirit," apparently referred originally to a stormy wind, a gale—the word may be onomatopoetic, imitating the

10. Calvin, *Institutes* 3.1.1; 1:537.
11. Ibid. 3.21.2; 2:920–21.
12. Karl Barth, *Church Dogmatics* I/1, trans. G. T. Thomson (Edinburgh: T. & T. Clark, 1936), 535.

"whoosh" sound of the strong wind. It is a *ruach* from the east that drives back the sea so that the Hebrew people can cross and escape the Egyptians (Exod. 14:21). Such an uncontrollable force could be seen as the power of God, and the meaning of *ruach* could then be extended to any situation in which God was dramatically at work. Thus within a few verses in Numbers 11, *ruach* rests on Eldad and Medad to enable them to prophesy and goes out from the Lord to bring quails from the sea and let them fall so that the people will have food (Num. 11:26, 31). Most English translations render the first case "spirit" and the second "wind," but the Hebrew is *ruach* both times.

The Hebrew people also saw wind, breath, or the movement of air as a sign of life, and *ruach* thus came to refer to the principle of life. God animates the dry bones in Ezekiel's vision with *ruach* to bring them to life (Ezek. 37); if the Lord were to take back his *ruach*, all flesh would perish and we would return to dust (Job 34:14–15).

Ruach could describe not just life but particular skills or gifts. Those who make garments for the priests have the "*ruach* of wisdom" (Exod. 28:2); craftspeople have the "*ruach* of God" (Exod. 35:31). Their particular skills come as God's gift. In contrast, the *ruach* that comes upon Samson might best be described as "berserk frenzy":[13] under its influence he tears apart a lion (Judg. 14:6), slays three men (14:19), snaps ropes (15:14), and kills a thousand Philistines with the jawbone of an ass (15:15).

From the start, then, the Spirit can be helpful and life-giving but also unpredictable, uncontrollable, potentially terrifying. Metaphorically, the strong wind could be an internal one, some experience that shakes the foundations of one's ordinary life. In Euripides' *Trojan Women*, Helen, brought home in disgrace after the war she had sparked by abandoning her husband to go off with Paris the Trojan prince, muses:

> And yet how strange it is. . . .
> What was there in my heart, that I forgot
> My home and land and all I loved, to fly
> with a strange man? Surely it was not I
> But Cypris, there. . . .[14]

13. Alasdair I. C. Heron, *The Holy Spirit* (Philadelphia: Westminster, 1983), 13.

14. Euripides, *The Trojan Women*, lines 946–48, trans. Gilbert Murray, *The Complete Greek Drama*, ed. Whitney J. Oates and Eugene O'Neil Jr. (New York: Random House, 1938), 995. See John Wisdom, "Gods," *Philosophy and Psycho-analysis* (repr. Berkeley: University of California Press, 1969), 166.

Some force she cannot explain, but only name as the goddess of love ("Cypris" is another name for Aphrodite), motivated her act. A Hebrew Helen might well have spoken of the *ruach* that blew her to Troy, the divine force that drove her to an action that her examination of her own rational motives cannot explain.

Ruach also descended on the judges of ancient Israel—Othniel (3:10), Gideon (6:34), and Jephthah (11:29), as well as Samson—and it is not always clear how much this should be seen as like the skill of craftsmen and how much like Samson's berserk frenzy. The Spirit inspires and guides, but also overwhelms. Paul Tillich talked about "ecstasy," or "standing outside oneself," as the appropriate human response to encounter with the Spirit: I am shaken up, driven into an abyss, pulled out of my accustomed ways of thinking and believing, both elevated and annihilated by a sense of divine presence.[15]

In the best chapter of a fine book on the Holy Spirit, Michael Welker emphasizes that the experience was at least as much communal as individual. Israel faced some sort of crisis, occasioned by external or internal threat. But thanks to a particular person, on whom God's Spirit was said to have come, the people found themselves unexpectedly united and able to act in a way that overcame the threat.[16] The Spirit does not act by magic, rushing down in the midst of battle; rather, somehow thanks to the Spirit, the people emerge from "insecurity, fear, paralysis, and mere complaint" to find that they can face the threat and triumph.[17]

The particular person through whom the Spirit's work is begun need not be a humanly powerful figure; indeed, these people are often outsiders who for one reason or another do not fit in. Othniel violates custom by urging his wife to ask her father for land (Josh. 15:18); Gideon begins as a skeptic about the whole Spirit business and later erects an idol (Judg. 6:13ff.; 8:27); Jephthah is the son of a prostitute and an unknown father (Judg. 11:1ff.).[18] Samson, to take the extreme case, is an "informer, brawler, and arsonist," who nevertheless manifests the work of the Spirit.[19]

15. Paul Tillich, *Systematic Theology*, 3 vols. (Chicago: University of Chicago Press, 1951–63), 1:111–13; 3:112. Karl Rahner talks about "the sober intoxication of the Spirit." Karl Rahner, "Experience of the Holy Spirit," *God and Revelation*, trans. Edward Quinn, Theological Investigations 18 (New York: Crossroad, 1983), 191.

16. Michael Welker, *God the Spirit*, trans. John F. Hoffmeyer (Minneapolis: Fortress, 1994), 52–54.

17. Ibid., 56.

18. Ibid., 59.

19. Ibid., 66–67; see Judg. 13:25.

The stories of Saul give us an even more concrete, certainly more vivid, image of the working of the Spirit. On the road to Gibeah, Saul meets a band of prophets, "and the *ruach* of God possessed him, and he fell into a prophetic frenzy along with them" (1 Sam. 10:10). Much later, now king but fearing the rising power of David, he sends a series of messengers to Samuel and David, but the messengers fall into a frenzy. So Saul finally goes himself, but "the *ruach* of God came upon him. As he was going, he fell into a prophetic frenzy. . . . He too stripped off his clothes, and he too fell into a frenzy before Samuel. He lay naked all that day and all that night" (1 Sam. 19:23–24).

Strange stories! The Spirit's workings lie beyond control or prediction, but their effects are visible enough. They seize people, transforming them, making leaders of outsiders and reducing kings to comatose nakedness. They bring communities together under unexpected leadership.[20] With David, the Spirit comes to rest on one king and his descendants (1 Sam. 16:13; 2 Sam. 7), but the idea of a strange divine presence remains.

So too in the accounts of the prophets, "because no prophecy ever came by human will, but men and women moved by the Holy Spirit spoke from God" (2 Pet. 1:21). While *ruach* is the usual term for the force inspiring the earliest prophets and becomes common again after the exile, prophets from roughly Amos to Jeremiah tended rather to say that the "word" (*dabar*) came to them. Jeremiah can even dismiss prophets who are "nothing but wind (*ruach*), for the word (*dabar*) is not in them" (Jer. 5:13).[21] In early texts, though, and consistently after the exile, prophets have received the *Spirit* and promise an ongoing work. The promise of the Spirit is the promise of God's blessing on the community (Isa. 44:3). The Spirit will bring justice and righteousness (Isa. 32:16–17). As in the time of the judges, the Spirit chooses unexpected leaders who bring about justice not by force but in a strangely powerful kind of powerlessness (Isa. 42:1–4). Indeed, the work of the Spirit contrasts with what is accomplished by might or power (Zech. 4:6). As Cyril of Jerusalem would remark centuries later, while the devil "comes like a wolf upon a sheep, ravening for blood, and ready to devour. . . . Such is not the Holy Spirit; God forbid. . . . His coming is

20. Ibid., 65, 99.

21. The reasons for these changes remain obscure. See Gerhard von Rad, *Old Testament Theology*, trans. D. M. G. Stalker, 2 vols. (New York: Harper & Row, 1962–65), 2:56; Heinz-Josef Fabry, "*rûaḥ*," *Theological Dictionary of the Old Testament*, ed. Johannes Botterweck, Helmer Ringgren, and Heinz-Josef Fabry, trans. David E. Green (Grand Rapids: Eerdmans, 2004), 13:372.

gentle."[22] God will pour the Spirit on male and female, old and young alike, "even on the male and female slaves" (Joel 2:28–29).

It is a mixed blessing. Jeremiah (referring to "word" rather than "spirit," but I think the distinction does not matter here) grew sick of the unpopularity and persecution to which his call as a prophet subjected him, and yet discovered,

> If I say, "I will not mention him,
> or speak any more in his name,"
> then within me there is something like a burning fire
> shut up in my bones;
> I am weary with holding it in,
> and I cannot.
>
> (Jer. 20:9)

The idea of divine presence, powerful, uncontrollable, remains.

The earliest Christians felt such a presence. Acts 2 describes the day of Pentecost, fifty days after Easter, on which the sound of the rush of a violent wind (it sounds like *ruach*) filled the house where Jesus' followers had gathered. They began to speak to the Jews gathered in Jerusalem for the festival from all over the world; some thought them drunk, while others were amazed to hear themselves miraculously addressed in their own languages. Peter addressed the crowd, evoking Joel's prophecy of the pouring out of the Spirit (now, in Greek, *pneuma*) and promising that those who were baptized would receive the "gift of the Holy Spirit" (Acts 2:38). Whatever we make of the details of the story, its connection with its first readers surely drew on memory or experience in their own communities of dramatic moments of the work of the Spirit.

In his first letter to the Corinthian Christians, Paul specified the nature of some of the gifts of the Spirit:

> To each is given the manifestation of the Spirit for the common good. To one is given through the Spirit the utterance of wisdom, and to another the utterance of knowledge according to the same Spirit, to another faith by the same Spirit, to another gifts of healing by the one Spirit, to another the working of miracles, to another prophecy, to another the discernment of spirits, to another various kinds of tongues, to another the interpretation of tongues. All these

22. Cyril of Jerusalem, *Catechetical Lectures* 16:15–16, trans. Edward Hamilton Gifford, Nicene and Post-Nicene Fathers, 2nd ser., 7:119.

are activated by one and the same Spirit, who allots to each one individually just as the Spirit chooses. (1 Cor. 12:7–11)

As in the Hebrew Scriptures, what the Spirit makes possible ranges from practical skills to dramatic and uncontrollable forces. Some can have the Spirit within them without even knowing it (1 Cor. 3:16; Gal. 5:25; 1 Thess. 4:8). Other gifts are publicly visible. As with the work of the Spirit in the period of the judges, the Spirit serves community. Paul emphasizes that community is the goal of all spiritual gifts. The Pentecost story reverses the Genesis account of Babel—where there different people suddenly lost the ability to speak to one another, here that ability is suddenly restored. Similarly in the Gospel stories, where the presence of demons isolates people, Jesus uses the Holy Spirit to restore those he has cured to community, integrating the weak and the outsiders.[23]

Having the Spirit is crucial to being a Christian: "No one can say 'Jesus is Lord' except by the Holy Spirit" (1 Cor. 12:3). The God revealed in Jesus is revealed as a mystery. Human eyes see a wandering teacher executed on a cross. Human reason cannot think of him as God. We need some other gift. Therefore, "these things God has revealed to us through the Spirit, for the Spirit searches everything, even the depths of God. . . . So also no one comprehends what is truly God's except the Spirit of God" (1 Cor. 2:10–11). "Likewise the Spirit helps us in our weakness; for we do not know how to pray as we ought, but the Spirit itself intercedes for us with sighs too deep for words" (Rom. 8:26). The unknown tongues spoken by the first Christians, and by charismatic and Pentecostal Christians today, speak of and to God in a way beyond human capacity or comprehension. For Paul the Spirit shapes every stage of our lives as Christians. When we begin a new life, it is "the new life of the Spirit" (Rom. 7:6). We are sanctified by the Spirit (2 Thess. 2:13). And the Spirit is the God-given guarantee of our hope concerning what awaits us when what is mortal is swallowed up in death (2 Cor. 5:5).

The tension between present and past in the work of the Spirit becomes more dramatic in the Gospel of John. As John tells the story, Jesus and his disciples already have the Spirit (John 6:63; 14:17), but "as yet the Spirit had not been given, because Jesus was not yet glorified" (7:39)—here the Spirit is both already present and yet to come. In the activity of the Paraclete (defender, helper, comforter, assistant,

23. Welker, *God the Spirit*, 201.

lawyer, advocate, counselor, mediator, one who exhorts or makes urgent appeals—all are possible translations of a word derived from "standing alongside"[24]), the future becomes present to Christians while still remaining future—something clearest in Jesus' "farewell discourses" in John 14–17. The same things related to the Spirit seem to be happening both in the present and in the future, in a way that appears at first just confused but turns out to make an important point about how the Spirit works. As the New Testament scholar Gail O'Day writes, "That the Paraclete crosses temporal boundaries within the narrative structure of the farewell discourse provides literary confirmation of a theological reality."[25] Like Paul, the author of John had experience of the activity of the Spirit in the Christian community, and one can suppose that he struggled with the question of whether to think of this as a continuation of something already happening during Jesus' ministry or a new, postresurrection development. The key passages are those in John 14–16 referring to the "Paraclete."

The Johannine community faced difficult challenges in defending their beliefs about Jesus, and they may have sensed a particular need for an advisor to stand beside or rest within them.[26] Jesus promises his disciples "another Paraclete" (14:16–17, the phrase assumes that he himself is also a Paraclete), who will "teach you everything and remind you of all that I have said to you" (14:26); "will prove the world wrong about sin and righteousness and judgment; about sin, because they do not believe in me; about righteousness, because I am going to the Father and you will see me no longer; about judgment, because the ruler of this world has been condemned" (16:8–11); and "will guide you into all the truth" (16:13). This promise seems not in principle different from the Synoptic account in which Jesus tells his disciples that the Spirit will tell them what to say when they are on trial (Mark 13:11; Matt. 10:20; Luke 12:12).

This other Paraclete is distinct from Jesus, but, in addition to reminding people of what Jesus said, will "testify on my behalf" (John 15:26) and "glorify me, because he will take what is mine and declare it to you" (16:14). Later theologies in which the Spirit adds new revelations to Jesus' message—from the Montanists in the second century to Joachim of Fiore in the eleventh—have been judged heretical. They do

24. Yves Congar, *I Believe in the Holy Spirit*, trans. David Smith (New York: Seabury, 1983), 1:53.
25. Gail R. O'Day, "I Have Overcome the World," *Semeia* 53 (1991): 161.
26. Raymond E. Brown, *The Churches the Apostles Left Behind* (New York: Paulist Press, 1984), 106–7.

not fit the picture John gives us here, in which the Paraclete's role is to affirm and support *Jesus*. Similarly, elsewhere in the New Testament the Spirit is "the Spirit of his Son" (Gal. 4:6), the "Spirit of Jesus" (Acts 16:7), and the "Spirit of Christ" (Rom. 8:9).

This Spirit also shapes the lives of Christians. Peter's Pentecost sermon describes how, "having received from the Father the promise of the Holy Spirit," Christ "has poured out this that you both see and hear" (Acts 2:33). Without the Spirit, God's work would not be visible or audible. This "pouring out," moreover, is not a one-time-only event—again and again the Spirit is poured out in the life of the early church (Acts 4:31; 8:15ff.; 10:44ff.; 11:15ff.; 15:8ff.; 19:2ff.). The "Spirit searches everything, even the depths of God," so that, having received the Spirit, "we may understand the gifts bestowed on us by God" (1 Cor. 2:10, 12). Further, it is not as if the Spirit presents us with something and waits to see what we will do with it. "When we cry 'Abba! Father!' it is that very Spirit bearing witness with our spirit that we are children of God" (Rom. 8:15). Not only the gift but our response to it is generated by the Spirit.

From the rich and complex biblical material concerning the work of the Holy Spirit, I want to focus on the epistemological function of the Spirit—its role in bringing us to faith. This might seem an intellectualistic narrowing of the topic, a turning of the Spirit's work into purely a matter of the head, with no role for the heart. But I hope to argue that when the best elements of the Christian tradition talk about faith, they refer to matters of head, heart, and all of life. As I mentioned in the preface, I believe that the Reformed tradition, which can be a bit thin on other aspects of Trinitarian theology, has a particularly rich contribution to make when it comes to the Holy Spirit, so I will focus here on three great Reformed theologians—John Calvin, Jonathan Edwards, and Karl Barth—before turning to some general conclusions about the Holy Spirit and a note on one particularly problematic issue, the *filioque.*

CALVIN—KNOWLEDGE AND LOVE

"Faith," Calvin declared, "is the principal work of the Holy Spirit."[27] Just as "the invisible Father is to be sought solely in the image [Christ],"

27. Calvin, *Institutes* 3.1.4; 1:541. Certainly not the only work: "For it is the Spirit who, everywhere diffused, sustains all things, causes them to grow, and quickens them in heaven and in earth." Ibid., 1.13.14; 1:138.

so "we must be drawn by the Spirit to be aroused to seek Christ."[28] We cannot come to know God apart from God's self-revelation in Christ, and we cannot come to believe that self-revelation apart from the "inner testimony of the Holy Spirit":

> For as God alone is a fit witness of himself in his Word, so also the Word will not find acceptance in men's hearts before it is sealed by the inward testimony of the Spirit. The same Spirit, therefore, who has spoken through the mouths of the prophets must penetrate into our hearts to persuade us that they faithfully proclaimed what had been divinely commanded.[29]

As Basil had written in the fourth century, "He who does not believe in the Spirit does not believe in the Son, and he who has not believed in the Son does not believe in the Father."[30] We cannot know the Father apart from the Father's self-revelation in the Son, or believe in that self-revelation apart from the inner testimony of the Spirit.

But what sort of "knowledge" is this? "The knowledge of faith," Calvin declared, "consists in assurance rather than comprehension."[31] The inner testimony of the Spirit results not in a purely intellectual realization of the truth of which it persuades believers, but more in a heartfelt sense that, "Yes, this makes sense: I can trust this; I can live my life this way." As Calvin put it, "It is harder for the heart to be furnished with assurance than for the mind to be enclosed with thought. The Spirit accordingly serves as a seal, to seal upon our hearts those very promises the certainty of which it has previously impressed upon our minds, and takes the place of a guarantee to confirm and establish them."[32] To have faith is to *trust* in God, and trust, while it involves claims about how God has been and will be trustworthy, is not purely an intellectual matter.

One crucial form of such trust comes in the reading of Scripture. Calvin ran through a range of arguments for the trustworthiness of Scripture, yet he conceded that "they who strive to build up firm faith in Scripture through disputation are doing things backwards."[33] However much we ought to see the truth of Scripture, without the help of

28. Ibid. 3.2.1; 1:544.
29. Ibid. 1.7.4; 1:78–79.
30. Basil, *De Spiritu Sancto* 11.27, in *St. Basil: Letters and Select Works*, trans. Blomfield Jackson, Nicene and Post-Nicene Fathers, 2nd ser., 8 (repr. Grand Rapids: Eerdmans, 1955), 18.
31. Calvin, *Institutes* 3.2.14; 1:560.
32. Ibid., 3.2.36; 1:584.
33. Ibid., 1.7.4; 1:79.

the Spirit sin will lead us astray; alternatively, once we are guided by the Spirit, the truth is so clear that argument becomes superfluous. "No one can say 'Jesus is Lord,' except by the Holy Spirit" (1 Cor. 12:3). For Calvin, the inner testimony of the Holy Spirit replaced the magisterium of the church as that which gives Scripture authority. He denounced as a "most pernicious error" the idea "that Scripture has only so much weight as is conceded to it by the consent of the church. As if the eternal and inviolable truth of God depended upon the decision of men!"[34] A sociologist may note that the Bible takes on its character as "Scripture" because of its use in the church community, but, Calvin would insist, from a *theological* perspective Christians must claim that the church *recognizes* Scripture rather than *making* Scripture—and it recognizes thanks to the work of the Holy Spirit.[35]

The Spirit's guidance of the authors of Scripture has become a central theme in much subsequent theology; the guidance of *readers* of Scripture has tended to be neglected. Yet for Calvin it was just as important: "Without the illumination of the Holy Spirit, the Word can do nothing. . . . And it will not be enough for the mind to be illumined by the Spirit of God unless the heart is also strengthened and supported by his power."[36] "The same Spirit, therefore, who has spoken through the mouths of the prophets must penetrate into our hearts to persuade us that they faithfully proclaimed what had been divinely commanded."[37]

The Spirit who penetrates our hearts then also transforms them. To read Scripture faithfully, the contemporary theologian John Webster has written, I must be willing to, in the medieval term, "mortify myself," to repudiate "the desire to assemble all realities, including texts, including even the revelation of God, around the steady center of my will."[38] If I assume that these stories exist to serve purposes I had already decided I wanted to use them for—and that is very easy to do—then I will not be open to understanding them correctly. To break down such a self-centered perspective, the Spirit, Calvin said, "enflames our hearts with the love of God and with zealous devotion."[39] When I am inspired by the Holy Spirit, I recognize the trustworthiness of Scripture

34. Ibid., 1.7.1; 1:75.

35. A point John Webster makes against David Kelsey and others. John Webster, *Word and Church* (Edinburgh: T. & T. Clark, 2001), 39. See also Ronald F. Thiemann, *Revelation and Theology* (Notre Dame: University of Notre Dame Press, 1985), 61.

36. Calvin, *Institutes* 3.2.33; 1:580–81.

37. Ibid., 1.7.4; 1:79.

38. Webster, *Word and Church*, 43–44.

39. Calvin, *Institutes* 3.1.3; 1:540.

as what the Westminster Confession called "the rule of faith and life,"[40] and my life begins to be transformed. I "depart from myself," as Calvin put it, in order to direct myself wholly to the service of the Lord, submitting and subjecting myself to the Holy Spirit so that I may "hear Christ living and reigning within" me.[41]

Faith and life, knowledge and love, cannot be separated in such matters—this is a theme in Christian theology at least as old as Augustine. Recognizing Christ as God's self-revelation will lead me to change my life, but the process runs the other way too. It is only as I begin to change my life that I grow able to recognize Christ.[42]

Aquinas's appropriation of Aristotle's theory of knowledge gave him useful categories for explaining how this should be. According to Aristotle, when I know something, my passive intellect takes on the form but not the matter of the object known. For instance, if I am thinking about the Eiffel Tower, the tower's matter is not somehow crammed into my head, but my mind becomes formally like it. If my knowledge is somehow incorrect or inadequate, then my mind only partially takes on the tower's form. Since God is love, therefore, I know God more fully and truly to the degree that I become more loving.[43]

The Reformers worried that such a view implied that we come to know God better only as we became more worthy. Several strands of late medieval theology had downplayed the role of grace and emphasized the importance of human worthiness. In contrast, Luther insisted, "Sinners are attractive because they are loved; they are not loved because they are attractive."[44] Luther wanted to make clear that nothing we do can earn a better vision of God. Aquinas had understood that "the faculty of seeing God, however, does not belong to the created intellect naturally, but is given to it by the light of glory."[45] In other words, the love within us that enables us to see God more clearly is not our own accomplishment, but a gift from God. Recent scholarship suggests Luther might have found Aquinas more an ally than an enemy

40. *Westminster Confession of Faith* 1.2, in *Creeds and Confessions of Faith in the Christian Tradition*, ed. Jaroslav Pelikan and Valerie Hotchkiss, 4 vols. (New Haven: Yale University Press, 2003), 3:606.

41. Calvin, *Institutes* 3.7.1; 1:690.

42. Augustine, *On Christian Doctrine* 2.13.20, trans. D. W. Robertson Jr. (New York: Liberal Arts Press, 1958), 47.

43. Thomas Aquinas, *Summa Theologica* 1a.12.6; trans. Fathers of the English Dominican Province (Westminster, Md.: Christian Classics, 1981), 53.

44. Martin Luther, "Heidelberg Disputation," trans. Harold J. Grimm, in *Career of the Reformer*, vol. 1, ed. Harold J. Grimm, Luther's Works 31 (Philadelphia: Muhlenberg, 1957), 57.

45. Ibid.

had he been trained in the theology of Aquinas rather than that of the fifteenth century.[46]

Protestant theologians have struggled ever since—the struggles have often taken the form of debates on the relation between justification and sanctification—to say both that our good relations with God are purely the result of grace and that knowing God involves a transformation within us in which we become more loving, more like God. The fundamental answer is surely a point on which Luther and Aquinas would have agreed: yes, we must be ethically transformed in order to know God better, but the ethical transformation too is God's gift. As Luther put it, "For if any man feel in himself a love towards the Word of God, and willingly hears, talks, writes, and thinks of Christ, let that man know that this is not the work of man's reason, but the gift of the Holy Ghost."[47]

When it comes specifically to the reading of Scripture, then, proper understanding of the text (which is part of the path to knowing God) will involve cultivating appropriate practices, attitudes, and dispositions, what Nicholas Wolterstorff calls "practices of the heart as well as the head, of devotion as well as reflection."[48] As John Webster has written, "Sanctification is the anthropological correlate of revelation."[49] That is, what happens to human beings when we are the objects of revelation is that our lives change. At the core of our changed practices will be a transformation of love, from self-love to love of God. Kevin Vanhoozer puts it this way: "Self-love can pervert the course of interpretation as it does every other human activity. It is the Spirit of understanding who enables us to transfer attention away from ourselves and our interests to the text and its subject matter. Understanding . . . is a matter of ethics, indeed of spirituality."[50] The ethical and spiritual transformations are gifts that follow our reception of revelation, not accomplishments that earn it, but the understanding that revelation brings is inseparable from such transformations. We cannot understand aright without becoming different persons. Whether or not we follow Aquinas in using Aristotle's philosophy to explain why this should be so

46. The classic text is still Otto Pesch, *Theologie der Rechtfertigung bei Martin Luther und Thomas von Aquin* (Mainz: Matthias-Grünewald-Verlag, 1967).

47. Martin Luther, *Lectures on Galatians* (1535) (on Gal. 4:6), trans. Jaroslav Pelikan, Luther's Works 26 (St. Louis: Concordia, 1963), 376.

48. Nicholas Wolterstorff, *Divine Discourse* (Cambridge: Cambridge University Press, 1995), 239.

49. Webster, *Word and Church*, 95.

50. Kevin Vanhoozer, "The Spirit of Understanding," in *Disciplining Hermeneutics*, ed. Roger Lundin (Grand Rapids: Eerdmans, 1997), 161.

(and most Protestants have been nervous about linking their theologies too much to one philosophy), the theological point remains.

EDWARDS—SENSING AND SEEING PATTERNS

Of those following Calvin, few if any have developed the epistemology of the Spirit as insightfully as Jonathan Edwards. "Illumination," Edwards said, is "the proper work of the Spirit of God,"[51] and the Spirit accomplishes that illumination in us by "discovering the excellency [one of Edwards's favorite words] and glory of divine things."[52] To see the world as God's creation, for instance, is simply to have it look different to us. So, Edwards reports, as his "sense of divine things gradually increased . . . the appearance of everything was altered: there seemed to be, as it were, a calm, sweet cast, or appearance of divine glory, in almost everything. God's excellency, his wisdom, his purity and love, seemed to appear in everything; in the sun, moon and stars; in the clouds, and blue sky; in the grass, flowers, trees; in the water, and all nature."[53] Even in lowly spiders, the teenaged Edwards famously observed "wondrous animals . . . from whose glistening webs so much of the wisdom of the Creator shines."[54]

But it was not just nature. Reading 1 Timothy 1:17 ("Now unto the King eternal, immortal, invisible, the only wise God . . ."), Edwards found that there came into his "soul, and was as it were diffused through it, a sense of the glory of the Divine Being; a new sense, quite different from anything I ever experienced before."[55] Contemplating the doctrine of God's absolute sovereignty, he resisted it for a time but then found his objections melting away as divine sovereignty appeared "an exceedingly pleasant, bright and sweet doctrine to me."[56]

Whether natural objects, Scripture passages, or doctrines, then, things manifest their spiritual qualities, according to Edwards, by simple inspection. How do I know that these cherries are red? I just look at them. I might be persuaded that my impression was wrong (my eyesight

51. Jonathan Edwards, Miscellany #732, *The Miscellanies 501–832*, ed. Ava Chamberlain, Works 18 (New Haven: Yale University Press, 2000), 359.

52. Ibid., #628, 156.

53. Jonathan Edwards, "Personal Narrative," in *A Jonathan Edwards Reader*, ed. John E. Smith et al. (New Haven: Yale University Press, 1995), 285.

54. Edwards, "The Spider Letter," ibid., 8.

55. Edwards, "Personal Narrative," 284.

56. Ibid., 283.

is distorted, or a red lamp is shining on white cherries), but it takes a good argument to overcome the immediate evidence of my senses. Similarly, Edwards would say, he knows the truth of Scripture and doctrine because, thanks to the work of the Holy Spirit, it just manifests itself when we contemplate it. A true Christian's idea of and delight in God's loveliness "is peculiar and entirely diverse from anything that a natural man has, or can have any notion of."[57] Preaching on Matthew 16:16, where Jesus tells Peter that only God, not flesh and blood, has revealed his recognition of Jesus as the Messiah, Edwards declares that God, "and none else," is the source of spiritual knowledge: "He imparts this knowledge immediately, not making use of any intermediate natural causes, as he does in other knowledge."[58]

Thus, "There is such a thing, as a spiritual and divine light, immediately imparted to the soul by God, of a different nature from any that is obtained by natural means."[59] This light is not some impression of "outward beauty or brightness" made on the imagination. It is "not the suggesting of any new truths, or propositions not contained in the Word of God."[60] Rather, it is "a sense of the heart," not like knowing the truth of the proposition "Honey is sweet," but like *tasting* honey's sweetness.[61] Honey in fact provided a favorite image: "Something is perceived by a true saint, in the essence of this new sense of mind, in spiritual and divine things, as entirely diverse from anything that is perceived in them, by natural men, as the sweet taste of honey is diverse from the ideas men get of honey by only looking on it, and feeling of it."[62] Here too, someone might persuade me that I had been misled by my sin or tricked by the devil into thinking that I had perceived such a light, but it takes a good argument to challenge an apparently clear impression, and the real thing is unmistakable: "He is certain that what he sees and feels, he sees and feels."[63] The sense of divine excellency in

57. Jonathan Edwards, *Religious Affections,* ed. John E. Smith, Works 2 (New Haven: Yale University Press, 1959), 208.

58. Jonathan Edwards, "A Divine and Supernatural Light," *Sermons and Discourses 1730–1733,* ed. Mark Valeri, Works 17 (New Haven: Yale University Press, 1999), 409.

59. Ibid., 410.

60. Ibid., 412. "Religion is not a way of looking at certain things, but a certain way of looking at all things." Douglas Elwood, *The Philosophical Theology of Jonathan Edwards* (New York: Columbia University Press, 1960), 23.

61. Ibid., 413–14. "There is not only a belief of what the gospel declares . . . but there is also a sense of it. . . . There is a difference between being convinced that it is so, and having a sense that it is so." Jonathan Edwards, *Notebooks on Faith,* in *Writings on the Trinity, Grace, and Faith,* ed. Sang Hyun Lee, Works 21 (New Haven: Yale University Press, 2003), 435.

62. Edwards, *Religious Affections,* Works 2:205–6.

63. Edwards, Miscellany aa, *The Miscellanies a-z, aa-zz, 1–500,* ed. Thomas A. Shafer, Works 13 (New Haven: Yale University Press, 1994), 178.

things is the "conviction of the truth of religion," and is "saving faith."[64] And this is the work of the Spirit.

Edwards was suspicious of those who "are principally taken and elevated with . . . not the glory of God, or the beauty of Christ, but the beauty of their experiences. They keep thinking, with themselves, what a good experience is this!"[65] He did not focus on individual "mystical experiences," but on a *way* of experiencing *anything* in the world. And he was convinced that those who concentrated on the character of their own experience were not really subject to the work of the Spirit, which would manifest itself in focusing attention on God.

Like Calvin, Edwards saw the Spirit's cognitive work as inseparable from its affective work. "The essence of all true religion," he insisted, "lies in holy love."[66] More specifically, "faith arises from a charitable disposition of heart, or from a principle of divine love,"[67] and it evokes from the soul "an answerable inclining of the heart."[68] In saving faith, our hearts incline to Christ himself, and this love in turn inspires humiliation, holiness, and renouncing the world.[69] The work of the Spirit cannot transform our knowing without also transforming our loving.

Recent work on Edwards, especially Amy Plantinga Pauw's marvelous *Supreme Harmony of All*, makes clear just how central the Trinity was to Edwards's theology.[70] However much the Holy Spirit became, for later American evangelicals, an independent contractor doing spiritual works without regard to any claims about the triune God, that was not true for Edwards. For Edwards the beauty and excellency so fundamentally characteristic of God involve the "consent" of one thing to another, and that implies a plurality. "One alone cannot be excellent, inasmuch as in such case, there can be no consent. Therefore, if God is excellent, there must be a plurality in God."[71] Similarly, if John says that "God is love," then there must be more than one person in God in order for there to be love.[72] In Edwards's earlier works, he can seem to fall victim to an error to which those who follow Augustine in matters

64. Edwards, "Divine and Supernatural Light," Works 18:415.
65. Edwards, *Religious Affections*, Works 2:251.
66. Ibid., 107.
67. Edwards, "Notebook on Faith," *Works* 21:428.
68. Ibid.
69. Ibid., 458.
70. Amy Plantinga Pauw, *The Supreme Harmony of All: The Trinitarian Theology of Jonathan Edwards* (Grand Rapids: Eerdmans, 2002).
71. Edwards, Miscellany #117, Works 13:248; see also "The Mind," *Scientific and Philosophical Writings*, ed. Wallace E. Anderson, Works 6 (New Haven: Yale University Press, 1980), 362.
72. Edwards, "Discourse on the Trinity," Works 21:113–14.

Trinitarian are prone: the Father and the Son are persons really doing things, while the Spirit is simply the bond of love uniting them. But at least by the mid-1740s, when he wrote his "Discourse on the Trinity," Edwards had a strong doctrine of the Spirit too as a personal agent—he described the Spirit as "the principle that as it were reigns over the Godhead and governs his heart and wholly influences both the Father and the Son in all that they do."[73]

Edwards was philosophically a Lockean, and so his paradigm of knowledge was the immediate awareness of a sense experience.[74] At one point, he even identified the spiritual sense with Locke's "new simple ideas,"[75] the basic building blocks of experience like colors or sounds or tastes we cannot imagine unless we have experienced them. According to Locke we can imaginatively put those building blocks together in different patterns, but the raw material itself comes to us, uninterpreted. Philosophers and psychologists alike these days doubt the possibility of such uninterpreted experience.[76] Take some simple experiments: draw a checkerboard of alternating red and white squares and another of alternating red and black squares. Paint all your red squares from the same bucket of paint; put them next to each other and see that they are the same color—nevertheless, the squares alternating with white will look darker than those alternating with black. Jerome Bruner and Leo Postman performed a particularly famous experiment in the 1940s. Flash a series of playing cards briefly on a screen, and ask the experimental subjects to identify them. Slip in an occasional black seven of hearts or red jack of spades. Some subjects will "see" a seven of hearts and not notice its anomalous color. Others will somehow combine the color they expect with the color on the card and report "seeing" it as brown or purple. One poor fellow ended up saying, "I don't know what the hell it is now, not even for sure whether it's a playing card."[77]

73. Ibid., 147. See Sang Hyun Lee, "Editor's Introduction," Works 21:19; and *The Philosophical Theology of Jonathan Edwards*, 195. See also Edwards, *Treatise on Grace*, Works 21:181, in contrast to Edwards, Miscellany #94, Works 13:260.

74. John Locke, *Essay concerning Human Understanding*, 2 vols. (New York: Dover, 1959), 4.2.1; 2:177. For Edwards, "the Northampton experiment proved that grace comes not as argumentation or as interposition, but as idea. Conversion is a perception, a form of apprehension, derived exactly as Locke said mankind gets all simple ideas, out of sensory experience." Perry Miller, *Jonathan Edwards* (Cleveland: Meridian, 1959), 139.

75. Edwards, *Religious Affections*, Works 2:205. Though he can also say that the Spirit's work is "to bring the world to its beauty and perfection, out of the chaos," which sounds more like finding a pattern. See Edwards, *Miscellany* #293, *Works* 13:384.

76. In what follows, I am repeating some of what I said in *Unapologetic Theology* (Louisville: Westminster John Knox, 1989), especially 26–29. Already in Locke's lifetime, Berkeley was raising these questions. See A. D. Ritchie, *George Berkeley* (Manchester: Manchester University Press, 1967), 14–18.

77. Jerome S. Bruner and Leo Postman, "On the Perception of Incongruity: A Paradigm," *Journal of Personality* 18 (1949): 214.

"Seeing," then, or any kind of experience—even something as simple as noting the hue of a patch of color—is always already an act of interpretation, shaped in some measure by context and previous experience. As the philosopher Hans Reichenbach noted, even a statement like "This appears white" already involves comparing "this" with some previously seen white object.[78] If the relevant stock of memories includes standard decks of playing cards, confusion results when confronted with a nonstandard example, but such an example only makes vivid the element of interpretation already present in all our perception.

"*X* is above *Y*" might seem another instance of a straightforward sense experience. But if I strap on complicated glasses that invert what I see, then everything looks upside down for a few days but then turns right side up. If I take the spectacles off after a few more days, everything initially looks upside down when viewed normally.[79] One might say that the problem here is just these odd glasses—but my eyes *normally* project an upside-down image on my retinas, which my brain automatically reverses. So what is up and down, above and below, in my visual experience? Even here, the answer involves interpretation.

Similarly with more sophisticated levels of interpretation. The physicist enters the lab and sees complex data registered. The non-physicist sees only odd dials and lights. Norwood Russell Hanson explains, "The visitor must learn some physics before he can see what the physicist sees."[80] One might protest that there must be two events here—the act of seeing itself, and a separate act of instantaneous interpretation—but Hanson has no sympathy. Why postulate two different acts when our experience is so clearly of a single one—this is what I see, always already interpreted?[81] The trained scientist will not say that the visitor to the lab sees what is there, while the expert interprets it, but that the expert sees what is there to be seen, and the visitor misses it.[82] As that greatest of all postmodern analysts of human experience, Marcel Proust, wrote,

78. Hans Reichenbach, *Experience and Prediction* (Chicago: University of Chicago Press, 1938), 176.

79. Michael Polanyi, *Personal Knowledge: Towards a Post-Critical Philosophy* (repr. New York: Harper & Row, 1964), 97.

80. Norwood Russell Hanson, *Patterns of Discovery* (Cambridge: Cambridge University Press, 1958), 17. Polanyi makes the same point about medical students learning to read X-rays. Polanyi, *Personal Knowledge*, 101.

81. "Instantaneous interpretation hails from the Limbo that produced unsensed sensibilia, unconscious inference, incorrigible statements, negative facts and *Objective*. These are ideas which philosophers force on the world to preserve some pet epistemological or metaphysical theory." Hanson, *Patterns of Discovery*, 10.

82. Polanyi, *Personal Knowledge*, 101. The twentieth century's two greatest philosophers of science, Karl Popper and Thomas Kuhn, disagreed on many things, but they agreed on the impossibility of uninterpreted experience. Karl Popper, *Conjectures and Refutations* (New York: Harper & Row, 1963), 46; Thomas S. Kuhn, *The Structure of Scientific Revolutions*, 2nd ed. (Chicago: University of Chicago Press, 1970), 46.

> Even the simple act which we describe as "seeing someone we know" is, to some extent, an intellectual process. We pack the physical outline of the creature we see with all the ideas we have already formed about him, and in the complete picture of him which we compose in our minds those ideas have certainly the principal place. In the end they come to fill out so completely the curve of his cheeks, to follow so exactly the line of his nose, they blend so harmoniously in the sound of his voice that these seem to be no more than a transparent envelope, so that each time we see the face or hear the voice, it is our ideas of him which we recognize.[83]

Edwards talked about the "inner testimony of the Holy Spirit" in the idiom of Lockean empiricism, the cutting-edge psychology of his day: things could have an observable quality of "excellency," and the Holy Spirit enabled us to make the observation. Psychologists and philosophers today would be more apt to talk in terms, for instance, of recognizing patterns, or "seeing as," and the Spirit's work can be described just as easily in this idiom.[84] Yet the reasons for holding the belief remain the same, a belief that, while corrigible in the light of compelling evidence, still seems, apart from such evidence, just clear to the one who believes. In Alvin Plantinga's words:

> I believe a thousand things, and many of them are things others—others of great acuity and seriousness—do not believe. Indeed, many of the beliefs that mean the most to me are of that sort. I realize I can be seriously, dreadfully, fatally wrong, and wrong about what it is enormously important to be right. That is simply the human condition: my response must be finally, "Here I stand; this is the way the world looks to me."[85]

Plantinga represents the tradition of "Reformed epistemology" in its most sophisticated current form—a tradition represented in earlier generations by Dutch philosophical theologians like Abraham Kuyper and Herman Bavinck. That tradition has often treated belief in God as, for

83. Marcel Proust, *Swann's Way*, trans. C. K. Scott Moncrieff (New York: Random House, 1934), 21.

84. Such description should resist linking the theological point to the philosophical/ psychological idiom in which it is expressed; future generations may modify us just as we modify Edwards. Calvin's own brief comments come fairly close to the impossible ideal of making the theological point without borrowing the terms of a particular philosophical or psychological theory, but are on that account cryptic, so that it is helpful to work them out in terms of whatever theories are handiest at a given time.

Bruce Marshall uses a somewhat different contemporary idiom: "The Spirit sees to the holding true of any sentences whose truth conditions are met by the Father and presented to the world by the Son." Bruce D. Marshall, *Trinity and Truth* (Cambridge: Cambridge University Press, 2000), 280. But—a point misunderstood by several of his critics—Marshall is also not committed to any one philosophical conceptuality.

85. Alvin Plantinga, *Warranted Christian Belief* (New York: Oxford University Press, 2000), 437.

Christians, a self-evident foundational truth, one of the things I "just know," like the fact that I am now sitting here at a computer terminal.[86]

Maybe I have a different theory of knowledge, or maybe my faith is just not as strong as theirs (I do not say that sarcastically), but I rather think of belief in God as one part of my web of beliefs, not resting on other, more basic beliefs but also not privileged as that which rests on no other beliefs. So it is with many of the most important beliefs in my life: deciding that I have regularly been experiencing hallucinations, or that most of my best friends are fundamentally untrustworthy, would require such fundamental changes in the way I look at, and live in, the world that only the most overwhelming of evidence could persuade me. But it could happen. Nothing is absolutely beyond reexamination.[87] No small set of beliefs provides the foundation to hold up all the others; rather, everything in the web helps support some of the other things in the web, though changes in some places would require bigger subsequent changes than others. "I have arrived at the rock bottom of my convictions," Wittgenstein once wrote. "And one might almost say that these foundation-walls are carried by the whole house."[88]

So, simply put, Christians read or hear the Bible's stories about Jesus, and about God's engagement with Israel and with the community of Jesus' first followers. It is a grab bag of stories, some of them quite mysterious or horrifying, as well as hymns, prayers, proverbs, and so on. But we may begin to see a pattern in it. How loving is this Jesus, how welcoming of outsiders, how forgiving of any who recognize their need of forgiveness. He speaks and acts with an authority that makes sense only if God is speaking and acting in and through him. Even as evil people arrest and execute him, it seems that God's plan is at work, that Jesus occupies the place of a sinner in a way that, in a mysterious but blessed exchange, brings light and freedom to all the places where we sinners stand. Seeing such patterns at work in stories about Jesus, we then also see them in the interaction of the God of Israel with the Israel of God, and in the life and thought of the first Christians.

To see a pattern is to have some features come to the fore while others move to the background, look different than they did at first

86. See Herman Bavinck, *The Doctrine of God*, trans. William Hendriksen (Grand Rapids: Eerdmans, 1951), 78–79; Alvin Plantinga, "The Reformed Objection to Natural Theology," in *Rationality in the Calvinian Tradition*, ed. Hendrik Hart, Johan van der Hoeven, and Nicholas Wolterstorff (Lanham, Md.: University Press of America, 1983), 364.

87. See Willard Van Orman Quine, *From a Logical Point of View*, 2nd rev. ed. (New York: Harper & Row, 1963), 41.

88. Ludwig Wittgenstein, *On Certainty*, #248; ed. G. E. M. Anscombe and G. H. von Wright, trans. Denis Paul and G. E. M. Anscombe (New York: Harper & Row, 1969), 33.

because we now see them in a different context, or even sit to the side, like a piece in a jigsaw puzzle that must fit somewhere, but not in a way we can discern at the moment. Israel's liberation from Egypt seems more central to the pattern than the slaughter of the Amalekites (1 Sam. 15). The joyful inclusiveness of Third Isaiah, which the Gospels report Jesus as quoting at the beginning of his ministry, seems a kind of culmination of the covenant made so long before with Abraham, that in him "all the families of the earth shall be blessed" (Gen. 12:3). Ezra's rules about foreign wives or Nahum's glee at the destruction of Nineveh move to the side as less important in understanding the meaning of Israel's history. The joy and sharing of the earliest Christians seems more important than the way Ananias and Sapphira drop dead (Acts 5:1–11). And so on.

More broadly, Christians find that the patterns they see in Scripture provide a clue for their understanding of every aspect of their world, and this in at least two ways. First, the Bible offers a kind of framework within which we can place everything else. It can, in a phrase of George Lindbeck's, "absorb the universe."[89] My sometimes apparently meaningless life is part of a meaningful whole that begins with God's creation of all things; is transformed in the life, death, and resurrection of Jesus; and will culminate in the judgment of a gracious God.

Second, in what is called *typological* interpretation, episodes in my own life or elsewhere in the world make a different kind of sense when seen as somehow analogous to stories in the Bible. Typology first developed in Christian interpretations of the Hebrew Bible or Old Testament. Joseph's rescuing of the brothers who sold him into slavery is a *type* of Christ, who died to save all his sisters and brothers. But one can extend the idea of typology to see events in our lives as fitting biblical patterns. Our vote to risk putting more of the church budget into mission work, even though we will have to give more to make this possible, seemed, perhaps, an isolated and trivial decision until we read again how the first Christians shared their possessions, and glimpsed the possibility that we were, however inadequately, conforming to a pattern as old as the church itself.

Up to a point, I can help someone see a pattern. Consider the figure reproduced in N. R. Hanson's *Patterns of Discovery*[90] that contains an image of Christ:

89. George A. Lindbeck, *The Nature of Doctrine* (Philadelphia: Westminster, 1984), 117.
90. Hanson, *Patterns of Discovery*, 14.

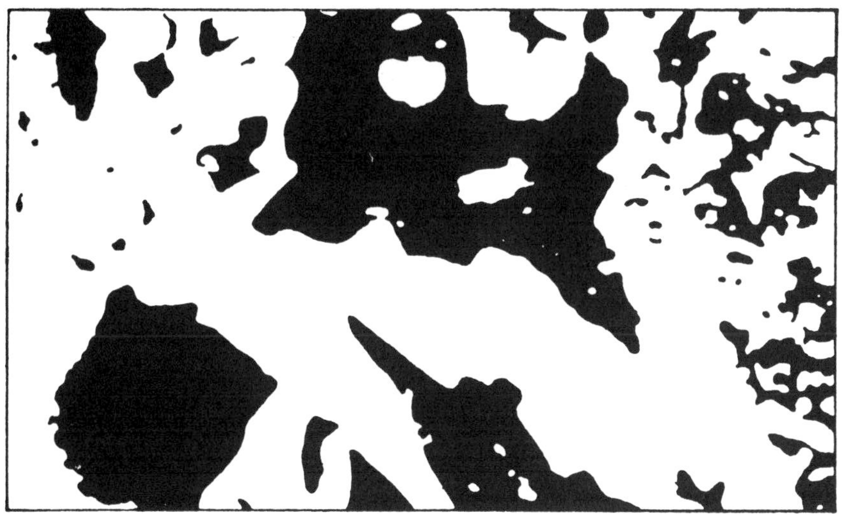

I can point to an eye or the chin in hopes of evoking the figure to someone who "does not see it" (two eyes in black at the center top, the curved line of the nose between them, with white on our right and black on our left . . .). But they may still not see the figure in this new way; neither of us can force the coming-to-vision of the pattern. So in the case of Christian faith, a sermon (or a work of theology) can take the biblical stories or the world around us and direct our attention to certain features, particular relationships. Works as substantial as Augustine's *City of God* or Barth's *Church Dogmatics* do this on a very large scale. But either the moment of "seeing" comes or it does not. One can admire the intellectual achievement of either of these works immensely and still not see the world according to the pattern they limn. One can read the Gospel of Mark as a powerful, haunting text that nevertheless leaves all its readers on the outside of its world.[91]

Alternatively, one does recognize the pattern, and then of course one sees it, without any sense of having arrived at this insight by suddenly trying harder or more sincerely. One may try to reproduce one's own insight in others, but one does not attribute their failure to see to lack of effort or intelligence. The insight comes as a gift, without any label from its giver—except that, as Christians reflect on the overall pattern of things disclosed to us, we can find that one feature of the pattern is

91. See Frank Kermode, *The Genesis of Secrecy* (Cambridge: Harvard University Press, 1979).

to attribute such gifts to the work of the Holy Spirit.[92] We should be grateful rather than proud that we see a Christian pattern in things, for the seeing is finally not our doing; the doctrine of the Holy Spirit here comes close to the doctrine of election in its significance for Christians.

My example from Hanson is in one respect misleading. The picture of Christ, once seen, does seem to be "there" in the drawing, but a tough-minded skeptic could insist that, after all, it is only an ink splotch that is "really there"; everything else is just in the imagination of observers. But there are other cases of seeing patterns. If you fail to see the pattern of the mottled snake there in the tall grass, it may bite you. If you see the pattern of the serial killer's criminal behavior, you may be able to make an arrest. Such patterns may be "interpretations," but they fit every useful definition of reality. So Christians would claim for the patterns they discern: we are seeing features that matter of the world as it is.

Such talk is frustratingly abstract; perhaps a few examples can make it less so. Consider Phyllis Trible's accounts of *Texts of Terror* in the Hebrew Bible in which truly horrible things happen to women.[93] It is not unreasonable to think that the God putatively disclosed in the narratives of which these stories are a part is not merely "patriarchal" in the worst sense of the term but positively sadistic, and to be rejected. Trible rightly insists that we have not read the stories seriously if we dismiss such an interpretation out of hand. Yet she herself finds that the horror of these stories, real though it is, seems finally less central to the scriptural narratives than the vision of a God of mystery and love.[94] She sees a pattern in which the terror of these stories does not lie at the center of things.

Basil Mitchell offers a good example of how such arguments work among literary critics:

> Scholar A takes a certain passage to be the clue to the author's overall meaning. The sense of this passage seems to him quite obvious and also its importance in the work as a whole. However, he recognizes that some other passages are on first reading difficult to reconcile with this one, as he has chosen to interpret it. So he has to bring these apparently recalcitrant passages into line by finding an interpretation of them which will fit; or, failing that, by conceding that they are discrepant, but dismissing the discrepancy as compar-

92. "The Spirit will not persuade by adding something to the totality of belief, by giving us reasons or evidence we do not already have, but by eliciting our assent to a way of structuring the whole." Marshall, *Trinity and Truth*, 204.

93. Phyllis Trible, *Texts of Terror* (Philadelphia: Fortress, 1984).

94. Phyllis Trible, "The Pilgrim Bible on a Feminist Journey," *Princeton Seminary Bulletin* 11 (1990): 232–39.

> atively unimportant. If he can explain why these passages should be in this way discrepant (why Plato nodded *here*) so much the better. In extreme cases he may declare these passages spurious or emend the text; in that case he would benefit from some independent evidence on the point.[95]

Good preaching involves helping a particular congregation think of how the biblical stories illumine the patterns of the world. So the prophet Nathan (a good preacher indeed) told King David nothing he did not already know about his betrayal of Uriah, but by putting David's life into the context of a story he enabled David to recognize the reality of his sin. Struggling at once with the text and with the world in which the congregation lives, the preacher attempts to show that that world fits into the biblical patterns and to deal with puzzling elements of both text and world. But for some listeners (on dark days, even for some preachers) the pattern does not fit. This is why we pray for "illumination" before the reading of Scripture: in the realization that only the inner testimony of the Spirit can enable us to see things in the pattern God intends.

Martin Luther King Jr. insisted that the arc of history is very long, but it bends toward justice. He did not, I am fairly sure, reach this conclusion simply by reflection on his own life experience or on the history of African Americans in the United States. The evidence there would have been ambiguous at best. Rather, he considered the biblical stories, in which darkness never closes out hope, exile is followed by return, and crucifixion by resurrection. Looking in the light of those stories at the history in which he was so important a participant, he could discern in that history a pattern like that in the biblical stories—a pattern he could not have seen without the illumination of the biblical texts.

On a much smaller scale, ordinary preachers sometimes face a tough task in a funeral sermon. Sometimes one can speak of accomplishments, and of family and friends who will treasure the deceased's memory. But suppose the old woman lived poor and died poor, had no family, alienated those who tried to help her as she suffered the bitterness of what may have been the onset of Alzheimer's. Those who would have remembered her kinder self preceded her in death. What comfort is there to speak at the end of such a life—unless somehow her life fits into a larger story that embodies God's will, and in which nothing that

95. Basil Mitchell, *The Justification of Religious Belief* (New York: Oxford University Press, 1980), 46.

is good is ever lost. But, if one starts with that story, then the values of her life emerge, and imposing a Christian pattern does not seem to be a distortion. The resulting sermon might indeed be more authentically Christian than one devoted to praising worldly accomplishment.

BARTH ON GRACE AND THE SPIRIT

Karl Barth never wrote the part of his *Church Dogmatics* dealing systematically with the Holy Spirit. The account of reconciliation, more than 2,700 pages and still incomplete when he died, which surveyed theology from a christological perspective, was to be followed by an account of redemption centered on the Holy Spirit. Yet Barth had already had a great deal to say about the Spirit. In particular, in the first volume of the *Church Dogmatics*, he discusses the triune God and each of God's persons, and then in the mammoth fourth volume each of the three parts develops an account of the Holy Spirit related to what it has to say about Christ. To present the whole schematically:

	IV/1	IV/2	IV/3
Christology	The Obedience of the Son of God	The Exaltation of the Son of Man	The Glory of the Mediator
Sin	Pride	Sloth	Falsehood
Overcoming of Sin	Justification	Sanctification	Vocation
Spirit and Community	Gathering of Community	Upbuilding of Community	Sending of Community
Virtues of the Christian Life	Faith	Love	Hope

Barth presented the sections on community and virtue in each part/volume under the rubric of the Holy Spirit. Moreover, even in the christological sections, the last subsection in each case (the verdict of the Father, the direction of the Son, the promise of the Spirit) turns out already to discuss the work of the Spirit, though this is made explicit in the title only in the third case.

Confronted with this mass of material related to the Holy Spirit, one might almost be grateful that the volumes on redemption never got written! Even a summary of all the riches to be found here is impossible in a short space, and I can only touch on themes relevant to my topic.[96] If one had to summarize the whole very briefly, it might do to say that for Barth the Spirit is always a principle of union, and in a threefold way. First, as in the tradition going back to Augustine, the Spirit is the bond of love that unites Father and Son.[97] Second, as in Calvin and others, the Spirit unites the believer with Christ: "The Holy Spirit is the awakening power in which Jesus Christ summons a sinful man to his community and therefore as a Christian to believe in him, to acknowledge and know and confess him as the Lord who for him became a servant."[98] Third, the Spirit brings the church together.

It is worth emphasizing how here, as so often in Barth's theology, everything is related to nearly everything else. It is through the Spirit that we are united to Christ, but that does not happen simply as a matter of an individual relation. We are joined to Christ only in that we are joined to the Christian community, the church. So, as my chart of volume four of the *Dogmatics* indicates, our individual justification is inseparable from the calling together of the church community, our sanctification inseparable from the building up of the church community, and our vocation inseparable from the sending out of the church community into the world.

Further, the bond of unity among us as a community is important not just for its pragmatic human values but because it mirrors the bond of unity among the persons of the Trinity. Barth insisted, "There is no special or second revelation of the Spirit alongside that of the Son."[99] "The only content of the Holy Spirit is Jesus."[100] Conversely, "The relationship of this man to the Holy Spirit is so close and special that he owes no more and no less than his existence itself and as such to the Holy Spirit."[101] They do not accomplish two separate works, but one work in which Word and Spirit collaborate (as well as the Father).[102]

96. For the Spirit and creation, for instance, see Karl Barth, *Church Dogmatics*, III/1, trans. J. W. Edwards et al. (Edinburgh: T. & T. Clark, 1958), 58.

97. Karl Barth, *Church Dogmatics*, I/1, trans. G. W. Bromiley (Edinburgh: T. & T. Clark, 1975), 469–70, 483. For an account of the dangers of this, see Robert W. Jenson, "You Wonder Where the Spirit Went," *Pro Ecclesia* 2 (1993): 303.

98. Karl Barth, *Church Dogmatics*, IV/1, trans. G. W. Bromiley (Edinburgh: T. & T. Clark, 1956), 740.

99. Barth, *Church Dogmatics*, I/1, 469–70, 483.

100. Barth, *Church Dogmatics*, IV/2, trans. G. W. Bromiley (Edinburgh: T. & T. Clark, 1958), 654.

101. Barth, *Church Dogmatics*, III/2, trans. Harold Knight et al. (Edinburgh: T. & T. Clark, 1960), 333. Barth could even play with the idea of the Son proceeding from the Spirit. Karl Barth, *Church Dogmatics*, I/1, 485–86.

102. Robert Jenson argues that, indeed, for Barth the Spirit is not a personal agent at all but, denoted characteristically in impersonal terms, functions simply as a power through which Christ works. Jenson, "You Wonder," 303. I will return to the question of the Spirit's personal character in the next chapter. Here I would just concede that, whether Jenson is entirely right or not, this is certainly not one of the strongest aspects of Barth's account of the Spirit.

Barth maintained that Jesus' resurrection, the coming of the Spirit, and the Parousia, Christ's return, are "three forms of one event."[103] They are separated in time but one in God's eternity. Between the times of Jesus' earthly life and the end of all things in God, the Spirit functions principally to form the community of Christ.[104] This between-the-times work is always incomplete, and Barth used his quite considerable gift for imagery to convey the point. Consider, for instance, his discussions of faith. Our faith is "an infrequent, weak, uncertain and flickering glow which stands in a sorry relationship to the perfection of even the smallest beam of light." We are "wanderers who pass from one small and provisional response, from one small and provisional perception and love, to another."[105] We see only "the misty landscape, the luminous darkness, in which God is both known and unknown. In our time between the times the veil has not yet fallen."[106]

Barth also insisted, however, that the veiled truth now available to us suffices: "Not only was God glorious in the past and not only will he be glorious in the final fulfillment of his promise, but he is glorious *here and now* in the promise of his Spirit."[107] "The life of the Church and the life of the children of God is, as the work of the Holy Spirit, nothing but the unity of the Father and the Son in the form of time, among and in us men whose existence as such is not yet at home with the Lord but still in the far country, although in Jesus Christ it is no longer in the far country but already at home with the Lord."[108] Yes, we have only glimpses through a glass darkly of the faith and hope and love that await us. But what a wonderful thing to have such glimpses! The hidden God remains hidden even in self-revelation. To unaided human sight and reason Christ appeared only a failed preacher, killed on a cross. "Even in the New Testament and particularly there, the possibility of faith does not go automatically with the fact that Jesus takes the stage as the revelation of the Father." "Flesh and blood has not revealed this to you," Jesus says to Peter. Only with the Spirit is it possible to see

103. Barth, *Church Dogmatics*, IV/3/1, trans. G. W. Bromiley (Edinburgh: T. & T. Clark, 1961), 295.

104. George Hunsinger, *Disruptive Grace* (Grand Rapids: Eerdmans, 2000), 171.

105. Barth, *Church Dogmatics*, IV/2:286.

106. Barth, *The Christian Life*, trans. Geoffrey W. Bromiley (Grand Rapids: Eerdmans, 1981), 168. As Irenaeus had written much earlier, "We do now receive a certain portion of His Spirit, tending towards perfection, and preparing us for incorruption, being little by little accustomed to receive and bear God, which also the apostle terms 'an earnest,' that is, a part of the honor which has been promised us by God." Irenaeus, *Against Heresies* 5.8.1; trans. A. Cleveland Coxe, Ante-Nicene Fathers, 1:533.

107. Barth, *Church Dogmatics*, IV/3/1:359.

108. Barth, *Church Dogmatics*, II/1, trans. T. H. L. Parker et al. (Edinburgh: T. & T. Clark, 1957), 158.

who Jesus is as the Son of God.[109] "How else will God be recognised except by God Himself?"[110]

In distinctions that work better in German than English, Barth separated out three moments of faith: acknowledgment (*Anerkennen*), recognition (*Erkennen*), and confession (*Bekennen*). Most interesting is that acknowledgment precedes recognition. In contrast to what might seem the natural order, one must be obedient and compliant before one can recognize the truths of Christian faith.[111] Here again, transformation of life is inseparable from change in belief. And, here again, this does not threaten the priority of grace because acknowledgment is just as much a gift of the Holy Spirit as recognition is.

The Christian "may make the laborious and profoundly dishonest attempt to regard as true something which he cannot regard as true because it is too high for him. He may even make the further and still more painful effort to persuade himself that this convulsive acceptance is redemptive. But a self-fabricated faith is the climax of unbelief."[112] "The whole idea of a leap that we have made or are making is best abandoned. No one makes this leap. As Christians, we are all borne on eagles' wings."[113] Faith is purely the work of the Spirit, and is from our point of view tentative and uncertain. Being a Christian involves learning to accept that tentativeness and uncertainty in the odd confidence that how hard or passionately or intensely we manage to believe has nothing to do with our salvation anyway. The Spirit works in us, as Barth quoted Luther, whether we are at prayer or "drinking Wittenberg beer with Philip and Amsdorf."[114] Here and elsewhere Barth kept reminding us that we can come to know God only as we are transformed, but that the transformation is the result of grace and not our own efforts.

CONCLUSIONS

The Spirit brings about faith—faith that the one Jesus called Father has been revealed in the Word incarnate in Jesus, and that that self-revelation

109. Barth, *Church Dogmatics*, I/1 (1936), 449.

110. Barth, *Church Dogmatics*, I/2, trans. G. T. Thomson and Harold Knight (Edinburgh: T. & T. Clark, 1956), 521.

111. Barth, *Church Dogmatics*, IV/1:758.

112. Ibid., 745.

113. Barth, *Church Dogmatics*, IV/2:309.

114. Ibid., 632.

makes clear a pattern of God's presence in relation first to the history of Israel and the early church, and then to all things. We see that the beginning and end that give shape and meaning to all things are best understood in God's relation with Israel and the particular Israelite, Jesus of Nazareth, in whom the Word became flesh and lived among us. Knowing that this way of seeing things is not our achievement and is something we should be grateful for rather than proud of, we believe that that which is mysteriously within us, enabling us to see that the "Father" has been revealed in the Word, is just as much God as the "Father" and the Word are. But this Spirit is initially that by which we believe rather than part of the content of our belief. The Word has become flesh in Jesus of Nazareth, visible to human witnesses; the Spirit "has no face";[115] it is incarnate only in the hearts of those who have received it. We find ourselves believing; we do not observe the mechanism by which God makes this possible—thus Latin versions of the Apostles' and Nicene Creeds use the ablative, the grammatical form that indicates the means rather than the object of a verb, for the Spirit: "Credo . . . in Deum Patrem . . . in Jesum Christum . . . in Spiritu Sancto." In Balthasar's words, "The Spirit is not so much a divine object of faith as the divine medium of the gift of faith."[116]

Thus all our talk of the Spirit draws on necessarily imperfect images. Following Peter Lombard, Aquinas identified three names for this third person of the Trinity: Holy Spirit, Gift, and Love.[117] The term *Spirit* has several implications:

1. Spirit is, like breath, the principle of life. What the Spirit gives us is not just a pleasant bonus, but that without which we are finally dead. The Spirit so transforms us that we are "born again."

2. Word is inseparable from Spirit. I cannot speak without breathing.[118] My words come forth in breaths, but the breaths communicate nothing except my words.

3. "The wind blows where it chooses" (John 3:8). Likewise, the Spirit is beyond our control. We find ourselves seized by the Spirit. Saul stripped himself naked and lay as if dead for a day and a night. Since the Spirit lies so beyond our control or comprehension, we can, in what

115. Yves Congar, *I Believe in the Holy Spirit*, trans. David Smith, 3 vols. (New York: Seabury, 1983), 3:15.

116. Hans Urs von Balthasar, *Explorations in Theology*, vol. 3: *Creator Spirit*, trans. Brian McNeil (San Francisco: Ignatius, 1993), 118.

117. Thomas Aquinas, *Summa Theologica* 1a.36–38; 182–93.

118. Gregory of Nyssa, *The Great Catechism* 2, Nicene and Post-Nicene Fathers, 2nd ser., 5:477; John of Damascus, *The Orthodox Faith* 1.7, in *Writings*, trans. Frederic H. Chase Jr. (New York: Fathers of the Church, 1958), 174.

we know by the Spirit, at most bear witness, rejecting comprehensive theory or total vision in favor of the perspectival and fragmentary.[119]

The Spirit is thus always *gift*, never achievement. We do not earn a gift; we cannot calculate its appropriateness.[120] Authentic gifts come unexpectedly. If we come to possess the Spirit, Aquinas notes, our "own power avails nothing; hence this must be given it from above."[121] Yet the gifts of the Spirit are not random; as back in Judges, among Christians they still come to the individual for the good of the community. *We* cannot direct the Spirit, but *God does* direct the Spirit, so that a wider good is served. As Basil the Great put it, "Just as when a sunbeam falls on bright and transparent bodies, they themselves become brilliant too, and shed forth a fresh brightness from themselves, so souls wherein the Spirit dwells, illuminated by the Spirit, themselves become spiritual, and send forth their grace to others."[122]

Gifts come, grace comes, from love. In the Augustinian tradition, the Spirit has been identified with the bond of mutual love between the Father and the Son.[123] This is connected to the Western affirmation of the *filioque*, wherein the love that unites Father and Son must perforce proceed from both—a topic to which I will shortly return. Whether or not one accepts the *filioque*, however, there is scriptural reason for identifying the Spirit with love, just as the Word has to do with intellect. Paul wrote to the Romans, "God's love has been poured into our hearts through the Holy Spirit that has been given to us" (Rom. 5:5). He called on them "by our Lord Jesus Christ and by the love of the Spirit, to join me in earnest prayer to God on my behalf" (Rom. 15:30). And he identified love as the first of the fruits of the Spirit (Gal. 5:22). In the East, in spite of opposition to the *filioque*, Gregory Palamas acknowledged that the Spirit "is like an ineffable sort of love of the Begetter for that ineffably begotten Word, a love by which the very God and Son beloved of the Father responds to the Begetter."[124] The Spirit thus represents both the love that internally brings the persons of the Trinity together and the mutual love of divine grace and human response

119. See Acts 1:8; John 15:26; Raymond Brown, "The Paraclete in the Fourth Gospel," *New Testament Studies* 13 (1967): 129–32; Barth, *Church Dogmatics* I/2:224.

120. See Stephen H. Webb, *The Gifting God* (New York: Oxford University Press, 1996).

121. Aquinas, *Summa Theologica* 1a.38.1; 192.

122. Basil, *On the Spirit* 9.23, Nicene and Post-Nicene Fathers, 2nd ser., 8:15.

123. Augustine, *The Trinity* 5.3.12; trans. Edmund Hill (Brooklyn: New City Press, 1991), 197; 15.5.37, 424; Aquinas, *Summa Theologica* 1a.29.4; 159.

124. Gregory Palamas, *Physica, theologica, moralia et practica capita* 150:36; *Patrologia graeca* 150:1144–45; cited in David Coffey, *Deus Trinitatis* (New York: Oxford University Press, 1999).

through which we creatures can come to know the triune God. As Balthasar put it,

> Considered as the innermost fire of Love of Father and Son, he is absolute knowledge of love from within; but considered as the product, the fruit of this love, he is—as love—also the objective testimony to the effect that this love takes place eternally. . . . Since the Spirit is both things simultaneously, he can be regarded as the one who eternally arouses the divine love; and this love, in turn, can never be exhausted (as human love, alas, can be) because the divine Lovers are constantly aware that their Fruit is always above and beyond.[125]

As such, the Spirit discloses that the reign of God comes through the triumph of love and not the imposition of power. In Jüngel's words, "Love does not see power and weakness as alternatives. It is the unity of power and weakness, and as such is certainly the most radical opposite of the will to power which cannot affirm weakness."[126] Our human way is to seek victory through power—even in knowing, we often seek to subdue the object of our knowledge to ourselves. But this is not how God is, and certainly not how we can know God. Rather, we must bow humbly before God in love if we are to hope to understand, and within God the persons of the Trinity engage in mutual praise.

A loving God manifests divinity by self-giving. *Kenosis* means self-giving or self-emptying—that which is described in Philippians, where Christ "emptied himself, taking the form of a slave, being born in human likeness" (Phil. 2:7). The *kenosis* of the Son is visible enough, above all on the cross. It is harder to grasp the *kenosis* of the Spirit. In Balthasar's words,

> We have no words at all to speak of the indwelling of the Holy Spirit in that which is unholy. The Passion of the Son is something that can be looked upon, because it takes place in human form. . . . But what are we to say of the indwelling of eternal love in our loveless, hating hearts? What are we to say of the eternal, radiant Wisdom's taking her place in our dull, hopeless narrowmindedness? "With unutterable sighs": Who is sighing here? The Spirit.[127]

125. Hans Urs von Balthasar, *Theo-Logic*, vol. 3: *The Spirit of Truth*, trans. Graham Harrison (San Francisco: Ignatius, 2005), 243.

126. Eberhard Jüngel, *God as the Mystery of the World*, trans. Darrell L. Guder (Grand Rapids: Eerdmans, 1983), 206.

127. Balthasar, *Creator Spirit*, 115. On the *kenosis* of the Spirit, see also Sergius Bulgakov, *The Comforter*, trans. Boris Jakim (Grand Rapids: Eerdmans, 2004), 219–20, 255, 280–83, 341, 351.

But such is God's love: a love that will guide us by an inner testimony to see the christomorphic pattern of all things, even at the price of entering into our narrow, sinned-soaked souls.

A NOTE ON THE *FILIOQUE*

The Nicene Creed, as edited into a standard form at the First Council of Constantinople in 381, declared that the Holy Spirit "proceeded from the Father." In the West, as early as the sixth century, the creed was often recited with the addition that the Holy Spirit "proceeded from the Father and the Son" (in Latin "and the Son" is *filioque).* Subordinating the Son to the Father remained a threatening heresy much longer in the West, and adding this phrase seemed a way of affirming the Son's full equality with the Father—whatever the Father did, including breathing forth the Spirit, the Son did too. Moreover, in Augustine's theology, as already noted, the Spirit was the bond of love that united Father and Son, and that image seemed to require that the Spirit proceed from both of them.

Many Eastern theologians, however, reacted with horror. First, the West had unilaterally introduced a change in the most basic of ecumenical creeds. Second, the change challenged a characteristic Eastern way of thinking about the Trinity. For Augustine and the West, the Spirit, the love that united Father and Son, constituted the principle that united the Trinity. For Orthodox theologians in the East, the Father served as that principle of unity, giving birth to the Son and breathing forth the Spirit. Having the Spirit process from the Son as well seemed to lose sight of the Father's central role as the origin of the Trinity. Some even worried that Augustinians were really finding the divine unity in a sort of generalized Godhead, thereby introducing a fourth principle into the Trinity. On the other hand, they suspected that the Spirit as a bond of love was not really a distinct person. After all, if we say that Mary and John love each other, we would normally count two people as involved in the relationship, Mary and John, rather than counting their mutual love as a third person.

As often on such technical issues, the biblical evidence is ambiguous. In John 15:26, the most direct statement on the matter, Jesus declares, "When the Paraclete (the Spirit of truth who proceeds from the Father) comes, whom I will send to you from the Father, he will testify on my behalf" (my amateur translation). So the Spirit "proceeds from the

Father." But the Son sends him from the Father. In John 14:26 the Father sends the Spirit in the name of the Son. "Spirit of God" is the most common New Testament phrase about the Spirit, but Matthew 10:20 has "Spirit of your Father," Acts 16:7 refers to the "Spirit of Jesus," Romans 1:9 says "Spirit of Christ," Galatians 4:6 speaks of "Spirit of the Son," and so on. If any summary of this diverse material is possible, one could say that the Spirit has some sort of relation with the Son. (A relation of dependence? Perhaps. But one could also cite passages about the Son's dependence on the Spirit.) But the one passage that speaks explicitly of procession says that the Spirit proceeds from the Father.

Moreover, the theologians of the early church simply did not think in any technical way about the procession of the Spirit. The Cappadocians consistently referred to the Spirit as processing from the Father. Athanasius usually did the same, but he could also declare, "Whatever the Spirit hath, He hath from the Word."[128] Cyril of Alexandria regularly spoke of the Spirit proceeding from the Son as well as the Father,[129] and as Norman Russell puts it, "Of all the Greek Fathers Cyril is the easiest to accommodate to the Western position on the *Filioque*."[130] In a phrase that would become a common compromise position, John of Damascus described the Spirit as "proceeding from the Father through the Son"; "He is the Spirit of the Son, not as being from Him, but as proceeding through Him from the Father."[131] But many of these phrases are casual references to an issue that early Christians had simply not thought about very much, so it is misleading to identify them with *any* position developed after debate had solidified opposing views. Even as late as 809, when a controversy arose because Western monks on the Mount of Olives were saying the creed with the *filioque* and Orthodox monks down the road at St. Sabba were not, an agreement allowed each to continue in their own way, and the church did not divide.[132]

Things got worse when, in response to the Western change in the creed (and Western trespassing on the East by sending missionaries to Bulgaria), Photius, a patriarch of Constantinople later in the ninth century, proclaimed that the Spirit proceeded "from the Father *alone*" and

128. Athanasius, *Discourses against the Arians* 3.25.24, *St. Athanasius: Select Works and Letters*, trans. Archibald Robertson, Nicene and Post-Nicene Fathers, 2nd ser., 4 (repr. Grand Rapids: Eerdmans, 1991), 407.

129. For detailed references, see Congar, *I Believe in the Holy Spirit*, 3:34–36.

130. Norman Russell, "Notes," *Cyril of Alexandria* (London: Routledge, 2000), 214, n. 96.

131. John of Damascus, *The Orthodox Faith* 1.12; *Writings*, 196.

132. Bulgakov, *Comforter*, 92.

excommunicated the pope for the heretical *filioque*,[133] declaring it "the summit of evils" to say "that the Holy Spirit proceeds not from the Father alone but also from the Son."[134] In the short run the excommunication was withdrawn, but both sides grew ever more determined, and in 1054 the patriarch of Constantinople and the pope excommunicated each other, producing a division between Eastern and Western Christians that endures to this day. Many other issues—theological, political, and cultural—played their roles in the split, but the *filioque* was generally identified as the most important theological matter at stake.

Might we be near to resolving this ancient quarrel? Both Pope Benedict XVI and Rowan Williams, Archbishop of Canterbury, have put reconciliation with the East at or near the top of their agendas. In 1973 Greek Catholics—those who follow Eastern rites but accept the authority of the pope—were permitted to drop the *filioque* when they say the creed. In 1979 the Theological Commission of the World Council of Churches, representing the largest range of Protestant communities, unanimously voted that "the original form . . . of the Niceno-Constantinopolitan creed on the Holy Spirit [without the *filioque*] . . . should be recognized by all as the normative form of the creed and be reintroduced into the liturgy."[135] The Lutheran theologian Wolfhart Pannenberg flatly declares, "The theology of the Christian West has good cause not merely to regret the one-sided addition of the *filioque* clause to the third article of the Creed of 381, and to withdraw it as uncanonical, but also to recognize that the Augustinian doctrine of the procession of the Spirit from both Father and Son is an inappropriate formulation."[136] The Reformed theologian Jürgen Moltmann agrees.[137] Catholic theologians from Yves Congar[138] to Walter Kasper,[139] with varying degrees of caution, do likewise.

I leave negotiations to the specialists in ecumenical theology. For the purposes of systematic theology, it seems possible at least to make the following assumptions without posing problems for future ecumenical consensus:

133. See Richard Haugh, *Photius and the Carolingians* (Belmont, Mass: Nordland, 1975).

134. Photius, *Encyclical Letter of 867*, 33.8, quoted in Jaroslav Pelikan, *Credo* (New Haven: Yale University Press, 2003), 209.

135. Cited in Congar, *I Believe in the Holy Spirit*, 3:206.

136. Wolfhart Pannenberg, *Systematic Theology*, trans. Geoffrey W. Bromiley, 3 vols. (Grand Rapids: Eerdmans, 1991–98), 1:318.

137. Jürgen Moltmann, *The Spirit of Life*, trans. Margaret Kohl (Minneapolis: Fortress, 1992), 71.

138. Congar, *I Believe in the Holy Spirit*, 3:72.

139. Walter Kasper, *The God of Jesus Christ*, trans. Matthew J. McConnell (New York: Crossroad, 1986), 299.

1. When Christians claim to be saying the Niceno-Constantinopolitan Creed (which is what we mean when we refer to "the Nicene Creed"), we ought to say it, not a unilateral Western revision of it.

2. The Father is the ultimate origin of all things in the Trinity. Whatever the Son has is the Father's gift. Thus, if "from" means "*ultimately* from," then anything the Spirit has or is comes "from the Father."

3. Nevertheless, Scripture authorizes us to speak of the Spirit "of the Son," "of Christ," or "of Jesus." The Spirit has a relation to the Son, and at least part of that relationship is that the Spirit forms a bond of love between Father and Son.[140] The particular relation of Spirit and love is scriptural, and Eastern theologians too have mentioned the idea of the Spirit as a bond of love.

Fine-tuning remains to be done, but the Trinitarian disputes behind the oldest major division within Christianity do seem on their way to healing.

140. Pannenberg, *Systematic Theology*, 3:317. This is not, Pannenberg emphasizes, a statement about the Spirit's *origin*. From the other side: "The Spirit proceeding from the Father comes to rest in the Son who is begotten of the Father, and, like an arch, unites the Father and Son in one embrace." Dumitru Staniloae, *Theology and the Church*, trans. Robert Barringer (Crestwood, N.Y.: St. Vladimir's Seminary Press, 1980), 23.

4
These Three Are One[1]

O Blessed glorious Trinity,
Bones to philosophy, but milk to faith,
Which, as wise serpents, diversely
Most slipperiness, yet most entanglings hath,
As you distinguished undistinct
By power, love, knowledge be,
Give me a such self different instinct,
Of these let all me elemented be,
Of power, to love, to know, you unnumbered three.

—John Donne[2]

Love can never be an offense to Christ.

—Feodor Dostoevsky[3]

Reading about the Trinity used to bother me—so many theologians seemed to know so much about the inner character of God. The Trinity, so they declared, involves one substance, two emanations, three personal properties, four relations, and five notions[4]—and is an absolute mystery. If the mystery is so absolute, I wondered, where did we get all those numbers? Reflecting on some of the insights discussed in chapter 1 concerning talk about God, particularly those from Aquinas, however, gave me a different perspective. David Burrell, among others, explains that when Aquinas talks about God as simple, infinite, eternal, and so on, he is really engaged in a kind of negative theology—not defining God's attributes but specifying ways in which we cannot talk about God. That is, we cannot talk about any parts or divisions in God, we cannot set any spatial or temporal limits to God, and so on. Similarly, Victor Preller and George Lindbeck have emphasized Aquinas's distinction between the *significatum* and the *modus significandi* of our talk about God. To review this distinction one more time: if I say "God is good," then it is true that God is good (the *significatum*), but the *way* in which God is good (the *modus significandi*) is utterly beyond my

1. I borrow this title from a book of the same name by David S. Cunningham (Oxford: Blackwell, 1998).

2. John Donne, "A Litany," *John Donne*, ed. John Carey (Oxford: Oxford University Press, 1990), 162.

3. Feodor Dostoevsky, *The Brothers Karamazov*, trans. Constance Garnett (New York: Modern Library, 1996), 339.

4. See Bonaventure, *Breviloquium* 1.3.1; trans. Erwin Esser Nemmers (St. Louis: B. Herder, 1947), 27; Thomas Aquinas, *Summa Theologica* 1a.27–32; trans. Fathers of the English Dominican Province (Westminster, Md.: Christian Classics, 1981), 147–73.

imagination. If I were to encounter God, I would say, "Oh, yes, now I see why it is appropriate to call God 'good,' but, limited by worldly examples and imagination, I would never in a million years have thought of the form that God's amazing goodness actually takes."

With these analyses in mind, I started rereading some classical trinitarian texts in a new way. The great theologians often admit, when talking about the Trinity, that they do not know what the terms they use mean, or they refer to mysteries beyond their power to explain. I had previously taken such remarks simply as signs of pious humility; now I began to think that they meant what they said. The key terms were not intended as definitions, but rather served as placeholders in arguments designed to preserve mystery rather than explain it.

Like many Christians (at least in Western churches), I had also thought of Trinitarian theology as beginning with one God and then trying to explain how that one is also somehow three.[5] This approach too often seems to introduce the Trinity as an additional complication, something more we have to believe after we have managed to believe in God. As Dorothy L. Sayers once wrote, to the average churchgoer it therefore seems "The Father is incomprehensible, the Son is incomprehensible, and the whole thing is incomprehensible. Something put in by theologians to make it more difficult."[6]

As I have argued in previous chapters, however, Christians *start* knowing God in God's self-revelation in Jesus Christ, in Jesus' references to the one he called "Father," and in the Holy Spirit, the Paraclete Jesus promised, who forms and sustains our faith. The task of any doctrine of the Trinity is thus not to show how an abstract one is three, but to show that these three are one,[7] and this is not an unnecessary complication but something essential to what Christians believe.[8]

5. "The Augustinian-Western conception of the Trinity . . . begins with the one God, the one divine essence as a whole, and only *afterwards* does it see God in three persons." Karl Rahner, *The Trinity*, trans. Joseph Donceel (New York: Crossroad, 1999), 17. Recent debates have qualified this distinction in various ways; sometimes they risk losing sight of ways in which it remains true.

6. Dorothy L. Sayers, *Creed or Chaos* (New York: Harcourt, Brace, 1949), 22.

7. See Wolfhart Pannenberg, *Systematic Theology*, trans. Geoffrey W. Bromiley, vol. 1 (Grand Rapids: Eerdmans, 1991), 299. "The trinitarian distinctions of Father, Son, and Spirit are not hidden. They characterize the divine reality that discloses itself in the event of revelation. What is hidden is the universal of the divine essence in these distinctions." Ibid., 340–41. See also Jürgen Moltmann, *The Trinity and the Kingdom*, trans. Margaret Kohl (San Francisco: Harper & Row, 1981), 17, 19.

8. Peter Lombard's *Sentences*, the standard theological textbook of the Middle Ages, began with the triune God, a pattern still followed by Bonaventure. See Zachary Hayes, "Bonaventure," in *The History of Franciscan Theology*, ed. Kenan Osborne (St. Bonaventure, N.Y.: Franciscan Institute, 1994), 56. It was Aquinas who shifted the pattern, beginning with the one God and then following with a discussion of the three persons. Though Karl Rahner and others have seen this as a disastrous mistake, Aquinas was followed in it by the vast majority of theologians, Protestant as well as Catholic, until the twentieth century. See Karl Rahner, "Remarks on the Dogmatic Treatise, 'De Trinitate,'"

When Arius and others in the fourth century said that Christ was a lesser divine being and not fully God, the danger they posed was not just in denying the full divinity of Christ but in taking the first step into polytheism. If Christians had taken that route, they would have broken with monotheism. They would have made Christian faith vulnerable to beliefs like those that concerned squabbling gods of Greek and Roman religion. Moreover, they would have adopted the view characteristic of many gnostic systems, where only lower levels of the Divine can come in contact with the vulgarities of our world, to replace the miracle of Christian faith, in which the only God there is, in grace and humility, comes to live among us. More than anything else, it seems to me, this was the insight Christian orthodoxy captured in the fourth century: Christian faith cannot preserve God's transcendence by interposing great numbers of mediating beings between God and us. Rather, it is God's love that connects with us, directly and immediately, and a loving God is not a lesser being on account of loving, for it is in being loving that God is greatest.

So I start here with two principles: (1) Trinitarian terminology should function less to explain the mystery than to preserve it; (2) thinking about the Trinity should move from the three to the one rather than the other way round. These two principles provide a different angle for thinking about some classical problems in Trinitarian theology.

PRESERVING THE MYSTERY: TERMINOLOGY

In courses on the history of doctrine many of us have learned—and some of us have taught—the basic Trinitarian terminology: Greek Christians came in the fourth century to say that God was three *hypostaseis* in one *ousia*; Latin Christians, starting as early as Tertullian around 200, spoke of God as three *personae* in one *substantia*. In English (and most modern Western European languages use equivalent terms), we say "three persons, one substance."

Some contemporary theologians urge that we get away from these "Greek metaphysical categories"—arguing either that they were always

---

More Recent Writings, trans. Kevin Smyth, Theological Investigations 4 (Baltimore: Helicon, 1966), 83–84; Eberhard Jüngel, *The Doctrine of the Trinity*, trans. Horton Harris (Grand Rapids: Eerdmans, 1976), 4. Gilles Emery and others now argue that critics like Rahner have unfairly exaggerated Aquinas's separation of his discussions of God's unity and Trinity. See Gilles Emery, *Trinity in Aquinas*, trans. Matthew Levering (Ypsilanti, Mich.: Sapientia, 2003), 132–33.

a mistake, or that they were appropriate to an earlier historical context but no longer to ours.[9] Others celebrate the breakthrough these categories achieved.[10] But, whether criticizing or celebrating, many writers assume that early Christian theologians found, or at least thought they had found, a technical terminology that captured exactly what they wanted to say about what was three and what was one in God.

Augustine, however, the greatest of early Trinitarian theologians writing in Latin, frankly admitted that the Greek distinction between one *ousia* and three *hypostaseis* "is rather obscure to me." He knew just enough Greek to know that the distinction did not work in Latin. Translating the Greek terms *ousia* and *hypostasis* as precisely as possible, he concluded, would yield in Latin one *essentia* and three *substantiae*. (In very rough terms, *ousia* and *essentia* mean the essence of a thing; *hypostasis* and *substantia* mean a particular individual.) But "many Latin authors, whose opinion carries weight," used *essentia* and *substantia* interchangeably to refer to what was one in God, leaving Latin speakers, if they tried to follow the Greeks, without a term for God's threeness. Indeed, "when you ask 'Three what?' human speech labors under a great dearth of words. So we say three *personae*, not in order to say precisely, but in order not to be reduced to silence."[11] As Augustine elaborated a bit later in *On the Trinity*:

> And so, for the sake of talking about inexpressible matters, that we may somehow express what we are completely unable to express, our Greek colleagues talk about one *ousia*, three *hypostaseis*, while we Latins talk of one *essentia* or *substantia*, three *personae*, because, as I have mentioned before, in our language . . . "*essentia*" and "*substantia*" do not usually mean anything different. . . . So when the question is asked "Three what?" we apply ourselves to finding some name of a species or genus which will comprise these three, and no such name occurs to our minds, because the total transcendence of the godhead quite surpasses the capacity of ordinary speech.[12]

One thing here seems clear enough: Augustine did not find a technical terminology appropriate to expressing the distinction between what is one and what is three in God. He explicitly admitted both to having

9. See, for instance, Leslie Dewart, *The Future of Belief* (New York: Herder & Herder, 1966), 145–48.

10. See, for instance, Bernard Lonergan, *The Way to Nicea*, trans. Conn O'Donovan (Philadelphia: Westminster, 1976), 136–37.

11. Augustine, *The Trinity*, trans. Edmund Hill (Brooklyn: New City Press, 1991), 5.2.10; 196. "Perhaps we just have to admit that these various usages were developed by the sheer necessity of saying something." Ibid., 7.3.9; 227.

12. Ibid., 7.3.7; 224–25, translation revised.

failed to find such terminology and to having concluded that literal translations of the Greek terms would make no sense at all in Latin. So he used Latin terminology that had become common, by his time, for about two hundred years, "not in order to say precisely, but in order not to be reduced to silence."

The terms *substantia* and *persona* had been standardized by Tertullian, writing in North Africa about 200; there had been a few uses of the terms before then, but Tertullian established them in the theological mainstream. He was, at the time, attacking Praxeas, a Christian in Rome who insisted so much on the oneness of God that, in Tertullian's phrase, he "crucified the Father," holding that the one God had suffered and died on the cross. Tertullian argued that, while God is indeed one *substantia*, the divine *personae* differ, and it was only the Son, not the Father, who was crucified. Tertullian never offered a definition of either *substantia* or *persona*; however, he regularly used *persona* as an ordinary language term for "human being,"[13] but also employed it more specifically for the face[14] or the mask an actor wore in classical drama while playing a particular role.[15] Thus, if we try to analogize from Tertullian's other uses back to the case of God, the three *personae* could either be three individuals or one individual playing three roles—and that ambiguity avoids just the question that needed to be answered.

Substantia meant "substance," but "substance" could mean anything from an individual thing to a kind of thing to the stuff out of which things are made. Unfortunately, moreover, Tertullian seems to have been unable to think of "substance" except as corporeal, a kind of material stuff,[16] which most other Christian thinkers agreed was inappropriate in the case of God. As clarifying metaphysical categories, then, the standard Latin Trinitarian terms Tertullian introduced seem either confusing or just wrongheaded, for *persona* dodges the question of whether the divine threeness involves reality or appearance, and *substantia* has implications that do not fit the case of God.

Is the problem then that pragmatic Latin speakers were unable to understand the subtleties of Greek metaphysics?[17] No, for as it turns

13. Tertullian, *De Poenitentia* 11, *Patrologia latina* 1:1357; *De Corona* 1, *Patrologia latina* 2:95; *De Monogamia* 7, *Patrologia latina* 2:987; *Adversus Praxeam* 14, *Patrologia latina* 2:196.

14. Tertullian, *Adversus Praxeam* 14, *Patrologia latina* 2:196.

15. Tertullian, *De Spectaculis* 23, *Patrologia latina* 1:730.

16. See Edmund J. Fortman, *The Triune God* (Philadelphia: Westminster, 1972), 114.

17. See Catherine Mowry LaCugna, *God for Us: The Trinity and Christian Life* (San Francisco: HarperSanFrancisco, 1991), 250–55, 266–78, 390–400; Colin Gunton, "Augustine, the Trinity, and the Theological Crisis of the West," *Scottish Journal of Theology* 43 (1990): 33–34.

out, the key Greek theologians did not claim to know what these terms meant either. Augustine worried that *ousia* and *hypostasis*, which in the Greek theology of his time were used for what were one and three in God, could be translated into Latin only by two words that were synonyms. But they had originally been synonyms in Greek as well, and the most authoritative of all church creeds, that of the Nicene Council in 325, quite casually used them interchangeably.[18]

In four of the five appearances of *hypostasis* in the New Testament (2 Cor. 9:4; 11:17; Heb. 3:14; 11:1), it means something like "confidence" or "assurance." In the fifth and theologically most interesting case, Hebrews 1:3 declares the "Son" to be "the reflection of God's glory and the exact imprint of God's very being (*hypostasis*)."[19] To push the literal meaning of the metaphor "imprint," imagine a seal pressed into wax and the form of the seal exactly duplicated in the wax—so the Son exactly duplicates the *hypostasis* of the Father. The problem is that *ousia* would have worked in that sentence too. In its only New Testament occurrences (Luke 15:12 and 13), *ousia* refers to the "property" the prodigal son requested from his father and then, in the next verse, squandered in dissolute living.[20] Outside the New Testament, *ousia* can also mean, among other things, "existence," "category," "substance," "stuff" or "material," "form," "definition," or "truth."[21]

Athanasius, the great defender of Nicaea, started out using both *ousia* and *hypostasis* for what there is one of in the Trinity; *prosopon*, the Greek equivalent of *persona*, was his term for the three. Others, however, argued that *prosopon*—like *persona*, it had other meanings, including the part an actor played and the mask he wore to play it—too much suggested that God's threeness is a matter of appearance, even of play-acting. Athanasius understood the concerns of those who therefore wanted another word for the three, some of whom had settled on *hypostasis*. In 362, writing to the church in Antioch, he accepted *hypostasis* as appropriate for the three[22]—but in 369 he had returned to

18. The Nicene Creed, *Creeds and Confessions of Faith in the Christian Tradition*, ed. Jaroslav Pelikan and Valerie Hotchkiss, 4 vols. (New Haven: Yale University Press, 2003), 1:158.

19. The author of Hebrews may have in mind Wisdom 16:21, which also speaks of God's *hypostasis*. "As a piece of Trinitarian language, *hypostasis* is merely an item of linguistic debris knocked from Hellenistic philosophy by collision with Yahweh." Robert W. Jenson, *The Triune Identity* (Philadelphia: Fortress, 1982), 108.

20. One could make this a parable of how God's essence (love) is "squandered" by the Son who travels into the far country where we sinners live—but I suspect that runs too far from any meaning one could honestly assign *ousia* in this passage.

21. R. P. C. Hanson, *The Search for the Christian Doctrine of God* (Edinburgh: T. & T. Clark, 1988), 183. Basil was so worried about this vast array of meanings that he often tried to avoid using the term. Ibid., 698.

22. Athanasius, "Tome or Synodal Letter to the People of Antioch" 6–7, in *St. Athanasius: Select Works and Letters*, trans. Archibald Robinson, Nicene and Post-Nicene Fathers, 2nd ser., 4 (repr. Grand Rapids: Eerdmans, 1991), 484–85.

using it for God's oneness.[23] Far from wanting to insist on any particular terminology, however, he warned against those who "fight about words to no useful purpose" and "only stir up strife with such petty phrases." As long as others were willing to explain how what they meant did not conflict with the Nicene Creed, Athanasius proposed, let them use whatever terms they preferred.[24]

In the standard story of these matters, the Cappadocian theologians—the brothers Basil and Gregory of Nyssa and their friend Gregory of Nazianzus, writing in the fourth century—clarified these matters and introduced technical precision. They dealt with the problem by treating *hypostasis*, in a Trinitarian context, not as an equivalent to *ousia* but as an equivalent to *prosopon*.[25] Theology now had a word (*hypostasis*) for what there were three of in the Trinity that did not imply that the threeness was only a matter of appearance. (Too bad that Latin-speaking Christians messed everything up by going back to *persona* as the term for the three.)

The Cappadocians' goal, however, was not to make everything about God clear—quite the contrary. Their Arian opponents (recent scholarship makes Arius a less-important figure in the movement, but his name still provides a convenient label[26]), Eunomius in particular, who believed that the Son was lesser than the Father, insisted that God could be defined. The Arians argued that "ingenerateness," that is, being without origin, was the defining quality of God, "and anyone who argued (as the Cappadocians did) that God was obscure, or difficult to know, or only partly revealed, was merely being obscurantist."[27] Since the Son was, by definition, generate, the Son could not be God—which was the point these Arians wanted to make. In contrast, the Cappadocians maintained that God is incomprehensible, unknowable, impossible to define.[28]

Thus according to the Cappadocians, the Arians' neat syllogism (God is ingenerate; the Son is generate; therefore the Son is not God)

23. Athanasius, "To the Bishops of Africa" 4; Nicene and Post-Nicene Fathers, 2nd ser., 4:490.

24. Athanasius, "Tome or Synodal Letter to the People of Antioch" 8; Nicene and Post-Nicene Fathers, 2nd ser., 4:485.

25. See, for instance, Gregory of Nazianzus, Oration 39.11, in *S. Cyril of Jerusalem, S. Gregory Nazianzen*, trans. Charles Gordon Browne and James Edward Swallow, Nicene and Post-Nicene Fathers, 2nd ser., 7 (repr. Grand Rapids: Eerdmans, 1955), 355.

26. John Behr, *The Nicene Faith* (Crestwood, N.Y.: St. Vladimir's Seminary Press, 2004), 1:26.

27. John McGuckin, *Saint Gregory of Nazianzus* (Crestwood, N.Y.: St. Vladimir's Seminary Press, 2001), 283. See also Eunomius, *Apology* 7–8, in *Eunomius: The Extant Works*, trans. Richard Paul Vaggione (Oxford: Clarendon, 1987), 41–43.

28. See, for instance, Gregory of Nazianzus, Oration 28.10, Nicene and Post-Nicene Fathers, 2nd ser., 7:292; Pannenberg, *Systematic Theology*, 1:342.

broke down in the face of the divine mystery: one cannot define God as "ingenerate" or anything else. The purpose of terms like *ousia* and *hypostasis* was to preserve the mystery, not to get rid of it.[29] Gregory of Nyssa—who was, of the Cappadocians, *both* the one most inclined to precision in theory *and* the one most committed to preserving God's mystery—explained it this way:

> All things that exist in the creation are defined by means of their several names. Thus whenever a man speaks of "heaven" he directs the notion of the hearer to the created object indicated by this name, and he who mentions "man" or some animal, at once by the mention of the name impresses upon the hearer the form of the creature, and in the same way all other things, by means of the names imposed upon them, are depicted in the heart of him who by hearing receives the appellation imposed about the thing. The uncreated Nature alone, which we acknowledge in the Father, and in the Son, and in the Holy Spirit, surpasses all significance of names. For this cause the Word [Christ], when He spoke of "the name" in delivering the Faith, did not add what it is—for how could a name be found for that which is above every name?—but gave authority that whatever name our intelligence by pious effort be enabled to discover to indicate the transcendent Nature, that name should be applied alike to Father, Son, and Holy Ghost.[30]

"*Whatever* name our intelligence by pious effort be enabled to discover" should be applied equally to Father, Son, and Holy Spirit. Gregory is not here defining *ousia* or *hypostasis*, nor is he even insisting that they are the terms that must be used in Trinitarian discussion. He is, rather, identifying a *rule* for the use of *whatever* terms we use to point to that beyond what any of our language can express: whatever term we use should be used equally of Father, Son, and Holy Spirit. At least in this case, as George Lindbeck says of doctrines in general, the doctrine functions to specify rules for linguistic usage, not to make metaphysical claims whose meaning we could not know.[31] After all, Gregory insists, "Whoever searches the whole of Revelation will find therein no doc-

29. See the remarkable analysis by Jean-Luc Marion, "In the Name: How to Avoid Speaking of 'Negative Theology,'" in *God, the Gift, and Postmodernism*, ed. John D. Caputo and Michael J. Scanlon (Bloomington: Indiana University Press, 1999), 35–37.

30. Gregory of Nyssa, *Against Eunomius* 2.3, in *Gregory of Nyssa*, trans. William Moore and Henry Austin Wilson, Nicene and Post-Nicene Fathers, 2nd ser., 5 (repr. Grand Rapids: Eerdmans, 1954), 103.

31. George A. Lindbeck, *The Nature of Doctrine* (Philadelphia: Westminster, 1984), 18–19.

trine of the divine nature."[32] So let us not try to define "nature" or any of its approximate synonyms when it comes to God.

Early Christian writers likewise resisted giving clear definitions to the key terms used to describe the relations among the persons of the Trinity, begetting and processing. Everyone agreed that both Son and Spirit somehow come from the Father (and perhaps the Spirit from the Son too—that was the topic of the long debate over the *filioque*). But Scriptures identify Christ as the "only begotten Son," and therefore the Spirit could not also be begotten. Rather than looking for a precise alternative term, the Fathers settled on the most vague and general one they could find—"process." As John of Damascus put it, "We have learned there is a difference between begetting and procession, but what the manner of this difference is we have not learned at all."[33] "As to the manner of the begetting and the procession, this is beyond understanding."[34]

"What then is Procession?" Gregory of Nazianzus imagined someone asking. "Do you tell me what is the Unbegottenness of the Father, and I will explain to you the physiology of the Generation of the Son and the Procession of the Spirit, and we shall both of us be frenzy-stricken for prying into the mystery of God."[35] "Begetting" too was mysterious, for the begetting of the divine Son was an "eternal begetting"—there was no time when the Son was not already begotten. And what could "eternal begetting" possibly mean? Gregory of Nazianzus insisted, "The Begetting of God must be honored by silence. It is a great thing for you to learn that He was begotten. But the manner of His generation we will not admit that even Angels can conceive, much less you."[36] In the thirteenth century, Mark of Ephesus summarized the whole Eastern tradition: "We, together with St. John of Damascus and all the holy fathers, do not know the difference between birth and procession."[37]

Similarly Gregory of Nazianzus insisted that the nature of the Trinity lies forever behind a veil, "hidden by the Cherubim."[38] Therefore,

32. Gregory of Nyssa, *Answer to Eunomius' Second Book*, Nicene and Post-Nicene Fathers, 2nd ser., 5:261. For evidence of the chaos that results if one tries to get a philosophically consistent picture out of Gregory's trinitarian terminology, see Christopher Stead, "Ontology and Terminology in Gregory of Nyssa," in *Gregor von Nyssa und die Philosophie*, ed. Heinrich Dörrie, Margarete Altenburger, and Uta Schramm (Leiden: Brill, 1976), 107–27.

33. John of Damascus, *The Orthodox Faith* 1.8, trans. Frederic H. Chase Jr. (New York: Fathers of the Church, 1958), 184.

34. Ibid., 182.

35. Gregory of Nazianzus, Oration 31.8, Nicene and Post-Nicene Fathers, 2nd ser., 7:320.

36. Gregory of Nazianzus, Oration 29.8; Nicene and Post-Nicene Fathers, 2nd ser., 7:303.

37. Quoted in Pavel Florensky, *The Ground and Pillar of the Truth*, trans. Boris Jakim (Princeton: Princeton University Press, 1997), 89.

38. Gregory of Nazianzus, Oration 28.3; Nicene and Post-Nicene Fathers, 2nd ser., 7:289.

"the knowledge of the mutual relations and dispositions of the Trinity is a matter we are content to leave to the Trinity itself."[39] As his finest biographer remarks, "This apophatic turning away from speech is not merely a gimmick with Gregory, for it is constitutive of his whole mental and spiritual approach."[40] In sum, as the distinguished historian R. P. C. Hanson puts it, while the Cappadocians "were successful as no writers before them had been in finding a satisfactory and clearly defined vocabulary for working with their subject," they never insisted on any formula or set form of words. "There never has been a single formula adopted by the majority of Christians designed to express the doctrine of the Trinity, and the Cappadocians never imagined that there could be one."[41] Like Augustine on the Latin side, they used terms to talk about the Trinity while remaining very clear that, given the mystery of God, they did not and could not know what those terms meant. Rather, they were using them as placeholders in propositions whose real function was to establish rules concerning what could not be said about the triune God.

In the title of this chapter I followed the lead of my friend David Cunningham and attempted to dodge the terminological problem by referring to "the one" and "the three"—no nouns at all. Even that, however, fails to capture the full caution of the Cappadocians in the face of the mystery of God. The number "one," Basil insisted, applies to one thing that is material and circumscribed; since God is neither material nor circumscribed, "God is therefore not one in number."[42] Just so, Gregory of Nyssa noted, plurality in general and threeness in particular in any ordinary sense of the word cannot apply to the divine *hypostaseis*, since they "are not separated from one another by time or place, not by will or by practice, not by action or by passion, not by anything of the sort."[43] As Basil concludes, "Let the unapproachable be altogether above and beyond number."[44] Yes, if we are some day granted the

39. Gregory of Nazianzus, Oration 23.11, in *The Later Christian Fathers*, ed. and trans. Henry Bettenson (London: Oxford University Press, 1970), 118.

40. McGuckin, *Saint Gregory of Nazianzus*, 244.

41. Hanson, *Search*, 677.

42. Basil, Letter 2.2 (there is debate about whether Basil actually wrote this letter, but it certainly comes from his circle), *St. Basil: Letters and Select Works*, trans. Blomfield Jackson, Nicene and Post-Nicene Fathers, 2nd ser., 8 (repr. Grand Rapids: Eerdmans, 1955), 116. "Count, if you must; but you must not by counting do damage to the faith." Basil, *On the Spirit* 18.44; ibid., 28. The idea goes back to a remark in Aristotle's *Metaphysics* that only the material can be numbered. See J. N. D. Kelly, *Early Christian Doctrines* (London: Adam & Charles Black, 1958), 268.

43. Gregory of Nyssa, *To the Greeks* 24–25, trans. Daniel F. Stramara, "Gregory of Nyssa, *Ad Graecos* . . . ," *Greek Orthodox Theological Review* 41 (1961): 385.

44. Basil, *On the Spirit* 18.44; Nicene and Post-Nicene Fathers, 2nd ser., 8:28.

vision of God, we will see that we were right to speak of the threeness of Father, Son, and Spirit and the oneness of God as both applying to God—but not only the nouns we use to specify what is three and what is one, but even the numbers themselves do not apply to God in any way we can now imagine.

The Greeks thus did not have a clear metaphysics of *ousia* and *hypostasis* that Latin theologians messed up by shifting to *persona* for what there are three of in God. In the classic forms of both Greek and Latin theology, the key terms resist clear meaning in order to preserve God's mystery. In selecting *persona* as the term for the three, where Greek theology came to reject *prosopon*, however, Tertullian and his successors, by evoking the image of the actor's mask, did risk making God's threeness seem a matter of appearance rather than reality. In modern European languages things have arguably gotten worse, but in the opposite direction. The Latin *persona* did not convey *enough* reality in the three. But "person" and its equivalents in most modern languages suggest a center of consciousness—the "I," Descartes' "thinking thing." That gives *too much* "threeness" to God.[45] As Karl Rahner insists, "There can be no doubt about it: speaking of three persons in God entails almost inevitably the danger . . . of believing that there exist in God three distinct consciousnesses, spiritual vitalities, centers of activity and so on."[46]

Part of the problem lies in modernity's too individualistic understanding of "person"[47]—and by "modern" I here mean a period beginning in the seventeenth century that has now largely come to an end. The modern view of things tended to think of a "person" in terms of an initially isolated individual, certain of its own existence but not sure that anyone else exists. In such a context it is hard to grasp that persons are formed by their relations, much less that we might learn this better in the case of the perfectly related divine persons than we can in imperfectly related, curved-in-on-themselves human persons.

Both Barth and Rahner, who were in other contexts sensitive to the relational formation of persons, oddly decided that God cannot be "three persons" because persons would have to be unrelated

45. Bernard J. F. Lonergan, *Divinarium Personarum conceptionem analogicum* (Rome: Universitas Gregoriana, 1957), 133.

46. Rahner, *Trinity*, 43, 107.

47. The problem goes back to Boethius's sixth-century definition of "person" as "an individual substance of a rational nature," which became the starting point for most of the Middle Ages. For a critique see Lonergan, *Divinarum Personarum conceptionem analogicum*, 133.

individuals,[48] although much recent (postmodern?) philosophy and psychology rejects such an image of the person in favor of a much more relational one. Both therefore proposed replacing "person"—Rahner with "distinct manner of subsisting,"[49] Barth with "mode of being."[50] Depending on context, these usages may swing too far again in the other direction, overemphasizing God's pure oneness.[51] When Barth, for instance, asserts that the "personality" of God belongs to God's one single essence,[52] this risks losing the distinction between Jesus and the one he called his Father that is clearly part of the biblical witness. But in any event, given the degree to which contemporary philosophy and psychology emphasize the relational character of personhood, we need not avoid "person" because it is too individualistic a term.

Whatever confusions exist in modern usage, however, I am arguing here that any attempt to get back to the good old days of classical Greek (or Latin) terminology, when theologians knew what the key terms properly meant, rests on a misunderstanding. Too many historians of the Trinity talk, either in praise or in blame, about the "Greek metaphysics" on which it rests. The Orthodox theologian Paul Evdokimov rightly insists, "Trinitarian doctrine is an absolute stranger to all metaphysical speculation."[53] What the early theologians said was much more something like this: We know from Scripture that the Son is not the Father, for the Son prays to the Father with an intensity that cannot be playacting. We know that the Spirit is Another the Father will send, and not the same as the Son. We know that there is one God, and yet we pray to the Son and the Spirit, and count on them to participate in our salvation in a way that would be blasphemous if they were other than God. We need some terms in order to say that God is both one and three, and so we devise such terms, but it is only beyond this life, in the vision of God, that we will understand *how* God is both one and three.

48. As Amy Pauw points out, one of the oddities of Karl Barth's theology is that he has a wonderfully relational view of what "person" means in the case of human persons, but then adopts the Enlightenment notion of the person as isolated individual when thinking about the divine case—as a result of which he concludes that the three in God should not be called "persons." See Karl Barth, *Church Dogmatics,* II/1, trans. T. H. L. Parker et al. (Edinburgh: T. & T. Clark, 1957), 284; IV/1, trans. G. W. Bromiley (Edinburgh: T. & T. Clark, 1956), 205; Amy Plantinga Pauw, *The Supreme Harmony of All* (Grand Rapids: Eerdmans, 2002), 79. Moltmann makes the same point about Rahner. Moltmann, *Trinity and the Kingdom,* 145.

49. Rahner, *Trinity,* 110.

50. Karl Barth, *Church Dogmatics,* I/1, trans. G. W. Bromiley (Edinburgh: T. & T. Clark, 1975), 358–60.

51. Lonergan remarks, "Although . . . there are three divine conscious subjects, it does not follow that there are three consciousnesses, really distinct from each other. . . . Three subjects are conscious together through one consciousness which is had in one or another way by the three subjects." Bernard J. F. Lonergan, *De Deo trino,* vol. 2: *Pars Systematica* (Rome: Universitas Gregoriana, 1964), 193. I confess to finding this obscure.

52. Barth, *Church Dogmatics,* I/1:351.

53. Paul Evdokimov, *L'Esprit Saint dans la tradition orthodoxe* (Paris: Cerf, 1969), 43.

Thus the doctrine of the Trinity operates as George Lindbeck says that all doctrines operate—as a rule or set of rules. In this case the rules would be something like:

1. Do not say anything that would imply there is more than one God.
2. Do not say anything that would imply that the Son or the Spirit is less than the Father.
3. Do not say anything that would imply that the Son's prayers to the Father, or the distinction between the Son and the Spirit, are matters of appearance rather than reality.
4. Affirm that the threefoldness of God's self-revelation (since it is *self*-revelation) mirrors something threefold in how God truly is.

Such rules state what it means to believe in the Trinity. When the traditional terminology offers a shorthand that at least steers us away from badly misleading terminology, it serves a good theological purpose. When it implies that we know what terms like *ousia* or *personae* as metaphysical categories mean when we apply them to God, then it mistakenly leads us away from proper appreciation of God's mystery.

PRESERVING THE MYSTERY: ANALOGIES

To understand something complicated, we often begin with something similar yet simpler. The analogous case gives us a start in the process of understanding, although, to be sure, later on we have to do some deconstructing, discovering how the two cases are different as well as similar. In the case of God, Aquinas and others, even as they used analogical language, properly emphasized how radically any analogy breaks down.[54] With respect to the Trinity in particular, the theological tradition offers two analogies—one social, one psychological—that deconstruct each other, each giving hints at insight even while reminding us that all analogies break down well before we reach real understanding of God.

Scripture tells us that human beings are made in God's "image and likeness" (Gen. 1:27–28), so human beings are an obvious place to start in looking for analogies for God. Two obvious features of human beings are (1) that we exist in relations with others and (2) that we

54. See William C. Placher, *The Domestication of Transcendence* (Louisville: Westminster John Knox, 1996), 27–31, 71–76.

think and consciously pursue goals. In Aristotle's famous terms, we are at once "political animals" and "rational animals." He would not be human, Aristotle says, if he did not exist in relation to others humans, as part of a community.[55] He would also not be human if he did not engage in acts of knowing and willing—and at the core of willing is to desire or love something. From these two characteristics of humanity, theologians developed a "social analogy" and a "psychological analogy" to the Trinity.

The "social analogy" has been common in Trinitarian thinking in the Eastern church and appeared also in the West, particularly in the work of Richard of St. Victor in the twelfth century and Bonaventure in the thirteenth. God, Richard said, is love, and love needs an object: "As long as anyone loves no one else as much as he loves himself, that private love which he has for himself shows clearly that he has not yet reached the supreme level of charity."[56] But, he observed, it would be disorderly for God to love anything in creation supremely, for created things are not supremely good. "Therefore, so that fullness of charity might have a place in that true Divinity, it is necessary that a divine person not lack a relationship with an equally worthy person, who is, for this reason, divine."[57] Two persons locked in mutual love, however, have about them a kind of selfishness that manifests an imperfection in their love. So, Richard concluded, "Nothing is rarer or more magnificent than to wish that another be loved equally by the one whom you love supremely and by whom you are supremely loved. . . . So a person proves that he is not perfect in charity if he cannot yet take pleasure in sharing this excellent joy. . . . Thus you see how the perfection of charity requires a Trinity of persons, without which it is wholly unable to subsist in the integrity of its fullness."[58]

A difference arises between the human case and the divine case. In the case of human persons, each has a different body and thus a different spatial location. Further, they can disagree with one another and thus find themselves at odds, or they can turn inward on themselves and attempt to deny their essential relatedness. The divine three, however, are not embodied, are always perfectly in accord, and always glo-

55. Aristotle, *Politics* 1.2, 1253a3–6; trans. T. A. Sinclair (Harmondsworth, Middlesex: Penguin, 1981), 59–60.

56. Richard of St. Victor, *The Trinity* 3.2, in *Richard of St. Victor*, trans. Grover A. Zinn (New York: Paulist Press, 1979), 375.

57. Ibid.

58. Ibid., 3.11; 384–85. See also Bonaventure, *The Soul's Journey into God* 6.2, in *Bonaventure*, trans. Ewert Cousins (Mahwah, N.J.: Paulist Press, 1978), 103: "Unless there were eternally in the highest good . . . a beloved and a cobeloved. . . . it would by no means be the highest good because it would not diffuse itself in the highest degree."

rify one another in mutual love, so that they are inseparably one even while they are three.[59]

In contrast to this, Augustine proposed a psychological analogy, which was further developed by Anselm and Aquinas.[60] The human mind, this analogy begins, exists in knowing and loving. But knowing and loving are not activities in which the mind *happens* to engage; rather, since the mind lacks matter, it exists precisely in the doing of these activities.[61] Further, a person cannot truly love something without knowing it (or one would be loving only a figment one's own imagination), and cannot truly know something without loving it (for one needs the empathy of love to achieve full understanding): "And so you have a certain image of the Trinity: the mind itself and its knowledge, which is its offspring and its word about itself, and love as the third element, and these three are one."[62]

Aquinas developed this analogy in more detail. Consider a mind engaged in knowing itself. In order to know itself, it has to form a concept—an image or likeness—of itself, what Aquinas calls "a word of the mind" (*verbum mentis*). If it knows itself perfectly, then that word will be an exact likeness of the mind that knows.[63] In this case, furthermore, the word is brought forth by the mind and has the same substance as the mind; and, when one thing brings forth another that has the same substance as the first, we call that "generation" or "begetting." Hence the second element in the psychological analogy can be called not only the "word" of the first but also "begotten," "child"—or, in a masculine-oriented way of looking at such things, "son."[64]

Loving, however, is different from knowing. The will does not create a *likeness of* that which it wills but rather has an *inclination to* the thing it wills. While perfect love involves knowing what one loves, it is the

59. Gregory of Nazianzus, Oration 42.15; Nicene and Post-Nicene Fathers, 2nd ser., 7:390.

60. Augustine also explored the social analogy, but ended up strongly preferring the psychological one. See Augustine, *On the Trinity* 12.2.5; 324.

61. "Love and knowledge are not in the mind as in a subject, but they too are substantially, just as the mind itself is." Ibid., 9.1.5; 273–74.

62. Ibid., 9.3.18; 282.

63. Thomas Aquinas, *Summa Theologica* 1a.34.1; trans. Fathers of the English Dominican Province (Westminster, Md.: Christian Classics, 1981), 178; Bernard J. F. Lonergan, *Verbum* (Toronto: University of Toronto Press, 1997), 207–8. "It is because of the knower's high degree of immateriality and self-subsistence that the knower does not regard the other [i.e., whatever is alien to it] as simply 'other.' . . . On the level of intellectual cognition, the intellect withstands and overcomes the alien-character of other beings, not by destroying the other in its otherness, but by preserving the other in its otherness. The intellect does this by *becoming* the other. Because of its greater degree of immateriality, the intellect can become the other while still remaining itself." Michael Baur, "Heidegger and Aquinas on the Self as Substance," *American Catholic Philosophical Quarterly* 70 (1996): 331.

64. Aquinas, *Summa Theologica* 1a.27.2; 148; Herbert McCabe, "Aquinas on the Trinity," in *Silence and the Word,* ed. Oliver Davies and Denys Turner (Cambridge: Cambridge University Press, 2002), 87–88; Lonergan, *De Deo trino*, 2:117.

knowledge rather than the love that creates the image of the object known and loved in the mind. "So," Aquinas explains, "what proceeds in God by way of love, does not proceed as begotten, or as son, but proceeds rather as spirit; which name expresses a certain vital movement and impulse."[65]

By this time the analogy looks rather impressive: it can explain why the second person of the Trinity is called "Word" or "Son" and why only the second person is "begotten" while we have to find another term ("proceeds") for the way the third person is produced, why that third person is called "Spirit," "Gift," or "Love," and why there cannot be additional processions.[66] Further, we have to know at least something about an object in order to love it, and so Aquinas finds in this analogy a support for the Western *filioque*: "For love proceeds from a word: we are able to love nothing but that which a word of the heart conceives."[67] Thus the third person must proceed from the second person as well as from the first. Moreover, while the analysis certainly goes beyond anything in Scripture as to detail, the equivalence of Son to Logos, or principle of understanding, and of Holy Spirit to love have solid scriptural bases.[68]

These two analogies have shaped much subsequent Trinitarian theology, including Barth's use of the psychological analogy, Moltmann's preference for the social, and beyond, into our own time. Each, however, reminds us of the limitations of the other. In the psychological analogy there is only one person—no element in God that could pray to another or feel abandoned by another—and this is at odds with the biblical witness. Moreover, for God to instantiate perfect love apart even from creation, there needs to be more of an "other" in God to be the object of

65. Aquinas, *Summa Theologica* 1a.27.4; 150. "Although in us love accomplishes only a kind of quasi-identification of the one loving with the beloved, in the divine Persons, love accomplishes a true and full identity of the one loving and the beloved." Lonergan, *De Deo trino*, 2:208.

66. Lonergan, *Verbum*, 216.

67. Aquinas, *Summa Contra Gentiles* 4.24.12; trans. Charles J. O'Neil (Notre Dame: University of Notre Dame Press, 1975), 140; Lonergan, *Verbum*, 110. "Since in divine persons to be intentional and to be natural are the same, the Word is God not only according to intentional existence but also according to natural existence. And therefore the other Persons are in the Word, since their natural existence is also their intentional existence. And according to this God is said to be in the divine intentionality of God understood, or in the Word. Also, although in us love accomplishes only a kind of quasi-identification of the one loving with the beloved, in the divine Persons love accomplishes a true and full identity of the one loving and the beloved; and according to this God is truly said to be loved in God loving. Therefore insofar as the Father and Son are loved by a love proceeding from them who is the Holy Spirit, they are in this very love. Again, although Father and Son are consubstantial by reason of divine generation, they are also consubstantial by reason of the love which joins the two into one. And according to this, the Holy Spirit is said to be the connection between the Father and the Son, *not* as if by procession he were intermediate, but because these who by nature are consubstantial, infinite love from eternity also makes one under another aspect." Lonergan, *De Deo trino*, 2:208.

68. As noted by Rahner, "Remarks," 85.

love than the psychological analogy provides. The social analogy, on the other hand, inevitably risks tritheism: if the analogy is to a case where we would clearly identify three human beings, why should we not speak of three Gods? So the social analogy gives us too much threeness, while the psychological analogy does not give us enough.

Calvin thought the use of such analogies more likely to lead astray than to illuminate and therefore judged it safer simply to avoid what he called "speculation."[69] I am inclined to follow Balthasar in thinking they can be helpful if used with extreme caution: "The creaturely image must be content to look in the direction of the mystery of God from its two starting points at the same time; the lines of perspective meet at an invisible point, in eternity."[70] As Aquinas noted, such analogies certainly cannot justify theological inferences;[71] we cannot say, "This is true in the human case, and the divine case is analogous, therefore it, or something like it, must be true in the divine case." The best justification of the explicit use of these analogies is that we implicitly use them anyway: the language in which we speak of the Trinity embodies a history in which these analogies are included. So better to get them out in the open, notice their limitations, and allow each to deconstruct the other.

Apart from their intrinsic inadequacies, the analogies also break down because of the imperfections of human beings, with whom they are drawing analogies. While I cannot be human except in relation to others, I am always curving in on myself and failing to be as fully open to such relations as I ought to be. While I exist as a thinking, willing being by knowing and loving the world around me, I never know or love perfectly, and therefore my knowledge and love never become identical with their objects. Reflection on these two imperfect analogies to the divine Trinity invites us to think how a community of fully loving persons not limited by bodies, spatial location, or the possibility of conflict in wills, and the perfection of an existing mind that fully knew and fully loved, might approach one another. But then of course we have to say

69. John Calvin, *Institutes of the Christian Religion* 1.13.18; ed. John T. McNeill, trans. Ford Lewis Battles, 2 vols. Library of Christian Classics (Philadelphia: Westminster, 1960), 1:142.

70. Hans Urs von Balthasar, *Theo-Drama*, vol. 3: *Dramatis Personae: The Person in Christ*, trans. Graham Harrison (San Francisco: Ignatius, 1992), 527. "This endeavor can never go beyond a convergence between two Trinitarian models whose common feature is to point upward toward an integration that cannot be achieved from within the horizon of the world. The interpersonal model cannot attain the substantial unity of God, whereas the intrapersonal model cannot give an adequate picture of the real and abiding face-to-face encounter of the hypostases." Hans Urs von Balthasar, *Theo-Logic*, vol. 2: *Truth of God*, trans. Adrian J. Walker (San Francisco: Ignatius, 2004), 38. See also Lonergan, *Verbum*, 204.

71. Aquinas, *Summa Theologica* 2a2ae.1.5; 1166.

that we cannot imagine that; at least in this life we cannot synthesize the two analogies but can only use them as mutual correctives.[72]

SO WHY BOTHER?

The traditional analogies used to understand the Trinity can only be suggestive, not least in that they deconstruct one another. Traditional Trinitarian terminology does not embody some appropriate theory of how the Trinity fits together; rather, the terms were developed to preserve the mystery of a God we cannot understand. So why try to talk about the Trinity at all? As I noted at the beginning of this chapter, it is hard to answer that question if we begin with one God and ask why we should think of that God as three. But that is not the logic of Trinitarian thought. Rather, Christians begin with three, and the doctrine of the Trinity is the explanation of their oneness.

As I also noted, the New Testament does not present a doctrine of the Trinity, and the language to say what the church came to feel needed to be said evolved only over several centuries. Yet, as J. N. D Kelly has remarked, a threefoldness in thinking about God "was embedded deeply in Christian thinking from the start . . . all the more striking because more often than not there is nothing in the context to necessitate it."[73] Long before the church worked out technical Trinitarian terminology, New Testament writers sometimes seemingly went out of their way to employ language that at least included three elements. The most explicit passages are the following:

1. The baptismal formula at the end of Matthew: "Go therefore and make disciples of all nations, baptizing them in the name of the Father and of the Son and of the Holy Spirit" (Matt. 28:19).[74]
2. Paul's benediction at the end of 2 Corinthians: "The grace of the Lord Jesus Christ, the love of God, and the communion of the Holy Spirit be with all of you" (2 Cor. 13:13).

72. Each of us has an "internally constituted 'self' that exists only through an engagement with the world of others; but that engagement is possible only in that the structure of interiority is already 'othered' and 'othering' in distinct moments of consciousness' inherence in itself. In the interdependence of these two ways of analogy, enriching and chastening one another, it becomes possible to speak, with immeasurable inadequacy, of the Trinitarian God who is love." David Bentley Hart, "The Mirror of the Infinite," *Modern Theology* 18 (2002): 547.

73. J. N. D. Kelly, *Early Christian Creeds* (London: Longman's, Green, 1950), 23.

74. Some scholars dismiss the passage as a later addition, but, having reminded us that we should not read too much later theology into it, many seem to accept with some caution its authenticity. "The concept of God as Father, Son, and Holy Spirit is clearly as old as the Messianic Community as it is known to us in the New Testament." W. F. Albright and C. S. Mann, *Matthew*, Anchor Bible (Garden City, N.Y.: Doubleday, 1971), 362; see also M. Eugene Boring, "Matthew," *The New Interpreter's Bible* 8, ed. Leander E. Keck (Nashville: Abingdon, 1995), 504.

3. Paul's contrast of variety and oneness in 1 Corinthians: "Now there are varieties of gifts, but the same Spirit; and there are varieties of services, but the same Lord; and there are varieties of activities, but it is the same God who activates all of them in everyone" (1 Cor. 12:4–6).

That each of these three passages begins with a different Trinitarian person is almost too neat, but it does at least indicate the lack of a necessary hierarchical order among the three.[75] None of these texts states the doctrine of the Trinity as it developed in subsequent centuries, but they do provide triune starting points that, in turn, led Christians to ask, "What has to be true, if it makes sense for us to say things like this?"

More fundamental than particular formulas, however, was a basic structure in what and how Christians believed. Christians had come to know God in Jesus, who was truly God as well as truly human. But, the New Testament tells us, Jesus prayed to someone he called his "Father," someone he said had sent him and to whom he was obedient, someone who raised him from the dead. He promised the coming of yet another, a Paraclete, the Spirit who had conceived him and descended upon him at baptism. Jesus' cry of abandonment from the cross leaves no doubt that there is distinction between him and the one he had always before called his Father—yet Christians prayed to Jesus and relied on him for their salvation. If that was not idolatry, then the one crying out as well as the one to whom he cried must be God.

Admittedly it was the relation between the Word and the one Jesus called his Father that first and foremost forced theologians to think about unity and diversity within God. The Spirit can actually sometimes seem something of an afterthought, perhaps unforgotten only because of the ubiquity of the Trinitarian baptismal formula. Yet it is hard to imagine a "binity" sufficing as a Christian account of God. For one thing, the Spirit figures so prominently in the New Testament stories of Jesus that it is hard to set out Jesus' identity as God apart from reference to the Spirit.

—Jesus is conceived by the Holy Spirit (Luke 1:35).
—The Spirit descends upon him at baptism (Matt. 3:16; Mark 1:10; Luke 3:22; John 1:32).
—The Spirit leads (or drives) him into the wilderness for temptation (Matt. 4:1; Mark 1:12; Luke 4:1).

75. See also Acts 2:32–33; Rom. 8:15–16; Eph. 2:18; 4:4–6; 1 Pet. 1:2.

—Jesus begins his ministry "filled with the power of the Spirit" (Luke 4:14). He preaches when the Spirit is upon him (Matt. 12:18) and casts out demons by the Spirit (Matt. 12:28).

—Jesus is "put to death in the flesh, but made alive in the spirit" (1 Pet. 3:18; see also Acts 1:2 and Rom. 1:4), and thus Christ's resurrection, the vindication of his divinity, is accomplished "in the spirit."

Thus as Christians came to experience the fulfillment of Jesus' promise to send the Paraclete by the presence of the Spirit among them, the relation of that Spirit to Jesus implied that, if Jesus is God, then so must be this Spirit. That thought gradually became explicit.[76] As noted in the previous chapter, the divinity of the Spirit in turn implies that not only God's self-revelation but our response to it is ultimately God's doing.

Theologians traditionally define the threefold way in which God is known to us and works for our salvation as the "economic" Trinity, that is, the threefold way in which God "manages the household." But both Rahner and Barth, the two theologians most responsible for reintroducing the importance of the Trinity into twentieth-century theology, emphasized that that threefold self-revelation of God, if it is to be God's *self*-revelation, must somehow mirror a triunity in the essence of God, the "immanent" Trinity. Rahner, in fact, stated an "axiom": the economic Trinity is the immanent Trinity, and the immanent Trinity is the economic Trinity.[77] I sympathize with those who are more cautious than he. Yves Congar, for instance, accepts the first half but not the second half of Rahner's axiom.[78] God's self-revelation in the economic Trinity allows us to infer an immanent Trinity *of some sort*, but we can neither infer back from what has been revealed of the economic Trinity to any detailed analysis of the immanent Trinity nor claim to have enough understanding of the immanent Trinity to infer from it the realities of the economic Trinity had we not already encountered them.

The one Jesus called "Father" is preeminently the origin of all things within the Trinity; the second person is that which somehow goes out to be over against the first, and the Spirit binds these two together in

76. Explicit at the latest by the time Cyril of Jerusalem delivered his Catechetical Lectures in 348. Cyril of Jerusalem, *Catechetical Lectures* 16.4; trans. Edwin Hamilton Gifford, Nicene and Post-Nicene Fathers, 2nd ser., 7:116.

77. Rahner, *Trinity*, 22; Barth, *Church Dogmatics* I/1, 333. "God *reveals* himself *as* Father, Son and Spirit because he *is* God *as* Father, Son and Spirit." Jüngel, *Doctrine of the Trinity*, 30.

78. Yves Congar, *I Believe in the Holy Spirit*, trans. David Smith, 3 vols. (New York: Seabury, 1983), 3:13–17.

love. Thus it does seem somehow fitting that the "Son" become incarnate and the Spirit bind us to the triune God in love. In Rahner's words, "The Father is the incomprehensible origin and original unity, the 'Word' his utterance into history, and the 'Spirit' the opening up of history into the immediacy of its fatherly origin and end."[79] We learn something about the persons of the immanent Trinity from their economic roles.[80]

Here, however, one pauses. "Something," "somehow"—any sensible theologian moves further with greatest reticence, cautious of Calvin's warning, in another connection, against making claims "not less insane than if one should purpose to walk in a pathless waste, or to see in darkness."[81] We are asking about the very essence of God, and that essence is too great for our understanding. We must cling closely to Scripture and to the logic of salvation, flickering candles as it were against what seems such a great darkness but is in fact, of course, invisible to our minds' eyes because of the brilliance of its too great light.

Still, this much: the Scottish theologian T. F. Torrance tells how, as a young army chaplain, he held the hand of a dying nineteen-year-old soldier, and then, back in Aberdeen as a pastor, visited one of the oldest women in his congregation—and how they both asked exactly the same question: "Is God really like Jesus?" And he assured them both, Torrance writes, "that God is indeed really like Jesus, and that there is no unknown God behind the back of Jesus for us to fear; to see the Lord Jesus is to see the very face of God."[82]

When we encounter Jesus, or when the Holy Spirit enters our lives, there is no other God behind them waiting to be discovered. Such an alternative would mean that we could not finally trust the revelation we had come to know, and would potentially open up all the tensions among competing gods that was characteristic of ancient paganism, where to befriend Athena was to risk Poseidon's fury. On this the Christian tradition has been consistent. In the first century Paul or one of his followers proclaimed that there is "one hope of your calling, one Lord, one faith, one baptism" (Eph. 4:4–5). Cyril of Jerusalem put it like this in the fourth century: "The gifts of the Father are none other than those of the Son, and those of the Holy Ghost; for there is one Salvation, one Power, one Faith. . . . And it is enough for us to know these

79. Ibid., 47.
80. Rahner, "Remarks," 85.
81. Calvin, *Institutes* 3.21.2, 923.
82. Thomas F. Torrance, *Preaching Christ Today* (Grand Rapids: Eerdmans, 1994), 55.

things, but inquire not curiously into His nature or substance."[83] Heinrich Bullinger, the consolidator of the Reformation in Zurich, wrote in the sixteenth century of "one God . . . one Mediator between God and men, Jesus the Messiah, and one shepherd of the whole flock, one Head of this body, and, to conclude, one Spirit, one salvation, one faith, one testament or covenant."[84] If the Holy Spirit leads us to know that Jesus Christ, as we come to know him in the biblical stories, is the self-revelation of the one God, then Father, Son, and Spirit cannot be three separate Gods. Indeed, such a God cannot be just any one God, but must be the God whose identity we have come to know in the biblical narratives about Jesus. Thus, in Moltmann's formulation, "The doctrine of the Trinity is nothing other than the conceptual framework needed to understand the story of Jesus as the story of God."[85] The one God thus known does not hold power in reserve, apart from the love revealed in the crucified Jesus or the Spirit's indwelling in our hearts; there is no God beyond the God triunely revealed, a God of love.[86]

SOME PROBLEMS

In addition to the debates about the *filioque* discussed in chapter 3, the most common Western and Eastern ways of thinking about the Trinity each generate additional specific problems. For Augustine and much of the West, it is the Spirit as the mutual love of Father and Son that binds the Trinity together. For the Eastern tradition, it is the Father as the origin of both Son and Spirit that is the Trinity's principle of unity. The Eastern view implies, as John Zizioulas has written, that God "exists on account of a person, the Father, and not on account of a substance."[87] In other words, it is not that the substance, God, exists, and as a result the three (Father, Son, and Spirit) exist. Rather, the Father exists, begets the Son, and breathes out the Holy Spirit (all eternally, of course; the order is logical or ontological, not temporal). It is thus the "Father" who is the reason why there is a Trinity. This emphasis on the Father

83. Cyril of Jerusalem, *Catechetical Lectures* 16.24; Nicene and Post-Nicene Fathers, 2nd ser., 7:121.

84. Second Helvetic Confession 17.2, in *Creeds and Confessions of Faith in the Christian Tradition*, ed. Jaroslav Pelikan and Valerie Hotchkiss, 4 vols. (New Haven: Yale University Press, 2003), 2:492.

85. Jürgen Moltmann, "The Christian Doctrine of the Trinity," in Pinchas Lapide and Jürgen Moltmann, *Jewish Monotheism and Christian Trinitarian Doctrine*, trans. Leonard Swidler (Philadelphia: Fortress, 1981), 47.

86. See Pannenberg, *Systematic Theology*, 1:447.

87. John Zizioulas, *Being as Communion* (Crestwood, N.Y.: St. Vladimir's Seminary Press, 1985), 41–42; see also idem, "The Contribution of Cappadocia to Christian Thought," in *Sinasas in Cappadocia*, ed. Frasso Pimenides and Stelios Roïdes (London: Agra, 1985), 32; and Gregory of Nazianzus, Oration 42.15; trans. Charles Gordon Browne and James Edward Swallow, Nicene and Post-Nicene Fathers, 2nd ser., 7:390.

grew even more pronounced in the East after Photius, during the ninth-century debates about the *filioque,* insisted even more forcefully that the Son played no role in the origin of the Spirit.[88]

T. F. Torrance and others have pointed out that, by itself, making the Father the foundation of the Trinity risks subordinationism, making Son and Spirit less than Father. A theology which keeps emphasizing that the Trinity starts with the Father endangers that joyful mutual equality which is one of the valued characteristics of the Trinity.[89] Such criticisms can be countered, however, by thinking through the implications of Cappadocian personalism—the way in which *any* person derives identity from those with whom that person is in relation. It will not do to say that Son and Spirit are who they are because of the Father, while the Father, as cause of the whole Trinity, has an independent identity. That would make the Father not a person, and thereby defeat the whole argument. Instead, we have to say—as the Eastern tradition at its best does say—that the three mutually define one another's identities, so that none would have a particular identity without the others.

If the persons of the Trinity were competing for power the way most human beings would, Gregory of Nyssa admitted, then the priority of the Father would be a source of inequality. But in the Trinity there is always the "reversal of values" made known to us in Christ: lords are always servants.[90] The persons of the Trinity glorify one another, and, Gregory observed, "It is plain, indeed, that one who gives glory to another must be found himself in the possession of superabundant glory; for how could one devoid of glory glorify another?" That the Spirit, for instance, glorifies the Father is not a sign of the Spirit's lesser character. Rather, there is a "revolving circle of the glory moving from Like to Like. The Son is glorified by the Spirit; the Father is glorified by the Son; again the Son has His glory from the Father; and the Only-begotten thus becomes the glory of the Spirit. For with what shall the Father be glorified, but with the true glory of the Son; and with what again shall the Son be glorified, but with the majesty of the Spirit? In like manner, again, Faith completes the circle, and glorifies the Son by means of the Spirit, and the Father by means of the Son."[91] In that circle of mutual glorification, priorities simply do not matter.

88. See Congar, *I Believe in the Holy Spirit,* 3:58.

89. T. F. Torrance, *The Trinitarian Faith* (Edinburgh: T. & T. Clark, 1988), 240.

90. Hans Urs von Balthasar, *Presence and Thought,* trans. Mark Sebanc (San Francisco: Ignatius, 1995), 166–67.

91. Gregory of Nyssa, *On the Holy Spirit, Against the Followers of Macedonius,* Nicene and Post-Nicene Fathers, 2nd ser., 5:323–24.

On the other hand, when Western theologians defined the Spirit as the bond of love that unites Father and Son (thus, one could argue, making the Spirit rather than the Father the Trinity's principle of unity), Eastern critics regularly objected that this could lead to denying the real personhood of the Holy Spirit. Two persons bound by love, they argued, are two persons, not three; a *relation* is not a *person*.[92]

Partly in response to this challenge, Aquinas proposed that *all three* Trinitarian persons are "subsistent relations."[93] To understand what that means, consider some contrasting cases. Tim and Tom are identical twins. In Aristotle's terms, they both have the same form but differ in their matter and in other things like spatial location. (Tim is the twin made up of *this* protein, fat, water, etc., and located *here*; Tom is the twin made up of *that* protein, fat, water, etc., and located *there*.) Such distinctions, however, cannot distinguish among the divine persons, who do not have matter or physical location. In Aquinas's account of the angels, who also lack matter, there can be only one angel of each species; since angels also lack matter, there would be no difference between Gabriel and Raphael if they were of the same species, since they would have exactly the same form.[94]

In the case of the three persons of the Trinity, however, if we ask, "What is this?" the answer in every case is, "God." The Father is God, the Son is God, the Spirit is God. Yet the Father is not the Son is not the Spirit is not the Father. Like angels, the three in God lack matter, physical location, or other ways in which we might distinguish among different instances of the same essence, but they are all one God and therefore cannot differ in species.

Aquinas therefore proposed that they are distinguished only by their relations. If we say, "Who or what is the Father?" the answer is, "God," and exactly the same answer for the Son and Spirit. If we then ask how they differ, the answer is that they differ only in that the Father is the begetter of the Son, the Son is the one begotten by the Father, and (given Aquinas's acceptance of the *filioque*) the Spirit is the one breathed forth by the Father and the Son. "Since," Aquinas argued, "relation, considered as really existing in God, is the divine essence Itself, and the essence is the same as person, as appears from what was said above, relation must necessarily be the same as person."[95]

92. Moltmann, *Trinity and the Kingdom*, 168, n. 73.

93. Aquinas, *Summa Theologica* 1.29.4; 159; see also Barth, *Church Dogmatics*, I/1:364–66. As early as the fourth century, Gregory of Nazianzus defined "Father" as "the name of a relation." Oration 29.16, Nicene and Post-Nicene Fathers, 2nd ser., 7:306.

94. Aquinas, *Summa Theologica* 1a.50.4; 263.

95. Ibid., 1a.40.1; 204.

On the more or less standard interpretation, Aquinas therefore concluded that in the Trinity, relations do not merely define the character of the persons; the persons *are* relations. There are no *relata* or things related, but only relations.[96] The relations are "subsistent," meaning that they have their own existence, even absent any subsisting terms to relate.[97] As one contemporary philosopher of religion, Christopher Hughes, puts it, "The heart of Aquinas' theory of the Trinity is the claim that Trinitarian relations 'constitute and distinguish' (*constituunt et distinguunt*) the divine persons."[98]

If we understand "relation" in the ordinary modern sense, however, this does not seem to make sense. As Moltmann writes, "It is impossible to say: person *is* relation. . . . It is true that the Father is defined by his fatherhood to the Son, but this does not constitute his existence; it presupposes it. . . . There are no persons without relations, but there are no relations without persons either."[99] Part of what "relation" means is that there are two or more things being related, and so there just cannot be relations without things to relate. If a relation means "nothing other than the sheer bond between things," as Balthasar says, then how can there be relations without things other than the relations to be related?[100]

Before concluding that Aquinas was simply wrong, some explanations are in order. Modern logic generally makes a sharp distinction between properties and relations. The book is red (property); the table is brown (property); the book is on the table (relation). To stick to Aristotle's terminology we think of properties as *in*, or *belonging to*, substances, while relations are *between* substances. Aquinas, however, was using Aristotelian logic, in which a relation is a kind of property. Aristotle listed "quantity, quality, relation," and so on as different kinds of properties that substances can have.[101] But "relation" here is really a mistranslation; Aristotle does not have a noun meaning "relation" in our sense but talks about "relatives" and "correlatives."[102] Aquinas therefore quite naturally talks about relations in his sense as "in" things

96. For careful accounts of this standard view, see Jenson, *Triune Identity*, 123; Cunningham, *These Three Are One*, 62.

97. Aquinas, *Summa Theologica* 1a.40.2; 205.

98. Christopher Hughes, *On a Complex Theory of a Simple God* (Ithaca: Cornell University Press, 1989), 197.

99. Moltmann, *Trinity and the Kingdom*, 172.

100. Balthasar, *Theo-Logic*, 2:129. "Persons cannot be translated fully into relations. A person is always already outside of the relations in which he or she is immersed." Miroslav Volf, "The Trinity Is Our Social Program," *Modern Theology* 14 (1998): 410.

101. Aristotle, *Categories* 4; trans. E. M. Edghill, in *Basic Works of Aristotle*, ed. Richard McKeon (New York: Random House, 1941), 8; see also *Metaphysics* 5.15; trans. W. D. Ross, ibid., 768–69.

102. See J. L. Ackrill, "Notes on the Categories," in *Aristotle*, ed. J. M. E. Moravcsik (Garden City, N.Y.: Doubleday, 1967), 108.

rather than "between" things.[103] It might make better sense for us to talk about them as "relational properties." Most relational properties, Aquinas notes, are *not* part of a substance's essence. Ellen is the wife of David and the mother of Susan, but she would still be Ellen if she had not married David or given birth to Susan. But the relational properties of the persons of the Trinity are different: the Father would *just not be* the Father without begetting the Son and spirating the Spirit.[104] Furthermore, the relational properties of each person are the only ways in which that person differs from the others. Relational properties are a necessary part of a person's identity and the only thing that distinguishes one person from another—and that, I think, is what Aquinas means when he says that persons are subsistent relations. (At least I hope that is what he means—if he means more than that, and there are passages open to such an interpretation, then I cannot agree with him.) Once again, what looks like an odd metaphysical claim can be restated in terms of negative rules:

1. Do not specify any distinctive qualities of any of the Trinitarian persons except that person's relations to the others.
2. Do not identify any "essence" of any one Trinitarian person prior to that person's relations to the others.

Such rules preserve mystery rather than explaining it. Aquinas certainly did not change his mind about the mystery of God when he turned to discussing the Trinity. When we speak of the Trinity, he says, "we must proceed with care and with befitting modesty."[105] He draws the analogy of an oncoming thunderstorm: it is as if Scripture has provided us the first drop of the rain, but we "cannot in the state of this life behold the thunder of the greatness."[106]

Still, the very "threeness" in God might seem to contradict the divine simplicity he had earlier affirmed. "Simplicity" was the first attribute of God he discussed—meaning by it that none of the distinctions we normally use to break things down in order to understand them can apply to God.[107] How then to say that there are three persons in God? Like the Fathers before him, Aquinas insisted that even *numerical terms,* when applied to God, "are not derived from number, a

103. Aquinas, *Summa Theologica* 1a.29.4; 159.
104. Thomas Aquinas, *On the Power of God* 10.3; trans. English Dominican Fathers (Westminster, Md.: Newman, 1952), 3:193.
105. Aquinas, *Summa Theologica* 1a.31.2; 165.
106. Aquinas, *Summa Contra Gentiles* 4.1.10; 39.
107. Aquinas, *Summa Theologica,* 1a.3; 14–20.

species of quantity, for in that case they could bear only a metaphorical sense in God, like other corporeal properties, such as length, breadth, and the like."[108] Numbers are normally a subcategory of quantity, a way of counting or measuring things. But we cannot count or measure God. Therefore, if we say that God is "three," we are taking "three," he explained, "from multitude in a transcendent sense. Now multitude so understood has relation to the many of which it is predicated, as *one* convertible with *being* is related to being; which kind of oneness does not add anything to being, except a negation of division. . . . In the same way, when we speak of many things, multitude in this latter sense points to those things as being each undivided in itself. . . . Therefore the numeral terms in God signify the things of which they are said, and beyond this they add negation only."[109] When I say that God is one, therefore, I am not asserting some positive attribute of God, but am simply saying that there are no ways in which I can make divisions within God. When I say that God is triune (similarly, but this case is admittedly harder), the "three" indicates things we must not say of the persons of the Trinity, but it tells us nothing positive about what it is like for God to be three.

In the very complex medieval debates on these issues after Aquinas, the key figures were united in their caution concerning talking about God. A generation after Aquinas, John Duns Scotus argued that there was no "real distinction" in, for instance, the Father between being the first person and being the origin of the second person, but there was a "conceptual [or formal] distinction."[110] Thus in our thinking about God, given the way in which we have to break things down to think about them more clearly, we distinguish the essence of the Father from the Father's relation as origin of the Son, but that distinction does not correspond to any real distinction within God, within whose utter simplicity we cannot make distinctions at all.[111]

A generation later, William of Ockham rejected Scotus's talk of a formal or conceptual distinction. To simplify a complex argument, he

108. Ibid., 1a.30.3; 162.

109. Ibid., 1a.30.3; 163.

110. John Duns Scotus, Quodlibetal Question 4.61, *God and Creatures*, trans. Felix Aluntis and Allan B. Wolter (Princeton: Princeton University Press, 1975), 103.

111. I am oversimplifying a complex story. Scotus shifted his position on the issue during his career. A clear summary is in Marilyn McCord Adams, *William Ockham*, 2 vols. (Notre Dame: University of Notre Dame Press, 1987), 1:22–29. Still, with respect to the application of these categories to the Trinity, I am persuaded by Mary Elizabeth Ingram's argument: "There is no need to assert a radical shift on the part of Scotus. He is clearly at work [both early and later] to offer a basis for the relationship among persons which, he asserts, constitutes the personality but not the metaphysical *suppositum* for the relationship." Mary Elizabeth Ingram, "John Duns Scotus," in *The History of Franciscan Theology*, ed. Kenan B. Osborne (St. Bonaventure, N.Y.: Franciscan Institute, 1994), 214.

asserted that, if there is not a real distinction out there in the object known, then a "formal distinction" in our thinking would leave us thinking about the object in a way contrary to how the object really is—in other words, we would be thinking falsely.[112] Thus there cannot be a true formal distinction without a real distinction (and, of course, if there is a real distinction, then there is no need for the category of "formal distinction"). So how can God be triune if God is simple? Ockham says that we must simply accept, from Scripture and the teachings of the church, that God is both three and one and not try to understand the divine mystery.[113]

The debates among Aquinas, Scotus, and Ockham on these issues are among the most fascinating in medieval philosophy, but, surprisingly, they differ little in theological intent. All were seeking to affirm what they judged faith required them to say while also claiming to know as little as possible about the nature of God.

In one respect, medieval caution about speaking about God's inner nature seems to me to go too far, thereby denying something revealed to faith. From the time of Augustine to the beginning of the twentieth century, most Western theologians concluded from the fact that the three are distinguished only by their relations that nothing in any of the three implies that that one of them should engage in some particular activity *ad extra*. To quote Peter Lombard, the author of the standard medieval theological textbook, on the most dramatic case, "As the Son was made human, so the Father or the Holy Spirit could have been, or could be now."[114] "*At this precise point*," Robert Jenson writes, "the Western tradition must simply be corrected. The identities' agencies *ad extra* do not achieve an undivided work because they are indistinguishable but because they are perfectly mutual."[115] Twentieth-century theologians like Rahner, Barth, and Jüngel have likewise rightly returned to the pre-Augustinian conviction that becoming incarnate is the uniquely appropriate role of the Son.[116]

All the activity of the Trinity *ad extra* is the work of the whole Trinity. Because of the relations among the three in the Trinity, each has a particular role in this mutual work. As Gregory of Nyssa put it, "Every operation which extends from God to the creation . . . has its origin

112. See Adams, *William Ockham*, 2:935, 1003.

113. William of Ockham, *Ordinatio* 1, d.2, q.1, *Opera Theologica* (St. Bonaventure, N.Y.: Franciscan Institute, 1970), 2:78.

114. Peter Lombard, *Sententiarum Libri Quatuor* 3.1.3, *Patrologia latina* 192:758.

115. Robert W. Jenson, *Systematic Theology*, 2 vols. (Oxford: Oxford University Press, 1997–99), 1:113.

116. Rahner, "Remarks," 80; Jüngel, with reference to Barth, *Doctrine of the Trinity*, 39–40.

from the Father, and proceeds through the Son, and is perfected in the Holy Spirit."[117]

If God's self-revelation is *self*-revelation, then the way in which we know God in the Word made flesh thanks to the work of the Holy Spirit must correspond to some characteristics of the three as they are in the one, and the only distinguishing characteristics they have are their mutual relations. Something about the begottenness of the Word makes it fitting that, in the one work of God for our salvation, it should be the Word that is made flesh, just as something about the way the Spirit is breathed forth makes it fitting that the Spirit should be the one guiding our hearts to faith and thereby to loving union with God. But I would stop short of any attempt to define that "something" or otherwise here try to penetrate the mystery of the immanent Trinity. Aquinas's distinction between the *modus significandi* and the *significatum* again makes this point in more technical terms. I can say that these actions of the Son and Spirit are appropriate in some way I would see if I saw God, but, here and now, I cannot imagine the nature of that appropriateness.

This conclusion is significantly different in two respects from the traditional theory of "appropriations." As noted in chapter 2, that theory holds that, while all of the activities of God are the work of the whole Trinity, there is an appropriateness to assigning some of them particularly to each of the persons—creation, for instance, to the Father, our salvation to the Son.[118] But this says both too much and too little. To the extent that it implies that it can be appropriate to think of any activity of God as somehow, even as a kind of quasi-fiction, the unique activity of one of the three, it goes too far. The three are engaged in *different* ways in *all* the activities of God. For instance, Augustine says that the voice at Jesus' baptism was the voice of the Father and the tongues of fire at Pentecost were the Holy Spirit,[119] but the work of all three persons was in both cases required to produce the phenomena.[120] On the other hand, if it suggests that we can distinguish the contribution of each of the three to the divine acts only in a kind of quasi-fictional way, then this theory of appropriation does not go far enough, for the fact that God's revelation is *self*-revelation does imply a relation,

117. Gregory of Nyssa, *To Ablabius, on "Not Three Gods,"* Nicene and Post-Nicene Fathers, 2nd ser., 5:334.

118. See, for instance, Aquinas, *Summa Theologica* 3a.23.2 ad 3; 2142; Karl Barth, *Dogmatics in Outline*, trans. G. T. Thomson (Edinburgh: T. & T. Clark, 1949), 52; Jüngel, *Doctrine of the Trinity*, 36.

119. Augustine, *On the Trinity* 1.2.7; 69–70.

120. Ibid., 2.4.18; 110.

albeit a mysterious one, between the ways in which we know God and the ways in which God is.

It makes me nervous, I admit, that some version of the theory of appropriations seems embedded even in the creeds, where in particular the Father is associated with creation, but that should not divert us from the essential point. Christian interpretation of Genesis has quite consistently seen the Word in God's speaking and the Spirit in the mighty wind that sweeps over the face of the waters, so that all three persons are at work in creation.[121] The second person becomes incarnate; the third person is active in the life of the church and the lives of Christians (though elsewhere as well in unexpected ways), but the first person has no particular associated activity. All that we know is that Jesus calls this person "Father" and invites us to do the same.

All three persons are engaged in all of God's acts; such a claim leads into the philosophical thicket of what counts as an "act." If I get up from my chair, walk across the room, and turn on the television, how many acts have I performed? An extensive philosophical literature has established, I think, that there is no definitive way of answering that question;[122] one can only define what counts as "an act" for a particular purpose. In the case at hand, "becoming embodied in Jesus of Nazareth" is something the second person, but not the first or third person, has done. It would not count as something all three persons of the Trinity do. But, if we think of "the incarnation" as a divine act, then all three persons are involved: "The Holy Spirit will come upon you, and the power of the Most High will overshadow you; therefore the child to be born will be holy; he will be called Son of God" (Luke 1:35). The Spirit enacts the will of the Father so that the Son becomes incarnate. And similarly with all other divine activities.

CONCLUSIONS

It probably comes easiest to think of the Trinity in terms of *one agent* engaged in *three activities*. Robert Jenson has persuasively argued that the Cappadocians believed that such a picture gets things exactly backward, and that they were right. The wrongheaded picture comes easiest

121. See also Ps. 33:6 and 104:30.

122. See Thomas F. Tracy, *God, Action, and Embodiment* (Grand Rapids: Eerdmans, 1984), 21–44, for an account of some of the issues.

because it describes how things work with human beings: when three human persons engage in the "same action," Gregory of Nyssa explained, they go about their work individually. But God is different:

> In the case of the Divine nature we do not similarly learn that the Father does anything by Himself in which the Son does not work conjointly, or again that the Son has any special operation apart from the Holy Spirit; but every operation which extends from God to the Creation, and is named according to our variable conceptions of it, has its origin from the Father, and proceeds through the Son, and is perfected in the Holy Spirit. . . . Whatever comes to pass, in reference either to the acts of His providence for us, or to the government and constitution of the universe, comes to pass by the action of the Three, yet what does come to pass is not three things.[123]

We conceive Godhead, Gregory of Nyssa says, "as an operation."[124]

Gregory of Nazianzus uses the analogy of not three rays coming from the same sun but three suns producing the same ray.[125] "God" is a verb, the name for the common activity of the three persons, what John of Damascus calls "the one surge of motion."[126] As Jenson puts it, "There *is*, most strictly speaking, no *some*-thing, God. . . . The divine *ousia* is the infinity—and this is its sole characterization—of the work done between Jesus and the Father in the Spirit."[127] The "persons" are the three who do this work in perfect, mutual glorification. From the scriptural narratives we learn that the three are in some sense, albeit one incomprehensible to us, real personal agents. They are engaged in the common activity of being God.[128]

Yet the point is not that the divine persons are "personal" only in some secondary or inadequate sense. For the theology of the Trinity, human persons do not finally define "personhood," with the divine persons a

123. Gregory of Nyssa, *To Ablabius, on "Not Three Gods,"* Nicene and Post-Nicene Fathers, 2nd ser., 5:334. "The Persons of the Divinity are not separated from one another either by time or place, not by will or by practice, not by activity or by passion, not by anything of this sort, such as is observed with regard to human beings." Gregory of Nyssa, *To the Greeks*, 385.

124. Ibid., 335.

125. Gregory of Nazianzus, *The Fifth Theological Oration: On the Holy Spirit*, Oration 31:14, Nicene and Post-Nicene Fathers, 2nd ser., 7:322. "When I contemplate the Three together, I see but one torch, and cannot divide or measure out the Undivided Light." Gregory of Nazianzus, Oration 40:41; ibid., 375. See also Pseudo-Dionysius, *The Divine Names* 2.4, in *The Complete Works*, trans. Colm Luibheid (New York: Paulist Press, 1987), 61; and Basil, Letter 189.6, Nicene and Post-Nicene Fathers, 2nd ser., 8:231.

126. John of Damascus, *The Orthodox Faith* 1.8; *Writings*, 186.

127. Jenson, *Triune Identity*, 164. See also Fourth Lateran Council, "Definition Directed against the Albigensians and Other Heretics" 428, in Henry Denzinger, *The Sources of Catholic Dogma*, trans. Roy J. Deferrari (St. Louis: B. Herder, 1957), 169.

128. Eugene F. Rogers Jr., *After the Spirit* (Grand Rapids: Eerdmans, 2005), 22.

vaguely analogous case. Rather, it is the divine three that manifest what personhood truly is. We human persons are always failing to be fully personal. As persons, we are shaped by our relations with other persons. Yet we always deliberately raise barriers or cannot figure out how to overcome the barriers we confront. When those we most love come to die, or in the dementia of old age are no longer able to understand what we may most want to say to them, we realize how much there was in our hearts that we never shared with them. When we best articulate our ideas, we cannot escape the feeling that there was something there we never quite captured. When we most rejoice in sharing with someone different from ourselves, difference nevertheless scares us.[129] The doctrine of the Trinity, however, proclaims that true personhood, however impossible its character may be for us to imagine, involves acknowledging real difference in a way that causes not fear but joy.

The Trinity offers not only a model of relatedness but also a model of equality. The world, this doctrine tells us, is not a pyramid with a single Lord at the top. One can never go so high as to transcend equality and mutual sharing, and they are thus built into the structure of all that is. In Moltmann's words, "It is only when the doctrine of the Trinity vanquishes the monotheistic notion of the great, universal monarch in heaven and his divine patriarchs in the world, that earthly rulers, dictators and tyrants cease to find any justifying religious archetypes any more."[130] In a community in which no one is out to assert power over others (and only in such a community), moreover, equality measured in terms of the exact apportionment of rights becomes irrelevant, and equality means instead the sort of self-giving mutual glorification that provides Scripture's most common hints about the inner life of the Trinity. In Arthur McGill's words,

> The issue between Arius and Athanasius has nothing to do with whether God is one or two or three. It has to do with what quality

129. "Fear of the other is pathologically inherent in our existence. . . . We are afraid not simply of a certain other or others, but even if we accept certain others we accept them on condition that they are somehow like ourselves. Radical otherness is anathema. Difference itself is a threat." Metropolitan John (Zizioulas), "Communion and Others," *St. Vladimir's Theological Quarterly* 38 (1994): 349–50. Much contemporary "inclusivist" and "pluralist" theology of religions is dedicated to proving that the different is not really different, so that we need not be afraid of it. This still leaves the thought that it would be right to be afraid of the truly different.

130. Moltmann, *Trinity and the Kingdom*, 197. See also LaCugna, *God for Us*, 17. Behind much of this discussion, see Erik Peterson, "Der Monotheismus as politisches Problem," *Theologische Traktate* (Munich: Küsel, 1951), 45–148. I am not sure how much to make of it, but Bertrand de Margerie thinks it not accidental that the christianized Roman emperors were so consistently Arian. Trinitarianism challenges the ideology of absolute monarchy. Bertrand de Margerie, *The Christian Trinity in History*, trans. Edmund J. Fortman (Still River, Mass.: St. Bede's Publications, 1982), 89. And it is interesting that the rise of absolute monarchs in modern Europe corresponded to a decline in the doctrine of the Trinity.

> makes God divine, what quality constitutes his perfection. From the perspective of self-contained absoluteness and transcendent supremacy, Arius can only look upon God's begetting a Son as grotesque blasphemy. God, he observed, must be very imperfect if he must generate a Son in order to become complete. But from the perspective of self-communicating love, Athanasius can look upon the dependent denied Son, not as a blot upon God's divinity, but as a mode of its perfection.[131]

The last word about things cannot be power if God is love. And in love, equality need not imply identity. Too much contemporary thought starts by praising diversity but ends up denying real difference—those other folks are OK, it implies, because, deep down, they are really like us. In contrast, one of the central insights provided by the doctrine of the Trinity is that *difference is all right.*

"If I glorify myself," John has Jesus say, "my glory is nothing. It is my Father who glorifies me" (8:54). But the Son is glorified so that the Son may glorify the Father (17:1). Just as the Son could not exist without the Father, so, Gregory of Nyssa insists, "The Father is never without the Son; for it is impossible that glory should be without radiance, as it is impossible that the lamp should be without brightness."[132] More than that, the Spirit glorifies and is glorified by both the Father and the Son. The triune persons compete, not in seeking their own glory, but in glorifying one another. In Wolfhart Pannenberg's formulation, "The Father does not merely beget the Son. He also hands over his kingdom to him and receives it back from him. The Son is not merely begotten of the Father. He is also obedient to him and he thereby glorifies him as the one God. The Spirit is not just breathed. He also fills the Son and glorifies him in his obedience to the Father, thereby glorifying the Father himself."[133]

AFTER-WORD: *CHORA* OR *PERICHORESIS*

In that strange dialogue *Timaeus*, Plato at one point discussed first the eternal and unchanging forms that are the objects of knowledge and second the changing objects of the sensible world, concerning which

131. Arthur McGill, *Suffering* (Philadelphia: Westminster, 1983), 78.
132. Gregory of Nyssa, *On the Faith*, Nicene and Post-Nicene Fathers, 2nd ser., 5:338.
133. Pannenberg, *Systematic Theology*, 1:320.

we have only opinion, but which are as it were copies, made in the world of change, of the unchanging forms. But forms and their copies do not exhaust his inventory of the world, for there is a "third type":

> Space (*chora*) exists always and cannot be destroyed. It provides a location for all things that come to be. It is itself apprehended by a kind of bastard reasoning that does not involve sense perception, and it is hardly even an object of conviction. We look at it as in a dream when we say that everything that exists must of necessity be somewhere.[134]

Chora in Greek could mean a mother, a nurse, a receptacle, a winnowing sieve, space, or the base material to which ingredients were added to make a perfume.[135] Plato elsewhere (*Republic* 373d; *Timaeus* 23b) used the term to refer to the territory of a city-state. In *Timaeus* (and there is of course some sexism in the feminine connotations) he took it to convey a mysterious nonentity on which both reality and appearance can appear. John Sallis warns of the dangers of attempts at explanation:

> By insisting on a reading of the chorology in which the meaning of the χώρα [*chora*] would come to be determined, the resulting interpretations produced a reduction of the χώρα, situating it within a horizon of sense that it would otherwise both limit and escape, effacing its distinctiveness in the very gesture of interpretation, in the very demand that the chorology make sense, in the refusal to read in it, instead, a limiting both of making and of sense.[136]

With his unerring eye for the fault lines in philosophical systems, Jacques Derrida seized on Plato's *chora*.[137] How odd, he noted, this third element of the world, which shares the eternity of the forms and yet is apprehended, not by true reason or even sense perception, but by "a kind of bastard reasoning . . . hardly even an object of conviction," looked at "as in a dream." *Chora* is wholly other, beyond all standard categories, not active or passive, present or absent,[138] "this 'thing' that is nothing of that to which this 'thing' nevertheless seems to 'give

134. Plato, *Timaeus* 52a-b, trans. Donald J. Zeyl, *Complete Works*, ed. John M. Cooper (Indianapolis: Hackett, 1997), 1255.

135. Richard Kearney, *Strangers, God and Monsters* (London: Routledge, 2003), 193.

136. John Sallis, *Chorology* (Bloomington: Indiana University Press, 1999), 4.

137. For an alternative reading, see Julia Kristeva, "Revolution in Poetic Language," in *The Kristeva Reader*, ed. Toril Moi (New York: Columbia University Press, 1986), 93–98.

138. Jacques Derrida, *On the Name*, ed. Thomas Dutoit, trans. Ian McLeod (Stanford: Stanford University Press, 1995), 102.

place'—without, however, this 'thing' ever *giving* anything."[139] Plato sensed that he needed *chora* to complete his system, yet *chora* so radically does not fit into that system that it—well, deconstructs it. Here so near the beginning of Western philosophy is an anticipation of every recent realization, from Gödel to Derrida himself, that the systems that reasoning imposes always leave out something and somehow distort what they include.

Chora fascinated Derrida, John Caputo says, first because it disrupts and deconstructs Plato's system, but second because, "*khôra* is an outsider, with no place to lay her/its head, in philosophy or in mythology,"[140] neither a concept we can understand nor a person of whom we can tell stories. It is desert, place of wandering (place with affinities for an Algerian Jew like Derrida?), *tohu wabohu*, emptiness, surd, yet the place, Plato said, where "everything that exists . . . must of necessity be." If *chora* is the only space for things, then indeed the world

> Hath really neither joy, nor love, nor light,
> Nor certitude, nor peace, nor help for pain;
> And we are here as on a darkling plain
> Swept with confused alarms of struggle and light,
> Where ignorant armies clash by night.[141]

Chora, Derrida remarked, "anachronizes being."[142] It dooms our every effort to make sense of things. "It will never have entered religion and will never permit itself to be sacralized, sanctified, humanized, theologized, cultivated, historicized. Radically heterogeneous to the safe and sound, to the holy and the sacred, it . . . is neither Being, nor the Good, nor God, nor Man, nor History. It will always resist them, will have always been . . . the very place of an infinite resistance, of an infinitely impassible persistence <*restance*>: an utterly faceless other."[143] Thus, if "philosophy" means "system," then *chora* is philosophy's enemy, the radically other that resists all systematization.[144]

139. Ibid., xv.

140. John D. Caputo, *The Prayers and Tears of Jacques Derrida* (Bloomington: Indiana University Press, 1997), 35.

141. Matthew Arnold, "Dover Beach," *The Norton Anthology of English Literature*, 5th ed. (New York: Norton, 1986), 2:1384.

142. Derrida, *On the Name*, 94.

143. Jacques Derrida, "Faith and Knowledge," trans. Samuel Weber, in *Acts of Religion*, ed. Gil Anidjar (New York: Routledge, 2002), 58–59.

144. See Emmanuel Levinas, *Basic Philosophical Writings*, ed. Adriaan T. Peperzak, Simon Critchley, and Robert Bernasconi (Bloomington: Indiana University Press, 1996), 11.

This utterly other, Derrida emphasized, is not the God of negative theology, not one who turns out, for all his mystery, to be "the giver of good gifts."[145] "On the subject of *khōra,* there is neither negative theology nor thought of the God, of the One, or of God beyond Being."[146] Yet, tantalizingly, he could write, "'God' 'is' the name of this bottomless collapse, of this endless desertification of language"[147] (though one must take seriously the quotation marks not only around "God" but around "is"). Most postmodern of postmodernists, most loyal son of Nietzsche, Derrida was in one sense very much a religious thinker in the tradition of Aquinas, Luther, and Barth—all those who keep rejecting as idols our every effort to domesticate God—and he was convinced that we conventionally religious folk, and anyone who appeals to "God," much less to God, are already inevitably talking about a domesticated idol, a God fitted to our needs and understanding. Rather than fall into idolatry, Derrida remained in the desert. Neither complex engineering nor the magic of water dowsing can produce water in truly waterless wilderness, and philosophy cannot fit *chora* into a system any more than mythology can fit it into a coherent story. Derrida was perhaps the most radical of the kind of recent philosopher I discussed in chapter 1, who shows the inadequacy of our totalizing intellectual projects in a way that can open a space for revelation. But Derrida went one step too far. He was so concerned to avoid idolatry that he ruled out the possibility of any talk of God, not as a way of preserving silence in the mystery, but in a way that simply thrusts us back into a secular world.

But grace is like mercy. It drops as the gentle rain from heaven upon the place beneath. All our efforts to domesticate the wholly other are doomed to failure, and we should not, Derrida reminded us, try to hold back despair by pretending that the desert is really God. As Oswald Beyer, a fine Luther scholar, writes of Luther's views, "Whoever shuts himself off to the reliable word, the promise, loses the world as a home and trades it in as a wasteland. . . . If the world is not believed as something promised, then it becomes, as Nietzsche appropriately said, 'a thousand wastes, silent, cold.'"[148]

145. Jacques Derrida, "How to Avoid Speaking: Denials," in *Derrida and Negative Theology*, ed. Harold Coward and Toby Foshay (Albany: SUNY Press, 1992), 106–8. See also Caputo, *Prayers and Tears*, 11.

146. Jacques Derrida, *Prière d'insérer*, trans. Thomas Dutoit *On the Name* (Stanford: Stanford University Press, 1995), xvi.

147. Derrida, *On the Name*, 55–56.

148. Oswald Bayer, "Luther as an Interpreter of Holy Scripture," trans. Mark Mattes, in *The Cambridge Companion to Martin Luther*, ed. Donald McKim (Cambridge: Cambridge University Press, 2003), 81–82, quoting Nietzsche's "Der Freigeist," part 1, stanza 3.

A loving God, however, might unexpectedly reach out to us. We might live under promises revealed to us. Where *chora* means space or room, the verb *chorein* means (among other things) to make room for.[149] In Trinitarian theology, the three persons, in what the tradition has come to call their *perichoresis*,[150] make room for each other. In Daniel Migliore's lovely phrase, they "are incomparably hospitable to each other."[151]

The term *perichoresis* had earlier been used of the humanity and divinity in Christ, but the first significant use with respect to the Trinity came in John of Damascus, writing in the early 700s.[152] As Barth summarized the idea, in *perichoresis* "the divine modes of being mutually condition and permeate one another so completely that one is always in the other two and the other two in the one."[153]

We trust that the distance between Jesus crying out in abandonment on the cross and the one he had always before called his Father mirrors some sort of distance within God—though we cannot imagine what terms like "distance within God" can mean. A kind of space lies within the triune God—a space potentially inclusive of the space of sinners and doubters—and yet this space is no desert but a spiritual garden of mutual love and glorification.[154] In the incarnation, the three show that there is always within God a space large enough for the whole world, and even all its sin: the Word's distance from the one he calls Father is so great that no one falls outside it, and the Spirit fills all that space with love.[155] The Spirit maintains, Balthasar says, the space that Christ opens up "at our disposal, as a new, open space."[156] The Spirit fills the "space . . . between the Unbegotten and the Begotten," Gregory of Nazianzus wrote.[157] As Moltmann puts it, "In the event between the surrendering Father and the forsaken Son, God becomes so 'vast' in the

149. For Derrida on God and *chora*, see Jacques Derrida, "Dialogue on the Gift," in John D. Caputo and Michael J. Scanlon, *God, the Gift, and Postmodernism* (Bloomington: Indiana University Press, 1999), 78.

150. There is one reference in pseudo-Cyril, but the more important first use of *perichoresis* in a Trinitarian context is John of Damascus, *The Orthodox Faith* 1.8, in *Writings*, trans. Frederic H. Chase Jr. (New York: Fathers of the Church, 1958), 187.

151. Daniel L. Migliore, *Faith Seeking Understanding* (Grand Rapids: Eerdmans, 1991), 70.

152. John of Damascus, *Orthodox Faith* 1.8; *Writings*, 187.

153. Karl Barth, *Church Dogmatics,* I/1:370.

154. Hilary of Poitiers, *The Trinity* 3.4; trans. Stephen McKenna (New York: Fathers of the Church, 1954), 67–68; John of Damascus, *Orthodox Faith* 1.8; *Writings*, 187.

155. Eberhard Jüngel, *God as the Mystery of the World*, trans. Darrell L. Guder (Grand Rapids: Eerdmans, 1983), 368.

156. Hans Urs von Balthasar, *Explorations in Theology*, vol. 3: *Creator Spirit*, trans. Brian McNeil (San Francisco: Ignatius, 1993), 169.

157. Gregory of Nazianzus, "On the Holy Spirit," Oration 31.8, Nicene and Post-Nicene Fathers, 2nd ser., 7:320.

Spirit of self-offering that there is room and life for the whole world, the living and the dead."[158]

The Word's journey into the far country so separates Christ from the one to whom he cries out from the cross that there is space between them for every sinner, and that space is filled with the love of the Spirit,[159] whom both Augustine and Gregory Palamas called the bond of love.[160] To quote Balthasar, "Out of his love, God the Father gives that which is more precious to him, his Son, for us. Out of his love the Son goes into the utmost darkness of the world, of death and hell, in order to bear the guilt of all his human brothers and sisters. And this love is given to us as the fruit pours into our hearts: God's holy spirit of love."[161] "If I make my bed in Sheol, you are there. . . . Even there your hand shall lead me" (Ps. 139:8b, 10a). In Rowan Williams's words, "The divine life is what sustains itself as unqualified unity across the greatest completeness of alienation that can be imagined."[162] In both the love that reaches out into the darkness of alienation and the love that sustains God's oneness, God is God.[163]

158. Jürgen Moltmann, *The Church in the Power of the Spirit*, trans. Margaret Kohl (New Francisco: HarperSanFrancisco, 1977), 96. "This infinite distance between God and God, this supreme tearing apart, this agony beyond all others, this marvel of love, is the crucifixion. Nothing can be further from God than that which has been made accursed. This tearing apart, over which supreme love places the bond of supreme union, echoes perpetually across the universe." Simone Weil, *Waiting for God*, trans. Emma Crawford (repr. New York: Harper & Row, 1973), 72.

159. Hans Urs von Balthasar, *Theo-Logic*, vol. 3: *The Spirit of Truth,* trans. Graham Harrison (San Francisco: Ignatius, 2005), 74. "As the Spirit who is breathed back by the dying Son to the Father—the Spirit always comes from the most extreme point that God's fatherly and filial love could find in order to be God even in what is most ungodly in order to experience to its very depths the inconceivable profundity of mutual love in the abandonment of God (and this is always 'eternal' in terms of experience) that the Son experiences from the Father." Balthasar, *Explorations in Theology*, 3:124.

160. See Boris Bobrinskoy, *The Mystery of the Trinity*, trans. Anthony P. Gythiel (Crestwood, N.Y.: St. Vladimir's Seminary Press, 1999), 66.

161. Balthasar, *The von Balthasar Reader*, ed. Medard Kehl and Werner Löser, trans. Robert J. Daly and Fred Lawrence (New York: Crossroad, 1982), 192.

162. Rowan Williams, "Afterword: Making Differences," in *Balthasar at the End of Modernity*, ed. Lucy Gardner et al. (Edinburgh: T. & T. Clark, 1999), 176. "Our distance from God is itself taken into God, finds place in God. . . . In the Incarnation God distances himself from himself: the divine intra-trinitarian love is enacted and realized in the world by the descent of Christ into Hell. And the separation between Father and Son is bridged by the Spirit." Rowan Williams, "Barth on the Triune God," in *Karl Barth: Studies of His Theological Method*, ed. Stephen W. Sykes (Oxford: Clarendon, 1979), 177.

163. Concerning God's love, of course, I must recall once more Aquinas's distinction between *significatum* and *modus significandi*. We trust that, to one who understood God, "love" would turn out to be a good word to use, but we cannot imagine the form of its appropriateness. As Balthasar puts it, "No truth of revelation, from the Trinity to the Cross and Judgment, can speak of anything but the glory of God's poor love—which, of course, is something very different from what we here below imagine by the name love." Hans Urs von Balthasar, "Geist und Feuer," *Herder Korrespondenz* 30 (1976): 82.

Index